THE EDUCATIONAL RIGHTS OF STUDENTS

International Perspectives on Demystifying the Legal Issues

Edited by Charles J. Russo, Douglas J. Stewart, and Jan De Groof

Published in Partnership with the
Assocation of School Business Officials International

ROWMAN & LITTLEFIELD EDUCATION
Lanham • New York • Toronto • Plymouth, UK

Published in partnership with the Association of School Business Officials International
Published in the United States of America
by Rowman & Littlefield Education
A Division of Rowman & Littlefield Publishers, Inc.
A wholly owned subsidiary of The Rowman & Littlefield Publishing Group, Inc.
4501 Forbes Boulevard, Suite 200, Lanham, Maryland 20706
www.rowmaneducation.com

Estover Road
Plymouthe PL6 7PY
United Kingdom

British Library Cataloguing in Publication Information Available

Library of Congress Cataloging-in-Publication Data

The educational rights of students : international perspectives on demystifying the legal issues / edited by Charles J. Russo, Douglas J. Stewart, and Jan De Groof.
p. cm.
ISBN-13: 978-1-57886-509-3 (cloth)
ISBN-10: 1-57886-509-3 (cloth)
1. Educational law and legislation. 2. Students—Legal status, laws, etc. I. Russo, Charles J. II. Stewart, Douglas J., 1939- III. De Groof, Jan, 1953-

K3740.E38 2006
344'.0793—dc22 2006015218

∞™ The paper used in this publication meets the minimum requirements of American National Standard for Information Sciences—Permanence of Paper for Printed Library Materials, ANSI/NISO Z39.48-1992.
Manufactured in the United States of America.

To our wives,
Debbie, Christine, and Heather,
with all of our love and affection.
—Charlie, Jan, and Doug

Contents

Foreword

"EDUCATION" AND "LAW": Individually, each of these words encompasses a vast and complex subject. Put together as "education law," the scope and intricacy increase, making it a potentially daunting subject. Yet education law is an increasingly important concern to educators around the world, largely due to the emerging range of citizen rights—and more specifically, student rights—in certain nations.

What rights do students have? How are those rights similar—and different—around the world? And why is the subject of student rights so critical?

The Educational Rights of Students: International Perspectives answers these questions and many more in simple words, not legal terms. Each chapter addresses various student rights and concludes with best practices and strategies currently in use. The fact that contributions to this book come from individuals recognized as leading education law experts in their nations is yet another element that makes this such an outstanding resource.

The subject matter of this book is particularly significant and valuable because it has close parallels to some of Association of School Business Officials (ASBO)'s core organizational values—the essential and enduring principles that guide us as an association—including commitment to the following:

- Meeting the needs and differences of every child, every day
- Absolute integrity and accountability
- Change, innovation, and new ideas

As advances in technology continue to bring us closer together, it's no surprise that there is an increased awareness of obvious similarities in many of the education problems and issues facing international communities as well as a greater public demand to resolve those problems. Consequently, legislatures around the world draw increasingly on the knowledge and experience of other countries to better manage the problems that exist or emerge.

I am confident that your interest will be piqued by the comprehensive examination of student legal rights laid out in the pages that follow. Read them. Share them. By all means, use them for their intended purposes—to increase the breadth and depth of this vital international dialogue, and to ultimately ensure the educational rights of all children.

Melody E. Douglas, RSBO
President, Association of School Business Officials International
Chief Financial Officer, Kenai Peninsula Borough School District, Soldotna, Alaska

Preface

In light of growing interest in the international and comparative educational rights of students, this edited volume, which covers thirteen different nations, provides an overview for interested readers.

Readers are advised that rather than translate notes and other pertinent terms into English, we have ordinarily preserved them in their original languages. We have done this not only because the underlying documents are often unavailable in English but also since translating the names might have created difficulties for native speakers who wish to research the relevant material. In addition, since each of the nations covered in this book uses a different system of legal citation, we have left references in their original form rather than attempt to standardize them under one rubric. Finally, we have preserved minor variations in the different forms of English used throughout the world so that readers can get a flavor of how our seemingly common tongue is used throughout the world.

Of course, no single book can ever hope to cover the myriad of legal topics, or laws of nations, addressing the educational rights of students. Even so, we hope that these well-written and researched chapters, authored by leading scholars in the field, will serve as up-to-date and ready sources of information to help keep educational leaders abreast of the many changes in the ever-growing area of comparative Education Law.

Acknowledgments

As with any book, there are a number of people who must be thanked. Four sets of people were very helpful in helping put this book together. First off, thanks to Tom Koerner at Rowman & Littlefield Education who was most supportive of this project from its inception through its being published. Thanks also to Paul Cacciato and Molly Ahearn at Rowman & Littlefield. Second, it almost goes without saying that we are grateful to the authors for their valuable contributions to this book. Third, at the University of Dayton we would like to thank Charlie's assistant, Ms. Elizabeth Pearn, for her efforts in helping to prepare the manuscript for publication. Last, but certainly not least, we would like to express our deepest appreciation and love for our wives for their ongoing love and support, and without whom none of this work would have been completed.

1

Introduction

Douglas J. Stewart, Charles J. Russo, and Jan De Groof

Advocacy of Children's Rights

DEFINITIONS OF RIGHTS and of childhood are difficult concepts since both are social constructs relevant to particular eras and specific countries. Thus, while certain rights for children may have been recognized as an outcome of the political, social, and industrial reforms of the late nineteenth century in the United Kingdom, similar rights, including the one to an education, were recognized much later in other nations. It is also the case that recognition of the basic rights affecting the total physical and mental welfare of children have only received widespread international acceptance in very recent years. Even so, in many nations, the reality surrounding the need to protect children remains very different from the political rhetoric.

Debate over what rights should be accorded minors has fluctuated in recent decades with considerable development and discussion occurring in the 1980s as various organizations became involved in protecting the interests of children. This was the period during which the phrase "the best interests of the child are paramount" became commonly accepted as, for example, in the United Nations Convention on the Rights of the Child. The 1980s and 1990s also witnessed the establishment in many countries of such bodies as Commissions for Children, which have taken on the task of carrying out research into the rights of children and informing governments as well as their communities about the many issues to do with protection of children's interests and particularly in relation to the physical welfare of the young.

During this period, many advocates of rights for children continued to argue that children should be granted the right to participate in all matters that intimately involve them such as a right to be heard in matters to do with family law, health, or education issues. In this debate, pro-rights advocates have maintained that, at certain stages of childhood, children are equally competent as adults to participate fully in rights that adults take for granted. These rights might include, for example, those of fundamental concern such as political and free speech rights or the right to freely associate with whomsoever they wish, regardless of adult pressures. In brief, these advocates claim for children the same rights that adults enjoy and, as a consequence, the policy of "the best interests of the child" should, they postulate, become one of "the wishes of the child." While such debate appeared to be gathering momentum during the late 1980s, it appears more recently that there has been a return to a consideration and implementation of policies to do with the more basic rights associated with child protection.

While advocacy of children's rights may be thought of as having a long existence, only in relatively recent times has the movement become more sharply focussed in the minds, policies, and practices of nations around the globe. Perhaps as a result of the toll that modern warfare has had on children, a "children first" policy was enunciated in the League of Nations Declaration of 1924. This was followed in 1948 by the United Nations Universal Declaration of Human Rights in which, by the fact that they were not excluded, children were seen to have rights which they, "as all members of the human family," should enjoy.

The United Nations Declaration of the Rights of the Child in 1959 basically recognised that children have "protection rights" but did not generally recognise the right of children to participate actively in matters affecting them. During the International Year of the Child, in 1979, Poland took the lead in encouraging the United Nations to develop a set of principles to do with children's rights that would become binding on member states. The outcome of Poland's efforts was the United Nations Convention on the Rights of the Child, which only two nations, Somalia and the United States, have not yet ratified.

The children's rights movement was further enhanced in 1990 with the Declaration of the World Summit for Children which led to many countries agreeing to introduce programs that are largely concerned with children's protection from poverty, disease/illness, and from exploitation. Subsequently, the United Nations Conference on the Environment and Development (1992) resulted in the Rio de Janeiro Declaration, which included a range of proposals for developing the interests of children that were advanced in the policy document titled Agenda 21. This document recognises that while all nations are facing vast problems arising from globalisation and environmental developments, there is pressing need to implement programs that will provide for children in the future.

Definitions and Categories of Children's Rights

In general, rights may be categorised into welfare and liberty rights or, as more commonly stated in relation to children, protection, and participation rights. The former rights are most frequently accorded children, including those to do with being raised in a safe and caring environment, the provision of food and water, and access to appropriate health and education systems. Participation rights are those to do with the full enjoyment of rights granted adults. Issues surrounding these particular interests have aroused controversy with concerns expressed about the competency of children to engage fully in such rights as well as the extent to which adults might have to forego a right in order for a child to be accorded it. The arguments were effectively summed up in a decision of the United States Supreme Court in 1979 in which it advanced three reasons as to why the constitutional rights of children are not equal to those of adults: children have a unique vulnerability, they are unable to make critical decisions in an informed and mature manner, and the rights of parents to direct the upbringing of their children.[1]

It is also interesting to note that in relation to participation rights, the Supreme Court of the United States, despite holding that the right to equal application applies to children,[2] has accorded more and more authority to school officials as they regulate student behaviour. This reality is similar to positions taken by courts and legislatures in other countries where protection, rather than participation, rights are those most usually recognised and upheld.

The United Nations Convention on the Rights of the Child

The debate over rights as well as the reality experienced in many, if not all, countries, notwithstanding, the United Nations Convention on the Rights of the Child (Convention) makes provision for both protection and participation rights. Further, even though the United States is not a signatory to the Convention, few would argue that American schools do not afford students significant protections that meet virtually all international standards; the major exception is that some American states, like several other countries, permit school officials to employ the practice of corporal punishment on children.

In brief, the Convention contains articles to do with civil, economic, social, and cultural rights of children. The provisions may be seen as relating to rights to do with provision such as food, health, and education as well as protection from abuse and sexual exploitation, and rights to participate in such activities as freedom of expression and association.

The Convention is arguably the most expansive and, therefore, most important international document to achieve international recognition of the rights inhering in children. However, in reality, although the Convention was ratified by the vast majority of the world's nations, few have fully incorporated its provisions into domestic legislation. Indeed, children in many of the member nations suffer from poverty, illness, and exploitation. Other member states failed to ensure that the rights of children are recognised let alone protected their rights to participation. Australia, for instance, along with other nations, has an unacceptable record of infant mortality, illnesses, and education among its indigenous peoples. It also has, what is for many Australians, an immoral and unacceptable policy under which child refugees or children of refugees are incarcerated in what amounts to prison conditions.

The Convention and Schools

Of the Convention's fifty-four Articles, at least thirty may be seen to impact directly on students in schools. While schools do not have to recognise the full range of rights or implement policies in relation to these rights, there will be many that educational institutions are expected to embrace including those dealing with rights to an education, religious freedom, free speech, fair and just discipline/due process, and to the range of rights recognised for children with special needs or those with differing cultural, religious, or ethnic backgrounds.

In this introduction, it is not possible to discuss all of the provisions in the Convention that impact schools or to address the many interesting issues emanating from them. Rather, the provisions contained in the Convention that are related to the themes covered in the ensuing chapters of this book are, albeit briefly, introduced.

Right to an education

The right of all children to an education is clearly set out in Article 28 of the Convention. Yet, since not all member states are immediately capable of carrying out this provision, the Convention includes a principle of progressively moving to achieve this goal starting with a primary education that is free and compulsory. In addition, member states are required to encourage the development of various forms of secondary and higher education that is to be made accessible to all on the basis of capacity.

Freedom of speech

Article 3 provides that in "all actions concerning children . . . the best interests of the child shall be a primary consideration." It is unlikely that this provision can be adequately met unless schools are willing to allow children to speak for themselves on educational and other matters that affect them in school settings. Indeed, Article 12 expresses such a right: "[A] child who is capable of forming his or her own views" has "the right to express those views freely in all matters affecting" them. This principle is carried further in Article 13 which declares, "[T]he child shall have the right to freedom of expression. This right shall include the freedom to seek, receive, and impart information and ideas of all kinds, regardless of frontiers, either orally, in writing, in print, in the form of art, or through any other medium of the child's choice." This provision does, of course, have limitations such as in expressing themselves freely, children do not have a right to injure another person's reputation; this is specifically noted in the Article.

It can be readily seen that since the underlying principle of freedom of expression has the potential to impact severely on school policies and practices, educators must ensure that the rights of students and staff are adequately and appropriately protected. In addition, Article 13 raises issues to do with what constitutes the curriculum and whose interests are being served in traditional processes associated with curriculum construction. Are children, for example, involved in this process?

Religious freedom

To the extent that Article 14 declares that a child has the right "to freedom of thought, conscience, and religion," a key issue for schools is to whether this right is exercised.

Student discipline

Article 28 provides, "States parties shall take all appropriate measures to ensure that school discipline is administered in a manner consistent with the child's human dignity." In this regard, since many countries agree that corporal punishment in schools is inconsistent with a child's human dignity, they have forbidden educators from engaging in the practice. However, as noted above and in the following chapters, since other countries have not done so, there is considerable inconsistency regarding this provision.

Privacy rights

A major issue in contemporary societies is that of the right of every person to privacy. Yet, as is well known, schools gather a considerable volume of information concerning children. In this regard, Article 16 declares, "No child shall be subjected to arbitrary or unlawful interference with his or her privacy." This raises important issues that schools have to consider concerning how, when, and what information is gained as well as from whom it is gained and how it is stored and retrieved and, importantly, to whom the information might be divulged.

Right to a secure and safe learning environment

School violence, including bullying in various forms and sexual abuse, whether by students or staff, is now recognized as a major concern in many countries. In some of the more important provisions of the Convention, Articles 32 through 34 address the physical welfare of children against harms occasioned by economic exploitation, drugs, and "all forms of sexual exploitation and abuse." In a number of member nations, legislation has been introduced to provide enhanced protection to children to guard them against such harm. However, as court decisions in the United Kingdom, the United States, Canada, Australia, and New Zealand—and likely others—indicate, harassment, violence, sexual abuse, and exploitation continue to be a problem in schools. Consequently, there is a need to ensure that policies and practices to prevent the problem are implemented and enforced.

A growing concern in a number of countries is that of cyber bullying. While there is little research as yet into this insidious form of behaviour, schools need to be aware of its existence and to have systems in place to protect students and staff alike.

Children with special needs

Various Articles in the Convention provide for children who have particular physical or emotional needs and/or who come from a minority/ethnic background. Each of the provisions is designed so as to ensure as far as possible the attainment of a "full and decent life" in the community. Article 23 for example is to do with children with physical and or emotional needs and the major objective is to "ensure dignity, promote self-reliance, and facilitate the child's active participation in the community."

Conclusion

In light of this brief discussion on the nature of the rights of children, the editors and chapter authors hope that this book will whet the appetite of readers to work to ensure the safety and well-being of all children since, after all, they are the future of the world.

Notes

1. Bellotti v. Baird, 443U.S. 622, 634 (1979).
2. In re Gault, 387 U.S. 1 (1967).

2

Australia

Douglas J. Stewart

DURING THE PAST DECADE, there has been increasing awareness in Australia, and elsewhere, that all children under the age of eighteen have rights that should be accorded an appropriate level of recognition. Moreover, Australian children and their rights' supporters are more determined than ever before to ensure that their rights are not only recognised but are also protected. Nevertheless, as the then Governor General of Australia noted in 1997, "[W]e still have a considerable distance to travel between the actual and the ideal before there is adequate protection of the best interests of all children in all situations."[1]

There is, then, an interesting paradox in Australia in that while there is an increased acceptance that children have rights, the reality is that in many ways communities continue to pay little more than lip service to this concept. In this regard, only eight years ago a well-known Australian barrister and children's rights' advocate complained that there is "a thoroughly ineffective proliferation of laws, institutions, policies, and practices about children in this country."[2] Recent events in Australia, including the many instances of sexual abuse of minors by adults,[3] and the incarceration of refugee children in detention centres,[4] have resulted in a heightened community consciousness that children remain among the more vulnerable members of our society and have a right to a more adequate protection than many currently enjoy. While it can be argued that it is largely the right to physical protection that has brought about such community concern, it is important to remember, as noted in the introductory chapter, that the rights children have go far beyond that of physical welfare to include provision and participation rights.

Some Background Comments

Legal and Political Systems

The initial legal and political system in Australia, dating back to colonies established in the late eighteenth and early nineteenth centuries, was based on that of England but modified in 1901 when a Federal system of government was introduced. Today there is a Commonwealth government and six states (New South Wales, Victoria, Tasmania, Queensland, South Australia, and Western Australia) and two Territories (Northern Territory and Australian Capital Territory) each, with the exception of Tasmania and Queensland, having bicameral legislatures.

In essence, all Australian jurisdictions reflect the Westminster system of government and legislative powers, as between the Commonwealth and other jurisdictions, are set out in the Constitution of the Commonwealth of Australia Act. Matters not specifically recognised in the Heads of Power given to the Commonwealth or the States and Territories, such as education and health, became the legislative responsibility of the States and Territories. These matters aside, the Commonwealth, mainly through its funding powers, has become increasingly involved in education and particularly so since the late 1950s and more so during the present decade. Gradually, then, the differences created as a consequence of education being a State/Territory responsibility, such as age of entry, management, and curricula, are being removed as a result of Commonwealth as well as State/Territory initiatives.

Common Law

While legislative differences exist between each of the jurisdictions, the common law that was "imported" into Australia with the arrival of European settlers is the same for each jurisdiction. A hierarchy of courts exists in each jurisdiction and while no one jurisdiction is required to adhere to decisions reached in another jurisdiction all lower courts are bound by decisions of the High Court of Australia which was established by the Constitution of the Commonwealth in 1901. The High Court is now the ultimate court of appeal for both public and private matters.

It is generally recognised that in the past there has not been a widespread culture of litigation against educational organisations in Australia particularly in relation to injuries incurred by students in school settings. As a consequence, there has not been an overly large body of case law in relation to such matters as have been determined in other countries, although this is no longer the reality as students and their parents or guardians have increasingly used the courts and tribunals to define student rights and to seek redress across a widening range of matters.

Dual System of Schools

It is important to note that a dual system of schooling has existed in Australia since early colonial days and this is reflected in there being government and non-government (religious and non-religious independent) schools funded by Commonwealth and State and Territory revenues. Nonetheless, it is the Federal government that provides the greatest level of funding but, apart from a High Court appeal heard over two decades ago, *A. G. (Vic) (Ex Rel Black) v. The Commonwealth of Australia*,[5] such funding has not been legally challenged. Moreover, even when debated, it is never a question of whether non-government schools should be funded from public revenues, but rather is one of how much is reasonable.

Human Rights as a Concept in Australia

Human rights, which are perceived as being based on prevailing concepts of morality and justice, encompass civil, political, economic, social, and cultural categories. However, it is commonly argued that only civil and political rights are universal and enforceable. Nonetheless, a right does not have to be legally enforceable in order to be seen as a right since many are enforced or supported by social or cultural custom and pressures. Many such rights do though, over time, become legally binding.

While it is certainly not the case in all countries, Australia is fortunate in that, by and large, civil and political rights are recognised and protected. It will be readily recognised that rights of an economic, cultural, or social nature determine our quality and enjoyment of life and that in all countries achieving these will be goals to constantly strive to improve. They are goals to be achieved rather than goals to be legally enforced although of course some, such as a minimum wage, are so protected. This brief discussion underpins the reality that rights vary according to many circumstances and have to be balanced against each other and the overall welfare of the community at large.

Unlike a number of countries such as the United States or South Africa and, to some extent, New Zealand, Australia does not have a Bill of Rights that would identify and protect the rights that exist. Neither does Australia have a Charter of Rights and Freedoms such as exists in Canada. Indeed, each of the referenda held to determine whether a Bill of Rights should be introduced into Australia have been resoundingly defeated. Nonetheless, Australia has adopted a number of conventions, protocols, and declarations that recognise and provide some measure of protection to the rights we have. Basically, though, these, with the exception of a very limited number of rights recognised in the Constitution of the Commonwealth of Australia, are granted under specific legislation at Commonwealth, State, or Territory levels. The commonly agreed Constitutional rights Australian citizens have include trial by jury, freedom of religion, protection of ethnic and racial minorities, right to vote, freedom from arbitrary arrest, right to work, and the protection of persons with disabilities.

Children and Rights

Arguably, the most well known document that has served to enhance Australians' awareness of the rights inhering in minors is the United Nations Convention on the Rights of the Child (UNCRC) which was ratified by the Commonwealth Government in 1990. Although Australia is a signatory to the Convention's fifty Articles, they have not been directly implemented in domestic legislation by Commonwealth, State, or Territory governments. Even so, indirectly, the influence of the principles underpinning the UNCRC is readily observable in recent statutes, particularly those dealing with child protection. For example, the Child Protection Act 1999 (Qld) contains provisions and language reminiscent of Articles in the Convention and particularly the statement that in administering the Act "the welfare and best interests of a child are paramount."[6] In the UNCRC, this principle is expressed as "In all actions concerning children, whether undertaken by public or private social welfare institutions, courts of law, administrative authorities or legislative bodies, the best interests of the child shall be a primary consideration."[7]

In essence, the Convention emphasises the basic point that all children are entitled to the rights accorded to adult members of the community. Such rights will, of course, be exercised in accordance with a particular child's capacity and are not therefore viewed as being absolute. It is also the case however, that not all Australian children enjoy the range of rights others enjoy. Aboriginal children, children with special needs, homeless children, and children of refugee families provide examples of where Australia has not yet met its obligations under the principles of the Convention, particularly in relation to the provision of health, welfare, and education services.

Right to an Education

In relation to schooling, it is interesting to note that in Australia there is no expressed legal right to an education although various human rights conventions to which Australia is a party such as the 1948 Universal Declaration of Human Rights, the 1966 International Covenant on Economic, Social or Cultural Rights, and the Convention on the Rights of the Child, contain provisions that hold education to be a right of everyone. While there is an increasing incursion by the Commonwealth in educational matters, mainly through the financial arrangements with the states, education, under the Constitution of the Commonwealth of Australia, is a legislative responsibility of each State and Territory.[8] Thus, legislation ensures the provision or otherwise of education; it is therefore up to each jurisdiction to determine the type and extent of education that is offered. As a consequence, there is no one single curriculum and the resources including funding differ from state to state.

Article 28 of the UNCRC recognises that children have a right to a primary education that is compulsory and free as well as requiring member states to provide different forms of secondary education and to make tertiary education available to those with the capacity to undertake it. Parties to the Convention are also required to use every means possible to ensure children attend school.

Compulsory education from age five to fifteen exists in Australia and government policies aimed at encouraging students to stay on at school beyond the compulsory stage or to undertake vocational or university study exist in each State and Territory. Australians have the right to choose whether to send their children to government or non-government schools while an increasing number of children attend independent, religious, and non-religious non-government schools. Moreover, there has also been a trend to provide steady increases in the funding of non-government schools from both Commonwealth and State finances; this has created considerable concern that wealthy independent schools are being maintained at the expense of government schools.[9]

Notwithstanding the provisions of Article 28 of the Convention, no Australian State or Territory government has declared that children have an unfettered right to an education. It may be argued, nonetheless, that as education has become such a central part of our society it might well be considered a customary right. Indeed, since the early years of compulsory education in Australia, litigation, including court hearings to do with compulsory attendance, was relatively commonplace and clearly established the power of government to enforce the requirement. This emphasises the point that education enforced by the state and for state purposes may also be viewed as providing children with a benefit and consequently becomes a right that cannot be denied them. Moreover, the recent emphasis, recognised through such measures as anti-discrimination legislation, on providing children who have special needs with an education equivalent to that of other children, implies that education in contemporary Australia is recognised as a right and not merely a privilege. Further, there is the expectation that these children must be able to access education on a basis similar to children without such needs.

Increasingly decisions reached concerning complaints to do with equal access to educational benefits that have been decided in human rights tribunals and in appeals in courts, clearly indicate there are still great differences between children with and those without special needs. This point is illustrated by a decision reached in a recent case heard in the Federal Court of Australia.[10] Scarlett Finney, who has spina bifida, was denied enrolment at a non-government school on the basis that the school was unable to cater adequately for her. The school maintained that it was unable to accept the costs required to alter buildings, train staff, and cater for Scarlett's personal needs. The Human Rights and Equal Opportunity Commission upheld the complaint from Scarlett that she had been discriminated against by the school's refusal to accept her application for enrolment and this decision was later confirmed on appeal to the Federal Court. The case demonstrates the point that, despite their unwillingness to do so, schools may have to carry some level of hardship in order to meet the requirements of this group of students.

The extent to which schools and teachers must go to provide an equal education is well documented in a case[11] in which a severely physically and intellectually impaired student, "I," was not permitted by the school to attend an excursion which the rest of her class attended. The student's complaint, initiated under the Anti-Discrimination Act (1991) (Qld) that she had been directly discriminated against, was upheld by the tribunal on the grounds that she had been denied access to an educational benefit that other children who did not have her impairment were able to enjoy. It is important to note that the staff at Corinda State High School had gone to considerable trouble in their attempt to facilitate "I"'s inclusion on the excursion but were unable to provide the level of security that they believed was necessary after the company providing the transport declined to take responsibility for her safety and personal comfort.

Not only is the provision of education to all children a responsibility of the government, so too, is the standard of that education. In this regard, Australian teachers are required to be tertiary qualified and registered with the appropriate State or Territory Teachers' Registration Board, or other appropriate statutory body, before they can be employed in the nation's schools. Registration provides a process for checking that applicants are not only morally "fit and proper persons" for the profession but that they are also adequately qualified for the task. Another means of ensuring an appropriate standard of education is through the requirement for teachers to undertake a prescribed number of in service courses on pupil free days throughout the year. These measures all indicate that governments not only accept there is a duty to provide education to children, but that it will be provided at the best possible standards.

Regardless of whether children can be said to have a right to education, the inclusion of children with special needs in regular classrooms, those who in past years might have been educated in special educational settings, imposes considerable responsibility on teachers. Consequently, teachers must have an adequate understanding of each student's needs and the knowledge and pedagogical skills required to meet these needs. This task is made all the more difficult by the wide range of impairments that children with special needs have. This places considerable pressures on teachers when these children are enrolled in regular classroom settings as, by and large, Australian teachers, when undergoing their initial teacher education courses at university, are not provided with the specialist training required to meet all of the needs of children with differing impairments. Nevertheless, teachers are still expected to be able to bring to their classrooms the level of skill needed to provide for every child regardless of whether there is a physical or intellectual, social or cultural difference that makes the task difficult and thus it is largely through experience gained in the classroom that teachers acquire the requisite skills to meet the demands of children with special needs.

Children in Detention Centres

Although the great majority of Australian children do attend school for the compulsory years of education and approximately 80 percent stay longer at school, there are many children who do not. In this regard, an Inquiry into Children in Detention found that up to 1,700 children had been held for varying lengths of time, in some cases for over five years, in Detention Centres in Australia and offshore. This has been a shameful period in Australian history and is summed up by the National Inquiry statement that "Australia's immigration detention laws and practices create a detention system that is fundamentally at odds with the Convention on the Rights of the Child." The Inquiry concluded the "end result is the automatic, indeterminate, arbitrary and effectively unreviewable detention of children. No other country in the world has a policy like this."[12]

In relation to their schooling, it was found that children in Detention Centres suffered from a lack of educational infrastructure, that there are insufficient hours devoted to schooling and assessment of learning, there is a lack of an appropriate/adequate curriculum, and that children suffered as a result of both a shortage of as well as a very high turnover of qualified teachers. This situation has been ameliorated to some extent since 2002 by children in the Detention Centres being permitted to attend local community schools where these exist. Even so, it should be noted that at the time of writing the pressure placed on the Federal government against detaining women and children in these centres has resulted in a change of policy that will release them into local communities.

Right to Freedom of Expression

Article 13 of the UNCRC states that subject to certain restrictions, including respect for others' rights and protection of national security or public order, every child has the right to freedom of expression. Such rights are generally seen as encompassing the right to freely express ideas and this covers oral and written expression as well as symbolic expression including matters to do with dress, hairstyle, and adornments. Importantly, Article 13 includes the right to seek and impart information and ideas of all kinds in any medium of the child's choice. This provision is strengthened further by Article 17 which obliges member states to ensure that students have access to information by way of the mass media.

Matters to do with freedom of expression that are frequently litigated in the United States are generally not issues in Australian schools. This is largely the result of there being, by and large, a culture of acceptance among students and their parents of school policies and practices that reflect consideration for students. In general terms, Australian teachers have had the support of students, parents, and the community when it comes to determining what constitutes a proper curriculum. They have not had the problem of litigation in determining a student's right to self-expression such as has occurred in the United States where views contrary to those of the teacher or the schools' policies have frequently been contested.

In one of the few cases to do with the right to freedom of expression to come before an Australian tribunal,[13] a student's complaint of discrimination against the school on the grounds that he had been unjustly suspended for his refusal to conform to the school's policy regarding length of hair, was upheld. This action was taken under provisions of the anti-discrimination legislation extant in Victoria at that time. Although the regulated powers of schools in that State to do with conforming behaviour have been strengthened since Cope, the case illustrates the point that in the management of students, statutory provisions to do with students' rights must be adhered to. It further illustrates the point that school rules need to give recognition to a student's right to freely express him or herself when this does not result in any disruption to school routines or policies.

Under the various Education Acts, Australian schools have the power to require students to wear uniforms and to maintain a reasonable standard of dress. Although students may consider this irksome, there has been no major difficulty in compliance and infractions are generally punished by detentions or, on rare occasions, suspension. Such disciplinary measures have not been contested in Australian tribunals. Moreover, teachers are usually very careful in their management of those students who are unable to comply with uniform regulations as they are only too aware of the "costs" this involves to some families. However, again, school policies and practices must reflect carefully considered responses to students who consistently break school uniform, or other, rules. Teachers have the authority and responsibility to insist on students being dressed according to approved school requirements and these can quite legitimately include restrictions on what is considered unacceptable both in terms of safety, such as footwear appropriate to school workshops or sporting activities, and in terms of being non-offensive.

The right of students to be able to express themselves freely is one that needs careful consideration by classroom teachers and school administrators alike. While unbridled expression is not acceptable, responsible written, oral, or symbolic expression must be sympathetically considered. This point can be illustrated by an incident that occurred in a government high school in which a student sought approval from the school's principal to be given the opportunity, at morning assembly, to call a meeting of fellow students in order to arrange a protest demonstration against French nuclear testing on the Pacific island of Muroroa.

The principal did not allow the student to call the meeting on the grounds that the school assembly was not for this purpose and argued it was against the interests of the school. Although this incident was resolved at school level and did not attract legal contestation, it may be compared with *Tinker v. Des Moines Independent Community School District* in which the United States Supreme Court held that the school board policy of attempting to prohibit students' protesting against the war in Vietnam was against the student's right to freedom of expression and declared "it can hardly be argued that either students or teachers shed their rights to freedom of speech or expression at the schoolhouse gate."[14]

In terms that are equally applicable to Australian schools, the United States Supreme Court went on to add that there had to be more than a desire to avoid the discomfort and unpleasantness that always accompany an unpopular viewpoint and concluded there was no evidence that the behaviour of the student would materially and substantially interfere with the requirements of appropriate discipline in the operation of the school. This statement lies at the heart of what should constitute an appropriate policy in relation to children's rights in an Australian school setting; school policies and practices need to reflect genuine operational and disciplinary requirements that are implemented in the interests of students as well as staff and the orderly running of the school rather than requiring conforming behaviour for other purposes.

Although Australian students appear to be reasonably receptive to the way they are managed and treated, any failure to ensure that fair procedures are followed in disciplinary dealings with them has the potential to cause considerable legal difficulty. Such might be the case, for example, when a student is excluded from school as the result of a breach of discipline but has not been given a fair hearing and his or her side of the case is not heard, or heard adequately. Incidents such as this have the potential to result in protracted legal argument and this can be stressful to staff, students, and others. One of the complaints in *Purvis v. New South Wales*[15] which went through a long appeal process to the High Court of Australia was that the complainant student had not been treated fairly when he was suspended and eventually expelled from his school for repeated assaults on other students and school staff. While he eventually lost his case, the point is well made that in any dealing with students, due process practices must be meticulously adhered to if complaints of rights violations against students are to be avoided.

In relation to freedom of expression and the right expressed in Article 13 of the UNCRC to "seek, receive and impart information of all kinds," considerable concern in an age of fast developing technologies is the requirement to protect students' access to information through emails, websites, or the Internet and, yet, at the same time to prevent exposure to harmful materials. Importantly, schools must ensure students are protected from being identified and accessed by paedophiles through use of school-based computer programs involving the Internet. There is a conundrum here in that students, while being assured of access to a range of information, have also to be protected from aspects of the media they use in order to access that information. It can also be argued that schools are in a difficult situation in that students might be able to claim that the methods used to ensure their protection from undesirable aspects of online materials might unwittingly introduce forms of censorship that work against the principles advanced in the Convention.

Schools also need to be very mindful of the pitfalls associated with student use of online and email facilities. In one incident that attracted considerable public attention, allegations of sexual impropriety against two members of staff, including the deputy principal, were posted on a website by students. The staff members who were involved in the matter were totally innocent of the allegations but the incident caused them great stress and involved considerable outlays of time and expense in the subsequent investigations by the education authorities and the police. Despite the potential for litigation against the students and/or their parents, no legal action was taken. In this regard, it should be noted that there is generally a reluctance by school staff to take legal actions against students. Indeed, the vast majority of problems tend to be resolved within the school where punishments would include suspension and expulsion, as was the case in this incident.

Cyber bullying by students is becoming an area of considerable research interest in Australia. To date, there is a paucity of information on the forms that cyber bullyings take as well as their consequences. There is evidence, though, that students are using email and other electronic technologies in novel ways to bully other students or staff. In the absence of adequate research data, the harm caused by cyber bullying is not readily identifiable. Nonetheless, it might be realistically expected that, by its very clandestine and insidious nature, the consequences of cyber bullying are likely to be equal to traditional forms of bullying. Indeed, in some ways the outcomes have the potential to be more harmful. As Australian schools are aware of the need to ensure a hostility free learning environment, they are increasingly seeking ways to minimise incidents of cyber bullying and to provide counselling services to those traumatised by it. As with other forms of hostility, schools need to have systems in place that will inhibit if not prevent such behaviour. It is also necessary to ensure that these systems are enforced and reviewed frequently.

In addition, many schools include in their policy and practice documents statements indicating that penalties will be applied to any student who misuses a home computer to ridicule or threaten persons associated with the school. In this regard, students are increasingly advised that certain computer practices not only breach school regulations but, additionally, have the potential to involve them with the law. This would be the case, for example, where students threaten others, where they defame others, or where they breach copyright.

In essence, then, in relation to freedom of expression and use of computers and Internet facilities, it is important that schools have systems in place that will protect students from infringing a wide range of laws including those to do with broadcasting and communications law, consumer, trade practice, and copyright legislation, as well as the common law duty of care associated with accessing distasteful or objectionable matter and defamation.

Right to a Safe Learning Environment

Article 19 of the UNCRC states that every student has the right to expect, and receive, their education in a safe and accommodating learning environment. It has been noted that there is a culture in Australia that largely eschews litigation as a consequence of harms suffered in school settings. Nonetheless, over the past two decades or so, litigation related to physical injury incurred by students in school settings has increased noticeably. In many instances, since schools have been held liable for these injuries,[16] they are required to expend much time and energy ensuring systems are in place to achieve the highest possible level of physical security for their students.

Cases brought under the law of torts by students injured in school accidents illustrate that generally courts decided in favour of plaintiff students. This might be about to change with a recent four-to-one decision of the High Court of Australia [17] which held a school authority not liable for the injuries incurred by an eight-year-old student. This case has very important repercussions for all Australian schools as it helps define the level of care needed for protecting the physical welfare of students while they are on school grounds. Importantly, the majority opinion stated:

> Nor is it reasonable to have a system in which children are observed during particular activities for every single moment of time—it is damaging to teacher-pupil relationships by removing every element of trust; it is likely to retard the development of responsibility in children, and it is likely to call for a great increase in the number of supervising teachers and in the costs of providing them.[18]

Right to a Hostility-Free Learning Environment

A major aspect of providing for the physical welfare of school students is to do with ensuring their safety in relation to bullying and harassment. In this regard, every school is required to have systems in place to ensure as far as is possible that such practices are discouraged and hopefully prevented. In a ruling of the County Court in Victoria,[19] handed down on 20 June 2003, the plaintiff's claim for damages against teachers and the principal of the school she had attended was successful. Insufficient action had been taken to ensure the student's protection from constant verbal and physical bullying including death threats and intimidation carried out against her by a number of other female students. The court held that the plaintiff was owed a duty of care and that this had been breached by the lack of appropriate action on the part of two teachers and the school principal and as a consequence the student suffered serious psychological harm.

Sexual abuse of students by other students and staff occur in school settings and, as with bullying, a school must have a risk management plan in place to combat this problem. In one case,[20] considerable emphasis was given by the Court for the need for appropriate preventive risk management systems to be in place and the need for these to be adequately policed and enforced. This case resulted in the female plaintiff, who had been sexually abused by a master at the school's boarding residence, receiving considerable damages including a large sum paid as exemplary damages which were awarded as a measure of the displeasure of the court at the callous behaviour exhibited toward the former student by the school maintained by the defendant Synod. In order to avoid the court's disapprobation as well as to prevent stress and anxiety to students all staff have a responsibility to ensure the practices set out in school policies in relation to sexual and other forms of abuse are completely adhered to.

All Australian jurisdictions have some form of mandatory reporting of suspected incidents of child abuse and most of the statutes require reporting by teachers of suspected abuse of students off as well as on school grounds. It has been argued that legislation in the state of Queensland is rendered less effective by mandated reporting of suspected incidents of child abuse being required only in incidents occurring on school grounds.[21]

Searches of Students

To a very large extent, students in Australian schools have not given cause for searches of their person or property other than for the occasional allegation of missing money or belongings. When these events occur, students have been required to empty their pockets, school bags, or lockers. However, on occasion, teachers have gone further and required students to strip and in a few, fortunately, very rare, exceptional incidents, there have been body cavity searches. These searches constitute assault and have the very real potential for a teacher to be involved in criminal and or common law proceedings. In Australia, police and customs officers are the only persons with the power to conduct these and then only within clearly defined situations.

Although relatively rare, searches for drugs are becoming increasingly necessary in schools but are only carried out where there is a reasonable suspicion that students have drugs, or other unlawful objects such as knives or guns, in their possession or concealed in school bags or lockers. In such instances, the appropriate procedure is for the school principal to request a police officer to carry out the search although, when this is done at school, every attempt must be made to have a parent present. Where this is not possible, the principal needs to be present so as to ensure that the rights of the student(s) are not violated. Similar procedures are required where police initiate a request to carry out a search of a student on school premises. It is not a practice in Australia for random drug searching of students or their property to be carried out. Yet, in view of the increased incidence of drugs being found in schools it might be expected that such searches could eventually be accepted in Australia. In this context, it is more than a little depressing to learn that primary school children are being targeted by drug pushers and consequently teachers and school administrators are required to be very alert to signs of this in their school.

Right to Fair and Reasonable Punishment

It has long been recognised in both common and statute law that in order to maintain the orderly working life of the school some form of discipline is required and in the past this has included physical punishment. With few exceptions, statutes across Australia now prohibit corporal punishment and, in the few instances where it is still permitted such as some independent schools not covered by the legislation, school regulations and practices must provide appropriate safeguards to ensure punishment is not excessive. Nonetheless, many would argue that any physical form of punishment of students is undignified and not in keeping with Article 28 of the Convention on the Rights of the Child which requires "school discipline to be consistent with the rights of the child and reflect the child's human dignity."

The most common form of punishment is, of course, verbal but even here students need to be protected from language abuse such as slurs or innuendo about their abilities, background, or personal characteristics. Claims of defamation can so easily arise, although this usually occurs when there is a written comment (libel) about which a student takes umbrage such as might be on an end of year report card or a letter sent home to parents about a student's behaviour. Derogatory words spoken about a student in a staff room, or other place, which a third party overhears, may also be defamatory (slander) and must be guarded against. It is interesting to note here, that courts in the United States have held verbal chastisement of students by teachers is acceptable provided "disparaging remarks are not malicious or wanton" and the teacher's behaviour "is not shocking to the conscience."

Above all, teachers are increasingly being made aware that, in order to prevent claims of failing to follow equitable processes, each student's statement concerning a particular matter or incident, has to be heard. Due process is often forgotten in the heat of the moment but failure to follow the proper procedures has the potential of a student taking legal action against teachers and school administrators. Preventive management policies and practices are the most appropriate means of handling disciplinary problems, and avoidance of measures that are not well considered is in everyone's best interests.

It was pointed out at the commencement of this chapter that children, arguably, have a right to an education and any interference with this will be most closely examined. In this context, it is important to use the authority granted to principals to exclude a student, even for short periods of time, sparingly. Similarly, taking away a student's privileges, such as attending an excursion, or removing the privilege of participating in out-of-classroom activities including cultural and sporting events, should always be considered very carefully.

Right to Privacy

Articles in most of the human rights documents provide for individual rights to privacy. In the UNCRC Article 16 provides protection against "interference with his or her privacy." In Australia, this right is strengthened by Commonwealth and State legislation. In the case of the Commonwealth, the Privacy Amendment [Private Sector] Act 2000 requires private organisations, including non-government schools, to develop codes of practice that will ensure standards associated with the collection, security, storage, use, access, correction, and disclosure of personal information are met.

In relation to government organisations such as state schools, the various state and territory governments have also introduced or amended legislation so as to ensure rights of individuals including children are protected. In Queensland, for example, the state government in 2001 introduced a set of Standards replicating the federal legislation which requires schools to develop privacy policies and practices which are to be reviewed and updated annually. Essentially, the Standards mean that only essential information, that which is needed for lawful purposes, is collected and that it is then stored and retrieved and used in accordance with requirements set out in the regulations.

The various statutes do not differentiate between adults and minors and thus the rights of a student to privacy are recognised and protected. In order to prevent an individual student's right to privacy schools must however determine at what point a student is competent to be able to be requested to provide information. As with other areas of legal management, this necessitates schools establishing and following accepted policies and practices adequate to protect students from invasion of their privacy rights. This obviously includes ensuring that only essential information about a student is gathered. It then becomes incumbent on the school to ensure that any information such as medical records is securely stored and accessible on a very restricted basis.

In this regard, protection against computer stored information files has to be provided. Some information may need to be divulged to staff, for example health details needed when a student is taken on a weekend excursion or some details that might affect a student's classroom learning such as a behaviour problem. The necessity of establishing and enforcing privacy regulations in the school cannot be overemphasised as not only is it a breach of the UNCRC to fail to respect a student's privacy rights, it is also a breach of Commonwealth and State legislation.

Conclusion

Australian students have not, as this chapter has shown, legally contested, nor generally questioned, rights that are associated with such matters as freedom of speech, or privacy or religious freedom that have been issues in the United States. Moreover, rights accorded Australian students are largely those protected by legislation. While it might be the case that governments would be most averse to deny a right, such as that to an education, they do have the power through legislative means to do just that as is illustrated by denying immigrant children in detention access to facilities and resources that other students have.

As a signatory to the United Nations Convention on the Rights of the Child, Australia has to a large extent met its international obligations. There are, though, areas where problems remain to be solved including education for all indigenous children who, despite considerable effort on the part of various governments, do not access education to the same level or extent as non-indigenous children.

Given the compliant and generally non-litigious nature of Australians, debate on issues to do with extending the recognition of rights students might be accorded will be slow in developing. As noted elsewhere in this chapter, it is largely the provision and protection of rights for children that have been recognised in Australia and any move to accord students the right to participate in decisions relating to their well-being will likely be denied them for years to come.

Notes

1. Sir William Deane, Opening Address to the First Asia Pacific Conference on Children's Rights, Brisbane, Australia, April 1997.
2. Moira Rayner, Barrister. "Students Rights" Address to the Australia and New Zealand Education Law Association Annual Conference, Brisbane, 1996.
3. See Douglas J. Stewart & Andrew E. Knott "Australia" in C. Russo Ed. *The Yearbook of Education Law* 2002, Education Law Association: Dayton, Ohio.
4. "A Last Resort? The Report of the National Inquiry into Children in Immigration Detention," May 2004.
5. (1981) 55 ALJR 155.
6. Child Protection Act, 1999 (Queensland). S5(b).
7. United Nations Convention on the Rights of the Child, Article 3 (1).
8. As education was not an enumerated area of legislated concern it became, under s 107 of The Constitution of the Commonwealth of Australia, a State Responsibility.
9. See Douglas J. Stewart & Charles J. Russo "A Comparative Analysis of Funding Non-government Schools in Australia and the United States," *Education and the Law*, Vol 13 No 1, 2001.
10. Finney v. The Hills Grammar School (1999) Human Rights and Equal Opportunity Commission; Hills Grammar Sch. v. Human Rights and Equal Opportunity Commissioner & Others. (2000, Federal Court of Australia).
11. "I" v. O'Rourke and Corinda High Sch. and Minister for Educ. of Queensland (Queensland Anti-Discrimination Tribunal, 31 January 2001).
12. "A Last Resort? The Report of the National Inquiry into Children in Immigration Detention," May 2004.

13. Cope v. Girton School Ltd (1995) EOC 92-68) The Equal Opportunity Board Victoria.

14. 393 U.S. 503, 506 (1969).

15. Purvis v. New South Wales (Department of Education and Training) [2003] HCA 62, 11 November 2003.

16. See "Australia" in Charles J. Russo, Ed. *Yearbook of Education Law,* Dayton, OH: Education Law Association, 1999, 393–407.

17. Trustees of the Roman Catholic Church for the Diocese of Canberra and Goulburn (as St Anthony's Primary School) v. Hadba [2005] HCA 31, 15 June 2005.

18. Ibid., s 25.

19. Lisa Eskinazi v. State of Victoria No 06471 of 1999.

20. S v. The Corporation of the Synod of the Diocese of Brisbane, Supreme Court, Queensland No 72 of 2000.

21. See Matthews, B. & Walsh, K. "Issues in Mandatory Reporting of Child Abuse by Australian Teachers" *ANZJLE* Vol 9 (2) 2004, 3–17.

3

Belgium: The Legal Rights of Students in the Flemish Community

Jan De Groof

The World Conference on the Right to and the Rights in Education, organized from twenty-five to thirty November 2004 in Amsterdam, appealed to international organizations, multinational and regional organizations, UNESCO, and the Office of the High Commissioner for Human Rights to give greater importance to promoting the right to education, a right that is indispensable for the exercise of all other human rights. The right to education and human rights education are two distinct, though interrelated, dimensions of the right to education as provided for in the Universal Declaration of Human Rights. The World Conference invited states to make measures with a view to incorporating their international legal obligations into the domestic legal order while undertaking studies and research aimed at promoting the realization of the right to education. This promotion of the right to and rights in education requires urgent action at supra-national, international, regional, and national levels.

The Director-General of UNESCO stated on the occasion of Human Rights Day on December 10, 2003, that the right to education is fundamental for achieving human rights in general and that the realization of human rights for all is a common purpose which unites people from different continents, religions, and cultures. The relevance of the Universal Declaration of Human Rights is undimmed by the passage of time since people are generally much more aware of their rights and of the ways in which they can assert and protect them. The Director also spoke of the need to raise awareness on human rights as a key to their attainment. This is why the right to education is so fundamental for human rights in general. This is why knowledge and awareness are a condition of empowerment. Only persons who are aware that they have rights can better strive for those rights. As such, all children should have access to education since the right to education is a fundamental human right. As an empowerment right, education is the primary vehicle by which economically and socially marginalized adults and children can lift themselves out of poverty, and obtain the means to participate fully in their communities. No civil, political, economic, and/or social rights can be exercised by individuals unless they have received a certain minimum education.

Educational rights remain a core target of policies, even with more pressure after the constitutional reforms. Since the constitutional revision of 1988,[1] schooling has partly been the responsibility of the linguistically-defined but also territorial Communities.[2] The division of educational matters and the transfer of competence for education to the Communities were stimulated to a great extent by the fact that the two ministers of national education had restricted competence: one for the Dutch speaking schools, the other for the French speaking schools. Each educational policy was heavily mortgaged by an incoherent and inadequate distribution of authority.

The transfer of competence to the Communities and their consequent regulation in educational matters reflected that the required legal framework had been established. Some of the competencies in education remain at the national level. These competencies are meant to guarantee a common system with respect to the definition of the start and end of compulsory education and the retirement scheme, and the recognition of degrees, in particular the minimal conditions for the awarding of degrees.[3]

Article 24 of the Constitution contains obligatory neutrality of state education, freedom of choice for parents, free education during compulsory school time, the right to choose between religious or non-religious education, equality between all students, parents, teachers, schools with reservation of certain objectives, and the legality principle. Except for the principle of freedom of education, which was taken up in article 24 in its previous draft, the right to education is now also a right guaranteed by the Constitution: freedom of education as an individual right however is void if the authorities do not realise at the same time that Belgian legislation transformed the right to education from formal law into material law.[4]

All of these principles are, as a matter of fact, enforceable, not only before an ordinary court (these courts can refuse to apply the decrees and regulations that are in conflict with article 24, and the Council of State can annul these decrees and regulations) but also before the Court that can henceforth examine all decrees or laws for compatibility with articles 10, 11, and 24 of the Constitution. If the occasion presents itself, the Court may annul these decrees or laws. This modification was a *conditio sine qua non* for the transfer of competence in educational matters to the Communities in order to grant the ideological minorities true guarantees which before they drew from the School Pact.[5]

In the Flemish community, the right to education and particularly the right to basic education[6] are fully achieved. The right to education for everyone and the commitment of the government is reflected and implemented in legislation against which citizens have legal recourse.

On 20 November 1989, the General Meeting of the United Nations adopted the International Treaty Concerning the Rights of the Child. Belgium did underwrite this treaty by the law of 25 November 1991 and the decree of 15 May 1991, which means that it becomes a legally binding instrument, from which obligations result for the Belgian and Flemish governments. The International Treaty Concerning the Rights of the Child is sometimes classified on the basis of the three P's: Protection, Provision, and Participation. Rights on protection (right to education, on social security, health care, nursery) must protect citizens against unlawful actions of the government. This includes particular provisions with regard to specific vulnerabilities such as protection of minor political refugees, the rights of minor handicapped persons, etc.

The International Treaty Concerning the Rights of the Child also includes rights to participation. These rights are more than just the legal protection of minors as actors in social living.[7] Under this Treaty, a minor is entitled to active participation in the social environment. Articles 28 and 29 of the Treaty stipulate the rights to and the objectives of education. Besides these two articles, the general articles of the Treaty are also very important. Articles 12 and 13 define the participation rights of minors. They have the right to take part in social living, which means they do have the right to express their own opinions and this implies that these opinions are taken into account, and that minors do have access to information.

A democratic society is based on participation. To the extent that schools are a reflection of the larger democracy, they must be democratically organised with the participation and involvement of all citizens. Compliance with the values recognised in art. 29 clearly requires schools to be child-friendly in the fullest sense of the term and to be consistent in all respects with the dignity of the child. "The participation of children in school life, the creation of school communities and student councils, peer education and peer counselling, and the involvement of children in school disciplinary proceedings should be promoted as part of the progress of learning and experiencing the realization of rights."[8] We once referred to the education institutions as "a school for ethics" and at the same time stressed upon the "ethics of a school."[9]

Right to Education and Freedom of Choice

The most important fundamental rights of students in Belgium are listed in art. 24 of the Constitutional Law. Article 24 of the revised Constitution (formerly article 17) is the legal basis of educational freedom and justice in Belgium and reads as follows:

(1.1) Education is free; any preventative measure is forbidden; the repression of offenses is only governed law or decree.
(1.2) The Community offers free choice to parents.
(1.3) The Community organizes neutral education. Neutrality implies notably the respect of the philosophical, ideological, or religious conceptions of parents and pupils.
(1.4) The schools organized by the public authorities offer, until the end of mandatory schooling, the choice between the teaching of one of the recognized religions and non-denominational moral teaching.
(2) If a Community, in its capacity as an organizing authority, wishes to delegate competency to one or several autonomous bodies, it can only do so by decree adopted by a two-third majority vote.
(3.1) Everyone has the right to education with the respect of fundamental rights and freedoms. Access to education is free until the end of mandatory schooling.
(3.2) All pupils of school age have the right to moral or religious education at the Community's expense.
(4) All pupils or students, parents, teaching staff, or institutions are equal before the law or decree. The law and decree take into account objective differences, notably the characteristics of each organizing authority, that justify appropriate treatment.
(5) The organization, the recognition, and the subsidizing of education by the Community are regulated by law or decree.

The freedom of education secured by art. 24 §1 of the Constitutional Law does not merely guarantee the right to set up schools, and therefore to choose between them, based on different denominational or non-denominational ideologies.[10] In addition, it guarantees the right to set up schools which define their identity by means of one or the other given teaching concepts of educational trends.[11]

These non-state ("free") schools should meet quality standards set by public authorities. In order to ensure that school choice may be exercised without limitation based on socio-economic status, approved non-public schools receive public funding at quasi parity with the schools operated by community, provincial, and municipal governments.[12] Article 24 §3 of the Constitutional Law stipulates that everyone has a right to education, without prejudice to one's fundamental rights and liberties. Access to education is free of charge until the end of compulsory schooling, tuition fees in all types of primary and secondary education are impossible. This provision implies that exclusively the access to education must be free of charge such that access to education cannot be restricted in any way, whether by direct or indirect school fees, or by imposing similar financial conditions. However, this provision does not exclude that a contribution could be requested for educational material or specific activities, provided that such expenses would not exceed the cost of necessary, supplied goods.[13]

All students of school age have a right to moral and/or religious education at the expense of the community. Parents who register their child in official schools for primary or secondary education have to declare by means of a written and signed declaration whether the child will be informed with denominational or non-denominational ideologies. This must be a free choice. If parents object to this on the basis of religious or moral convictions, schools must inform them about their rights and duties, for instance the possibility to obtain exemptions. All students have the right to fulfil school tasks that fit their own particular philosophies. Government education has to be neutral: this means that the religious, philosophical, or ideological conviction of parents and students must be respected. Subsidised official education has not the uniform mutual characteristic as the (national) community schools but is moving to a pluralistic type of education.[14]

Subsidized non-governmental education includes denominational, non-denominational private education, and independent schools that apply specific instructional methods. Only official schools have a duty to offer optional instruction in the officially recognised faiths and philosophies of life and to respect the beliefs of every family with children in the school.

The principle of equal treatment for all Belgians and the ban on discrimination are stipulated in art. 10 and 11 of the Constitution specified with respect to education in art. 24 § 4.[15] The constitutional jurisprudence refined this principle in numerous judgments. The School Pact (SP) of 1959 states that "the right of parents to choose the education given to their children implies the possibility of having available, at a reasonable distance, a school corresponding to their choice" (SP art. 4, 1). Since parents have unequal ability to pay for schooling, this requires that public funds be provided to cover the costs.

With regard to freedom of choice, the Community is even compelled on request of the parents of sixteen pupils who do not find a public or a "free" confessional school within a range of four kilometres, either to subsidize "free" or public education, or else to participate in the transportation expense to such a school.[16] The Constitution guarantees that every educational institution will be treated on an equal basis. All receive money from the Community in relation to the number of pupils or students. Unequal treatment is only allowed when objective differences exist.

An "adapted" treatment, as the Constitution is currently understood, authorizes study grants (if necessary, loans) for financially weaker families; favourable standards for schools in rural areas (and for that reason with fewer students), facilities for handicapped students, and immigrant children; and a difference of financial treatment according to the level, the form of education, the geographical situation, and the distance between schools of the same network. In all of these cases, there is an objective reason that fully justifies different funding by the authorities.

Law Concerning Compulsory Education

In Belgium, compulsory education begins in the school year when children turn age six and lasts until they become eighteen years of age. All children who reside in Belgium are subject to compulsory education. This counts also for illegal minorities.[17]

From the age of fifteen, children can also attend part-time education or vocational training, and work part-time. Teachers and parents however must try to motivate students to obtain a diploma of secondary education and not quit school when they turn eighteen. An exemption from compulsory schooling for other reasons such as marriage or motherhood is not allowed. Children who suffer serious disabilities can in some cases be exempted from compulsory education.

The law of 29 June 1983 concerning compulsory education stipulates that the persons who exercise the parental authority are obliged to ensure that children are registered in a school and attend classes at a regular basis or that they are educated on a legal basis. Compulsory education doesn't mean compulsory schooling is necessary. Home teaching is allowed in Belgium and can be organised by the parents or in unsubsidized private schools. Home teaching means parents (or tutors) organise the education themselves and pay for it but it has to meet certain requirements in order to comply with those of compulsory education. The Flemish government stipulates the formal conditions which must be fulfilled at organising home tuition.

On the one hand, the development of the individuality and the skills of the youngster are core targets, on the other hand education has to prepare children for an active life as an adult. Respect for the fundamental human rights and for the cultural values of the youngster himself and of others must be promoted. Other substantive conditions are not imposed. The inspectorate checks whether the supplied home tuition meets the objectives and examines whether the development targets are being achieved. Parents must accept this external quality control.

If parents do not accept the education of their children as being controlled or if the inspectorate notices at two successive controls that home-schooling does not meet the objectives, parents are obliged to enrol their children in primary or secondary schools funded or subsidised by the government. Some private schools in Flanders are not recognised by the government and neither is their certificate of education. Students have to obtain certificates that are equivalent to the ones obtained in mainstream education, for instance by passing examinations for the examining board of the Flemish Community. It is forbidden to give students a job outside the framework of compulsory education. Under certain conditions, students can exercise a certain temporary activity when they are below the age of fifteen, for example, in the artistic world.

Right to Participation

On 2 April 2004, the Flemish government ratified the decree applying to participation on school. This decree regulates several aspects of participation in basic and secondary education and contains the regulation concerning the pedagogical and school councils, councils of students and parents, and the co-administration of college and conciliation procedures. Staff members, parents, and students in basic, primary, and secondary schools can ask for the establishment of an educational (pedagogical council), a students', or parents' council. From 1 September 2004, these councils must be set up if a sufficient number of persons is asking for them. Representatives of the educational council, the students' council, and the parents' council are a member of the school council. In this way, they participate in school policy.

There are some conditions for the establishment of these councils. If at least 10 percent of the staff members ask for it, an educational council is obligatory, if at least 10 percent of the parents ask for it, a parent council is obligatory. Regulations in primary and secondary education differ. In primary education, a student council has to be established if at least 10 percent of the regular students ask for it. These students are eleven to thirteen years of age. A student council is always obligatory in secondary education. If the involvement of students is guaranteed in another way and if less than 10 percent of the regular students ask for a student council, a derogation is allowed.

Locally, participation of all educational actors in community education is organised by the school council which has a general right to information and a well-defined scope of competence regarding advice and consultation. The school council comprises three members directly elected by the parents, two members co-opted from the local, social, economic, and cultural sectors, and three members who are directly elected by and among the staff.[18] The head teacher attends the meetings of the school council and has an advisory vote.

Participation and consultation in subsidised education is also set up via the school council. This council is composed of an equal number (between three and five representatives) of parental representatives , subsidised staff members of the schools concerned, representatives of the local community co-opted by the above mentioned groups, and students (in secondary education). It is also possible to delegate representatives of the educational council or students or parents' council to the school council. It can be stated in conclusion that the school council provides a forum for consultation between all the participants in school life.

The rights on information, recommendation, and consultation, guaranteed in the participation decree, do not affect the freedom of education; the rights on participation must be asserted taking into account the pedagogical project. The school governing board always takes the final decisions and assumes all responsibility.

Special Education for Students with Disabilities

Special primary education[19] is the education which, based on an educational project, provides teaching, care, and therapy for children whose overall personality development can be ensured either insufficiently or not at all by normal education, whether permanently or temporarily. For these purposes, special basic education is divided up in eight different types,[20] depending on whether the child is physically or mentally disabled, has emotional problems, suffers from learning disabilities, or stays in a hospital or in a sanitarium. Prior to a child's admission to special primary education, a report is drawn from which one can determine what type is most appropriate for the child.[21]

In integrated basic education, implying a form of co-operation between normal and special education with the purpose of integrating a student from the special education in the normal education system—an integration plan must be written up as well. Children must be able to attend a school that meets their needs and get the appropriate education. This special approach provides the disabled children education that develops their physical and intellectual abilities, encourages their social adjustment, prepares them for family life, and trains them to exercise a job in accordance with their handicap.

Temporary or permanent integration of disabled students in the regular education system can be organised (art. 4) to encourage their social adaptation. In order to guarantee the free enrolment of students the number of schools for special education set up or subsidised by the government must be sufficient and geographically spread. Disabled students can only be excluded from enrolment if the school governing board can show that the school cannot offer the approach and facilities for their specific needs to education, therapy, and care.

Equal Educational Opportunities

Article 24, § 1, first paragraph of the Constitution, guarantees the freedom of education, not only the active aspect such as the organisation of education, but also the passive aspect, namely the freedom of choice which entails that parents or students can choose the education that best fits their philosophy of life. At the same time, this second freedom does not mean that parents and students must have an unconditional right to registration in the school of their choice.[22]

In free education, a school board can deny admission provided that the grounds are not based on improper criteria by which human dignity could be at risk.[23] Parents must be informed of the refusal to admit their child in writing within four calendar days with the reasons given. In the event of a legal challenge, a judge decides on the basis of the concrete circumstances whether or not the refusal was justified. It is generally acknowledged that only serious grounds which are directly related to the pedagogical or denominational project of the school are acceptable. The refusal of students by "free" schools on the ground of their sex has been a controversial issue. Jurisprudence and the legal doctrine are divided on that issue.[24]

The principle of equal treatment and the ban on discrimination were as already mentioned stipulated in art. 10 and 11 of the Constitution[25] and should be respected by the schools. The Court of Arbitration declared that schools could treat certain categories of people differently, provided that there be an objective and sensible justification for the criterion of differentiation. The principle of equality is violated if it can be established that the means used do not reasonably tally with the aim pursued.[26] Non-public schools in a number of cities have entered, more or less willingly, into agreements designed to distribute minority children (children of large minority populations, especially from North Africa) more evenly. This involves accepting and even recruiting pupils who do not share the religious character of the school and who, in many cases, live at some distance.

Like most other European states, Belgium is facing a growing ethnic and cultural pluralism in addition to its traditional character as a trilingual state. Immigrants from Italy and Spain in the 1950s, from the Maghreb countries (chiefly Morocco) and Turkey in the 1960s and 1970s, and from Eastern Europe and from other European member-states in the 1970s and 1980s have provoked tensions. The arrival of refugees and the international status of Brussels strengthened further the multi-ethnic character of a country that always was a privileged encounter spot of the Latin and Germanic cultures and a world centre of Jews. Yet, integration problems relevant for the education sector exist mainly vis-à-vis Muslim immigrants.

In the 1990s, the Flemish government already encouraged primary and secondary schools to have an eye for equal opportunities in education for all children. Schools were granted extra means, supervision, and support. On 15 July 1993, the common Declaration on non-discrimination policy was signed by the governing bodies, the minister of education, the education syndicates, and the parents' associations.[27] This declaration, with a view to equal education chances for immigrants and autochthons, aims two objectives: non-discrimination at schools and the improvement of the admission policy. The declaration respects international treaties in which non-discriminatory education is recognised as a fundamental social right.[28] Funds have been appropriated under the terms of positive discrimination legislation which provides, in particular, for the provision of human and financial resources to institutions meeting certain socio-economic criteria.

Since 1 September 2002, all the temporary projects have been replaced by an integrated support provision, paying special attention to children from deprived backgrounds. This new provision provides full opportunities to all children to learn and develop themselves and counters exclusion, social separation, and discrimination.

The decree of 28 June 2002 on equal opportunities in education[29] sets out three major lines of action taking into account the aim of multicultural society, chiefly in the urban areas. In principle, parents, and students, if they are old enough, have the right to enrol their children in the schools of their choice. Only in a strictly limited number of cases, can schools refuse to enrol or refer newly enrolled students to other schools. There is the establishment of local consultation platforms with a threefold task.[30] The local consultation platforms ensure the rights of enrolment, act as intermediaries in cases of conflicts, and co-operate in implementing local policies on equal educational opportunities. The additional support must enable schools to develop extended needs provisions geared toward deprived children.

The decree concerning equal educational opportunities aims to promote *diversity* and reinforces the right of free enrolment. By virtue of art. IV.7 of the decree, a commission has been established concerning the individual rights of students.[31] This commission, which was set up by the Ministry of Education of the Flemish Community on January 1, 2003, gives advice, safeguards the right to free enrolment, and deals with complaints.

Exclusion, segregation, and discrimination will be avoided and social cohesion will be promoted. In theory, in Flanders all students are treated on an equal basis; their origin, skin colour, religion, or social background is not important. Nobody will be denied an enrolment on the grounds of sex, nationality, or religion. There is also a special care for underprivileged students and children with foreign backgrounds. Research has shown that these students are more likely to leave school early ("school outburst") and that they face specific problems due to their deprived social, cultural, and financial background. It is more difficult for these children to face the expectations of schools. Teachers must be aware of these difficulties and make sure these problems are not neglected. A real "equal education policy" must reinforce in the first place the position of these vulnerable students.

When students are being enrolled, school governing boards are obliged to inform them and their parents, or those with parental authority, about the school regulations and the pedagogical project. These documents respect the constitutional principles concerning human rights and those of the child in particular. For instance, students must be treated equally in their schools and discipline must be kept in an acceptable manner since the right to education develops respect for the cultural and national values of the child himself and of others. School regulations that are unilateral and oriented toward certain kinds of students are inconsistent with and in violation of the law. Parents who register their children must agree with the school regulations and the specific school project. A school governing board must stipulate how approval must be given, such as by a signature. This school governing board cannot determine itself whether a student can give satisfaction to the school's project.

School registrations of students last for their entire school career. Annual registrations in the same schools for the same students are no longer needed. This provides security for the parents. There is another special approach regarding registration. Some students have to be enrolled first. A school is obliged to enrol students who belong to the same "communal unit." The primacy for new students will be put into practice when they are related to a registered student already in the same school. Brothers and sisters, half-brothers and half-sisters, whether they live in the same house or not, and children who live in the same house but have no common parent(s), belong to a communal unit.

School governing boards must show favour to relatives above other students but they also may give preferential treatment to students whose situation corresponds to at least one of the "equal chance indicators."[32] This is the case if the parents belong to the benefits drawing population, when the mother has no diploma of secondary education, when the student lives temporarily or permanently outside his own family relation, when the family receives a replacement income, or when Dutch is not the official home-speaking language. If school governing boards decide to make some special efforts for these students, they have to do this for all the students who meet with at least one indicator.

Insofar as the social, cultural, and ethnic diversity in schools is a surplus value, there are measures to allow schools to keep this diversity. Schools can treat certain categories of people differently, provided that there be an objective and sensible justification for the criterion of differentiation.

By virtue of the decree, "local consultation platforms" have been established for primary and secondary education.[33] The cooperation within such a local consultation platform is very important. It is a prerequisite for receiving subsidies. The schools involved in the platform must stick to the agreements which are made; otherwise, they might lose subsidies.

The main actors of a local consultation platform are the school governing board, representatives of the employer's (teachers) association, the parents association and the students' union, representatives of organisations who stand up for ethnical and cultural minorities or poor people, and a representative of the local authority (or district council). Schools cooperate with local authorities to implement a local policy on equal opportunities in education. They also act as an intermediary in case of conflicts.

The local consultation platform has a few main assignments. In order to diminish all kinds of discrimination and exclusion of students, an analysis of the problem of unequal chances in education has to be made. There is a need for quantitative and qualitative figures. Special attention must be drawn to foreign students who do not speak Dutch at home.

School Regulations in Education

Each school governing body establishes a school regulation containing rights and duties of each student (art. 61).[34] The purpose of school rules is to achieve a balance between the rights and obligations of the educational consumer on the one hand and those of the education provider and his staff on the other hand. Regulation of the legal status of students and teachers is an attempt to defeat all forms of partiality. Every school has a specific policy that contains information concerning order and disciplinary policy, study organisation, and opportunities for appeal. The education project of the school is written down in that policy. Parents and students are informed.[35]

Before the first registration of a student in secondary education,[36] a governing body must inform the involved persons on the pedagogical project and the school regulation. The parents and students receive this regulation in writing. The registration is only valid after the parents and students have approved this project and regulation (art. 62). Measures are taken by the staff members of the institution in case of misbehaviour (art. 63). As a result of impudent behaviour, they must bring the student to improve his behaviour as well as to cooperate with fellow students and staff members. It could be that as a result of these measures a student is no longer able to attend lessons. When this situation arises, the class council must be consulted. Disciplinary measures are taken when the behaviour of a student endangers the realisation of the pedagogical project of the institution.

In the interest of the student disciplinary measures are not transmissible from one institution to another (art. 65 § 1). The disciplinary regulation stipulates how one can take legal action against these measures (art. 67).

The decree specifies the procedure applying to suspension or exclusion of students. The school board must stipulate in the school regulations what procedure is to be applied for a suspension of more than one day or for exclusion. At least the following must be foreseen: prior advice of the class council, parents have access to the student's disciplinary record and must be heard, the decision must be motivated and notified to the parents in writing.[37]

Study Grants and Loans

Each year the Flemish community gives financial support to students who come from financially deprived families. The study grants for secondary education and study financing for higher education aim at promoting the democratisation of education. They are designed to ensure that all young people are given full opportunities in the field of training and intellectual development, regardless of their origin, financial possibilities, or social and cultural environment. There are three pillars in the legislative system: the condition of nationality, the educational conditions, and the financial conditions.

The nationality condition requires that study grants be awarded to all students of Belgian nationality. Foreign students living in Belgium can also apply but they have to stay for a lengthy period in Belgium. In secondary education, minors subject to compulsory education always meet the educational conditions, even if they failed to pass the preceding school year. Once they become of age (and are no longer subject to compulsory education), they have to have passed the preceding school year if they want to apply for a study grant.

The financial support in secondary education varies depending on the family income and the number of persons in the family who live on the income.

Financial conditions define that the income is the basis for giving a study grant. If the income exceeds a certain maximum income, the student can no longer apply. The basis for defining this income is tax law.[38]

Protection of the Physical and Mental Integrity of the Child

Selected articles of the International Treaty Concerning the Rights of the Child aim to enforce the physical and mental integrity of the child. Article 19 stipulates that legal, administrative, social, and educational measures must be taken to protect children against all kinds of physical and mental violence, (sexual) abuse, and maltreatment as long as the parents, relatives, or guardian are taking care of the child.

Article 422*bis* of the Belgian penal code stipulates that the physical integrity of children and the protection of living must be guaranteed. Article 22*bis* of the Constitution adds that the moral, physical, mental, and sexual integrity of the child must be protected. The right to physical integrity implies the protection and promotion of one's personal development as a human being.

It is important that schools are aware of and draw attention to the physical and mental health of the youngsters and that they offer a wide scale of activities and entertainment. Students must be treated with the appropriate respect and be offered various possibilities for creative and cultural self-expression and participation. Schools must reinforce the social defensibility of young people. It belongs to their pedagogical freedom to choose which values they would like to impart with their students. The government however imposes certain objectives as basic social skills and attitudes, this with respect for the school's pedagogical project. At nursery school, little children are already being taught basic values such as respect for other opinions, and tolerance. They learn how to live together with other people, to search for non-violent solutions for conflicts, to take care of someone else, his belongings, and other social skills.[39]

There is a clear link between the well-being of students and their performances in school. Anti-social behaviour has been strongly linked with repeated failure and bad results at schools. Successful behaviour must thus be rewarded but in order to avoid conflicts and bad behaviour teachers must be aware of and take into account the different social backgrounds of students. Therefore, it is important to have a good communication with the students as well as with their parents. School rules must be decisively applied in order to reduce anti-social behaviour.

Parents do have the main educational authority but this implies obligations in the interest of the child. Attention must be paid to the personal needs and problems. Children must be able to build a truthful relation with the teacher. If social problems occur, and the child has been neglected, abused, or maltreated, this must be communicated.[40] Centres for student guidance are funded by the government and can be consulted by students, parents, teachers, schools, and governing boards. Confidentiality is guaranteed with regard to personal information. These centres maintain and promote the focus on children with specific problems.

Parents and teachers have to make decisions taking into account the individual development of children. Parents must protect, accompany, and help the child. Teachers must de-ontologically and didactically take into account the increasing autonomy, critical sense, and independence of the child. When the integrity of the child or his or her development is in danger, protective and repressive action is obliged. In this case, only the absolute right to social health, moral and physical integrity applies.[41] This covers a special issue on *violence at schools.*

Conclusion

Every person of school age has a right to education at the expense of the Community. This right has been incorporated into Belgian and Flemish legislation. In Flanders, all students are treated on an equal basis. The past years a big effort has been made to guarantee equal educational opportunities. The origin, religion, or social background of students should be of no importance. There are special provisions for disabled students and those from a deprived social, cultural, or financial background. Immigrants and autochthons have the same educational rights. Further, there is continuous attention for specific rights of students such as freedom of speech, religious freedom, protection of privacy, protection of the physical and mental integrity, and the right to participation.

Notes

1. Partly after the constitutional revision of 1968 to 1971; see De Groof, bevoegdheidsverdeling van 1970 inzake onderwijs: zienswijzen van de Raad van State en lessen voor de Constituante, Tijdschrift voor Bestuurswetenschappen en Publiek Recht, 1988, blz. 391–405; Verstegen, R., De gemeenschappen bevoegd voor het onderwijs, Tijdschrift voor bestuurswetenschappen en Publiek recht, 1990, 22; Veny, L., Onderwijs en Grondwet. De nieuwe grondwetsbepalingen inzake onderwijs, Tijdschrift voor bestuurswetenschappen en Publiek recht, 1988, 594.

2. After the 1988 Constitution revision still a few competences chiefly dealing with social security, labor organization are federal. De Groof, J. and Penneman, H., Artikel 127, § 1, eerste lid, 2∞ van de Grondwet. Een overzicht van de bevoegdheidsverdeling in onderwijsaangelegenheden, in Tijdschrift voor Onderwijsrecht en Onderwijsbeleid, 1997–1998, nr. 5–6.

3. Article 59bis §2 of 15 July 1988 reads as follows (see art. 127 of the revised Constitution):

> Community Councils shall settle by decree, each for the matters pertaining to them:
> 1 cultural matters;
> 2 education with the exception of:
> a) fixing the beginning and the end of the compulsory school attendance period;
> b) minimum conditions for granting diplomas;
> c) the pension system.
> 3 cooperation between the Communities as well as international cooperation.

4. De Groof, J., Droit à l'instruction et liberté d'enseignement, Brussel, 1985, 218p.

5. De Groof, J., De Schoolpactwet: Coördinatie en Annotatie, Brussel, 1995.

6. The term basic education refers to both pre-school/nursery education (age three to six) and primary education (age six to twelve).

7. Deli, D., De Handelingsbekwaamheid van de minderjarige in het schoolgebeuren in Tijdschrift voor Onderwijsrecht en Onderwijsbeleid, 1993–1994, nr. 2, 74–87.

8. Vandekerckhove, A., Leerlingenparticipatie: inspraak als mensenrecht voor jongeren in Tijdschrift voor Onderwijsrecht en Onderwijsbeleid, 2003–2004, nr. 1–2, 67.

9. De Groof, J., "The Legal Status of Pupils in Europe" in *Yearbook of the European Association for Education Law and Policy*, Den Haag, 1998, 13–52.

10. Primary and secondary education in Flanders is provided by three "networks." Free educational institutions (*vrij gesubsidieerd onderwijs*) are set up by private persons or institutions, mainly the Catholic Church, and subsidized by the Community. "Official" education can be divided into Community education (*gemeenschapsonderwijs*) and official subsidized education (*officieel gesubsidieerd onderwijs*). The official subsidized education is sponsored and controlled by local authorities—provinces and municipalities—but subsidized by the Flemish Community.

11. Court of Arbitration, no. 28/92, April 2, 1992, B.S., May 14, 1992, 10.991.

12. Glenn, C., De Groof, J., *Finding the Right Balance: Freedom, Autonomy, and Accountability in Education*, 45.

13. Court of Arbitration, no. 28/92, April 2, 1992, B.S., May 14, 1992, 10.991.

14. De Groof, J., Het levensbeschouwelijk karakter van de onderwijs-instellingen in België, Brugge, 1985, 190.

15. Ornelis, F., and Penneman, H. in *The Legal Status of Pupils in Europe, Yearbook of the European Association for Education Law and policy*, Den Haag, 1998, 274. Jan De Groof and Hilde Penneman Ed. *The Legal Status of Students in Europe*, 274.

16. Art. 25, Decree February 25, 1997; De Groof, J., De vrijheid van en het recht op onderwijs, ibid.

17. De Groof, J., Ornelis, F., Recht op onderwijs, ook voor "illegalen," Tijdschrift voor Onderwijsrecht en Onderwijsbeleid, 1999–2000, nr. 5, 333–334.

18. Education in Flanders, The Flemish Educational Landscape in a Nutshell, ministry of the Flemish community, 2005, 44.

19. Zie Wet op het buitengewoon en geïntegreerd onderwijs van 6 juli 1970 zoals gewijzigd door het decreet betreffende onderwijs XIII van 13 juli 2001, B.S. 27 November 2001.

20. Art. 3 of the Law on the Extraordinary and Integrated Education of 6 July 1970.

21. Ornelis, F., and Penneman, H. in *The Legal Status of Pupils in Europe, Yearbook of the European Association for Education Law and Policy*, Den Haag, 1998, 276.

22. Court of Arbitration, ruling no. 110/98, 4 November 1998, ground. B.3.2.

23. Art. 31 § 3, Decree February 25, 1997 (Elementary Education).

24. See Deli, D., De niet gemengde school heeft (gelukkig) nog bestaansrecht, in Tijdschrift voor Onderwijsrecht en Onderwijsbeleid, 1996–1997, nr. 6, 430; Verstegen, R., Gemengd onderwijs. Elementen voor het juridische debat, in Tijdschrift voor Onderwijsrecht en Onderwijsbeleid, 1994–1995, nr. 2, 131.

25. Besides the implementation of international law, cfr. Veny, L., De implementatie ven de internationale verdragen in de Belgische rechtsordening, in Tijdschrift voor Onderwijsrecht en Onderwijsbeleid, 1992–1993, nr. 5–6, 301; Hanson, K., Fundamentele rechten van leerlingen en het recht op toegang tot het onderwijs, in Tijdschrift voor Onderwijsrecht en Onderwijsbeleid, 1998–1999, nr. 5–6, 328.

26. Court of Arbitration, nr.38/91, December 5, 1991, B.S., December 21, 1991, 19, 160.

27. Verhellen, E., Verschelden, G., Vanthuyne, T., Kinderrechten en non-discriminatie, het plaatselijk overleg non-discriminatie in het Gentse onderwijs, in Tijdschrift voor Onderwijsrecht en Onderwijsbeleid, 1999–2000, nr. 5.

28. Bijvoorbeeld het Internationaal Verdrag inzake de uitbanning van alle vormen van Rassendiscriminatie van 1966, in België goedgekeurd door de wet van 9 juli 1975 (B.S. 11 december 1975) en Internationaal Verdrag inzake sociale, economische en culturele rechten (New York, 1966).

29. Het decreet gelijke onderwijskansen I van 28 juni 2002 zoals gewijzigd bij het decreet van 14 februari 2003, het decreet van 30 april 2004, de decreten van 7 mei 2004 en het decreet van 15 juli 2005.

30. Education in Flanders, the Flemish Educational Landscape in a Nutshell, ministry of the Flemish community, 2005, 40–41.

31. Zie ook Besluit van de Vlaamse Regering van 27 september 2002 betreffende de Commissie inzake leerlingenrechten, B.S. 31/10/2002.

32. Verstegen, R., Algemene Analyse. Gelijke onderwijskansen in de Vlaamse Gemeenschap. Verkenning van enkele principiële vragen, Tijdschrift voor Onderwijsrecht en Onderwijsbeleid, 2003–2004, nr. 4–5, 284.

33. Het besluit van de Vlaamse Regering van 28 juni 2002 betreffende de lokale overlegplatforms inzake gelijke onderwijskansen.

34. "Decision of the Flemish Government Concerning the Organisation of Full-time Secondary Education," 19 July 2002.

35. De Groof, J., "The Legal Status of Pupils in Europe" in *The Legal Status of Pupils in Europe, Yearbook of the European Association for Education Law and Policy*, Den Haag, 1998, 13–52.

36. As well as in primary education as defined in art. III.1§2 of the decree of 28 June 2002 concerning equal educational opportunities.

37. Penneman, H., "Synoptic Review of the Country Reports" in *The Legal Status of Pupils in Europe, Yearbook of the European Association for Education Law and Policy,* Den Haag, 1998, 61.

38. Education in Flanders, The Flemish Educational Landscape in a Nutshell, ministry of the Flemish community, 2005, 41.

39. Scheys, M., Dupont, C., Huylebroeck, K., Antisociaal gedrag op school voorkomen en oplossen in Tijdschrift voor Onderwijsrecht en Onderwijsbeleid, 1999–2000, 1–2, 17–30.

40. Besluit van de Vlaamse Regering betreffende de opdracht van het personeel in het basisonderwijs van 17 juni 1997, B.S. 11 September 1997.

41. De Groof, J., Noli me tangere, Tijdschrift voor Onderwijsrecht en Onderwijsbeleid, 1999–2000, nr. 1–2, 15–16.

4

China

Ran Zhang[1]

TRADITIONALLY, STUDENTS' RIGHTS is an under-developed notion in China. The educator-student relationship had been commonly analogized with the traditional Chinese father-son relationship (*yiri wei shi, zhongshen wei fu*),[2] both of which were asymmetrical in nature and emphasized the subordination of children. For a long period of time after the People's Republic of China was founded by the Chinese Communist Party (CCP) in 1949, party policies were the major governing rules for the state, and public interests took precedence over individuals' rights.

As China gradually changes from a state "ruled by ruler" into a state governed by the "rule of law" since the late 1970s,[3] student rights have been incorporated into the legal framework and are becoming a controversial area in the everyday life of students, teachers, and administrators as well as in academic discourse.[4] As such, this chapter reviews the concept of "right to receive an education" in the Chinese legal system, its manifestation in special populations, and some substantive and procedural rights of Chinese students. This chapter examines both the laws-on-the-books and the laws-in-practice while reflecting on emerging issues in each topic area.

Sources of Educational Law

China follows civil law tradition and maintains a code law system. The major sources of education law in China are briefly illustrated below.

Constitution[5]

- Under the chapter of "General Principles," the state establishes schools, develops educational facilities, and encourages non-public education.[6]
- Under the chapter of "Fundamental Rights and Duties of Citizens," citizens of People's Republic of China have the right and duty to receive an education.[7] Other citizen rights are also described in this chapter.[8]

Statutes[9]

- The Education Law (1995) and six other national educational laws.[10]
- Other statutes that deal with education in part, e.g. the Law on the Protection of Minors (1991), Juvenile Crime Prevention Law (1999), the Protection of Handicapped Law (1990), and etc.
- Basic civil, administrative, and criminal laws and their respective procedural laws.[11]

Administrative Regulations issued by the State Council.[12]

Local legislation[13]

Legislation in the Ethnic Autonomous Regions[14]

Administrative Rules:

- On the national level, issued by the Ministry of Education[15] alone or jointly with other ministries. In terms of the number of rules and the range of legal relationships adjusted, this is the major source of educational law.
- Issued by the government below the national level.

International Conventions:

- Universal Declaration of Human Rights.
- International Covenant on Civil and Political Rights.[16]
- International Covenant on Economic, Social, and Cultural Rights.[17]
- Convention on the Rights of the Child.[18]

Characteristics of Educational Law and Students' Right Protection in China

The legal framework of educational law in China is far from mature. Since the People's Republic of China was founded by the CCP in 1949, education has been governed by party policies. All educational statutes were passed after the Cultural Revolution (1966–1976), and the Education Law, the basic law outlining the educational system and defining legal relationships, was not enacted until 1995. In fact, some important educational reforms in the past twenty years are still initiated by party policies.[19] For example, the Reform of China's Educational Structure[20] launched significant educational reform in China; the Scheme for the Reform and Development of Education in China[21] set up the goals and strategies for educational development in the 1990s; most recently, the Several Opinions on Further Reinforcing and Improving the Moral Education for Minors started a round of efforts on moral education.[22]

In addition to the role of party policies, some legal provisions are "experimental" in nature. This is actually recognized by the legislation. When the conditions for enacting a statute are not sufficiently mature, on the delegation of power from the National People's Congress or its standing committee, the State Council can enact administrative regulations to deal with the legal relationships that a statute is supposed to adjust.[23] Absent relevant statutes or administrative regulations, the people's congress at the provincial level or in major cities can enact regulations in accordance with its specific situation and need, except for the legislative power reserved for the National People's Congress and its standing committee.[24] It is not clear from the wording of the law if the deprivation of the right to education could constitute an area where statutory regulation is necessary.[25] As noted in the sources of educational law, only seven statutes have been enacted in the area of education. In practice, many educational matters are regulated by the administrative rules enacted by the Ministry of Education such as the categories of disciplinary actions against students as discussed below.[26]

The lack of maturity of Chinese educational law is a double-edged sword with regard to the protection of student rights. On the one hand, the involvement of party policies and the experimental nature of legal provisions led to a low level of legitimacy and posed some serious threats to the stability and consistency of law. It is especially troublesome when the administrative rules enacted by the Ministry of Education are the major living laws in practice. Some of these rules lack constitutional and statutory bases or run counter to the basic citizen rights provided in upper-level statutes. For instance, college students were prohibited from marrying[27] even though they met age and other requirements under the Marriage Law. This prohibition was repealed in the new administrative rule issued in 2005.[28]

The rules have limited authority as a source of law. Unlike the regulations issued by the State Council and the local legislations, they cannot be directly cited in a court decision, they can just be used to inform the judges' decision.[29] While this deliberation by judges can provide some legitimacy, it may also result in inconsistent implementation of law and threaten students' stable expectation of their rights.

On the other hand, this immaturity of law must be viewed in light of the evolving nature of rule of law in China and leaves more room for local innovations and future development. As discussed below, some local regulations and rules provide more protections for the education of migrant children[30] and additional procedural safeguards in disciplinary actions.[31]

It is also important to acknowledge that some recent education cases contributed to the development of rule of law in China, and have challenged the traditional roles of Constitution and court cases in the Chinese legal system. Even though the Constitution occupies the top position in the legal hierarchy, it is generally not directly applicable in individual cases. This is due to the legal doctrine that prohibits direct application of general principles when more specific provisions are available, as well as two judicial interpretations issued by the Supreme People's Court in 1955[32] and 1986.[33] According to some Chinese scholars, this inapplicability was challenged by a 2001 education case, *Qi Yuling v. Tian Xiaoqi*,[34] in which the Supreme People's Court cited the Constitution.

Chinese scholars refer to this judicial reply as "China's *Marbury v. Madison*" and believe that it marks the beginning of direct applications of the Constitution and the starting point of judicial review in China.[35] Although not all scholars agree on the constitutional nature of this case,[36] the case generated a volatile discussion on judicial review and constitutionalism in general.

As a country that follows the civil law tradition, cases are not part of the official sources of law in China. Yet, in judicial practice, judges sometimes refer to their own judgments and other parallel or higher courts before rendering their opinions.[37] In addition, one of the efforts of the current judicial reform in China is for the Supreme Court to publish some selected typical cases in order to guide lower courts' decisions in similar situations.[38]

One of the influential educational cases from the Supreme Court is *Tian Yong v. University of Science and Technology Beijing*[39] in which the trial judges went beyond the text of legal code and held that students should be given a notice and a chance to defense in disciplinary action.[40] This case and a later similar case rendered by the same court, *Liu Yanwen v. Beijing University*,[41] attracted wide media attention and generated substantial academic and policy discourses. These, in part, resulted in a later revision of the administrative rule addressing the management of college students, affording them greater due process rights in disciplinary actions.[42] In short, some educational cases may affect later decisions and may trigger changes in the official sources of law.[43]

Right to Receive an Education

Education is often regarded as one of most important mechanisms of social mobility of individuals and public prosperity. Essential to this notion is the universal right to receive an education. This section discusses the right to receive an education in the Chinese context, with the following sections examining how this right is applied to some special populations.

As with constitutions in other countries,[44] article 46 of the Chinese Constitution stipulates, "The citizens of People's Republic of China have the right as well as the duty to receive an education."[45] Obviously, education is explicitly established as a fundamental right in the Chinese Constitution. The Education Law further establishes the principle of equal educational opportunity regardless of "nationality, race, gender, occupation, property, [and] religious belief."[46] Article 42 of the Education Law also provides a list of students' rights, including the right to participate in educational activities and use educational facilities, equipment, books, and materials; the right to obtain scholarships, student loans, and financial aid according to relevant state regulations; the right to fair assessment and the conferment of credentials and degrees upon completion of programs; the right to file a grievance for disciplinary actions and the right to bring a complaint or suit if the right of personal safety or property has been impinged upon by schools or teachers; and other rights or interests protected by statutes or administrative regulations.[47]

In terms of compulsory education,[48] children who have reached six years of age must attend school for nine years[49] regardless of their gender, nationality, or race.[50] This requirement can be satisfied in a private school but it is not very clear whether home-school is allowed in China.[51] Children of school age, their parents, or other legal guardians, related social organizations, and individuals all have the duty to enable students to receive and complete required years of education.[52] Child labor is prohibited in China.[53] Parents or legal guardians have the responsibility to provide necessary conditions for the education of minors. If parents fail to send children to schools, government officials can make them send the children to school.[54]

Corresponding to the notion of compulsory school attendance is the state's responsibility to provide education and to help students who have financial difficulty to attend schools. As mentioned above, the Education Law prescribes that students have equal educational opportunities regardless of their socio-economic status.[55] Chapter Seven in the Education Law sets forth the responsibilities of state and local governments for educational expenditures[56] while Article 10 of the Compulsory Education Law stipulates that "No tuition should be levied for students in compulsory education." Even so, it was not until 2006 that the state abolished miscellaneous fees.[57] Before that, compulsory education was indeed not free in China.[58] To assist students with financial difficulty to attend school, the Ministry of Education and the Ministry of Finance require local governments to establish a financial aid system and prohibit schools from denying enrollment of students due to their inability to pay miscellaneous fees, textbook fees, boarding fees, or other expense.[59]

Although the right to receive an education is a fundamental right under the Chinese Constitution, it has not been completely transformed into concrete legal protection. Several reasons contribute to this result. As discussed earlier, since the Constitution is not generally applicable to specific cases in China, the legal status of a fundamental right that it specifies does not lead to a particular review standard. Further, even if it can be agreed that the Constitution is only supposed to provide abstract principles, they still need to be translated into concrete rights and duties in statutes, regulations, and rules that are implemented in practice. Yet, for many reasons, this has not been true in China. As in many other nations,[60] there is a significant disparity between constitutional ideals and the actual practice in the provision of education. In the following sections, the legal rights and current landscape of their protection are examined for migrant children, girls, students with disabilities, and minority students.

Special Populations

Education of Migrant Children

Perhaps the most controversial issue about equal educational opportunity in China is the right to education of migrant children. In theory, although migrant children are not a legal category under the Constitution or the Education Law, discrimination against them might be a violation of equal educational opportunity with respect to occupation or property under article 9 of the Education Law. Migrant children are those children who are originally from the countryside but currently live in cities together with migrant-worker parents. Based on the fifth national census in 2000, there are about fourteen million migrant children of or under age fourteen in China.[61] Insofar as the right to attend neighborhood schools in China is conditioned on formal household registration, which for migrant families is fixed to their home villages,[62] migrant children do not have an entitlement to public education in the city where they currently live.

According to a 1998 administrative rule issued by the Ministry of Education,[63] in order to be enrolled in city public schools, migrant children must complete complex application procedures. They first need to obtain approval from educational agencies or the township governments in their hometowns, and then apply through city educational agencies or directly to city public schools. In addition, public schools could charge extra fees to the migrant students they admit; these fees are usually several times the amount of fees for regular students.

A 2003 rule replaces extra fees with the principle of equal charge and places more responsibilities on city governments to provide education for migrant children even though enrollment is conditioned on their capacity rather than the needs of students.[64] In practice, many city schools refuse to enroll migrant students. Due to lack of institutional support in implementation, the vast majority of migrant children are kept out of public schools and do not receive an education.[65] While the actual protection of the rights of migrant children to education is largely dependent on local policies and practices, some cities do much better jobs than others.[66]

Girls' Education

Girls' education is probably the most deeply entrenched equal educational opportunity issue in China. Unlike the rights of migrant children, the legal status of girls is clear in the legal framework. Equal rights for women are a fundamental right in the Constitution[67] and the Education Law.[68] The Law on the Protection of the Rights and Interests of Women[69] further specifies that females have equal rights in enrollment, placement, degree conferral, and overseas study. In terms of practice, China has achieved a fairly good participation level. In 1998, female enrollment in elementary, secondary, and post-secondary levels was 48 percent, 46 percent, and 39 percent, respectively.[70] The government also launched a "Spring Bud Project" to target poor girls' education specifically.[71]

On the other hand, girls have been more vulnerable to dropping out since the implementation of tuition fees in the mid-1990s. Gender discrimination is often obvious in educational policies and practices,[73] and while sexual harassment is another threat to girls, especially in poor rural areas.[74] In addition, "son preference" has been identified in Chinese culture and is believed to account for the "endangered" position of girls.[75] In this sense, girls' education is a social and cultural issue in addition to a legal one.

Special Education

China has the largest disability population in the world. It is estimated that more than fifty million people in China are handicapped[76] and more than 2 percent of children have disabilities.[77] The rights of students with disabilities to education are protected in the Constitution,[78] educational laws,[79] and disability laws.[80]

The development of protection for students with disabilities in China has four key features. First, the definition of disability is getting broader. In the Constitution of 1982 and the Compulsory Education Law of 1986, protection is primarily afforded to students with visual, hearing, and cognitive disabilities.[81] Under the Law on the Protection of Persons with Disabilities of 1990, the categories are expanded to include speech, physical, emotional, multiple, and other disabilities.[82] The Education Law in 1995 uses the general term of "persons with disabilities" without enumeration.[83] Second, the delivery of special education changes from special schools to a combination of general classrooms, special classes within regular schools, and special schools.[84]

Third, the laws do not mandate, but rather encourage, local governments to provide education to all students with disabilities;[85] correspondingly, education is not a full entitlement for students with disabilities. In the compulsory education stage, whether students with disabilities can gain access to education and what kind of education they can obtain are largely related to their physical or emotional "conditions" and if they can cope with study and life in school.[86] Accommodations are not readily available. Local governments are not required to provide necessary conditions to enable all students with disabilities to receive education, although they should gradually create conditions toward that direction.[87]

Fourth, students with disabilities face fewer legal restrictions to access post-compulsory education. In the past, wide varieties of students with disabilities were prohibited from post-compulsory education by national administrative rules on the basis of a notion of "physical ineligibility." Now, the new national guideline removes some of these restrictions in college admission and leaves more latitude to universities.[88] For example, students with amputations are now eligible for college admission if they meet other admission requirements and can handle their chosen programs of study.[89]

In recent years, the disabled population in China has become more assertive in claiming and defending their rights. In 1995, a student with infant paralysis brought a specialized upper secondary school to court for being denied admission. This was the first special education suit between student and school in China.[90] More recently, people who were carriers of the hepatitis B virus have begun to challenge educational and employment discrimination.[91] Under this social pressure, the standards of physical eligibility for both college admission and civil servant recruitment have been revised.[92] Even so, implementation remains a problem and litigation looms on the horizon.

Education of Minority Students

Besides Han, there are fifty-five ethnic-minority groups in China,[93] constituting about 8 percent of the total population.[94] All nationalities are equal[95] and citizens have equal educational opportunities without regards to their nationalities.[96] Regional autonomy is practiced where ethnic minorities live in compact communities[97] and education is one area of such self-governance.[98] The state subsidizes education in poor minority areas[99] and provides assistance for poor minority students to finish their study.[100]

A form of affirmative action exists for some ethnic-minority students in college admission. Twelve national minority institutes and one national minority university have been established in China, which are dedicated to minority education.[101] Special minority classes are also formed in general universities.[102] In admissions to higher education or specialized upper secondary schools, scores can be lowered for minority students while special considerations can be given for students from the ethnic-minority groups with very small populations.[103]

Language policy is often an integrated part of minority students' rights. In China, standardized Chinese (or Mandarin) is the language used in schools.[104] Since it is recognized that every minority nationality has the freedom to use and develop their own language,[105] in minority regional autonomous areas, minority language should be used in schools if conditions allow, and Chinese classes are offered in elementary schools.[106] Bilingual education is therefore provided.[107]

Substantive and Procedural Rights in Education

Thus far, this chapter has explored the rights of Chinese students to receive an education in general and for selected special populations. Equal educational opportunity defines who has access to education and is a crucial component in ensuring both social development and social justice in a rapidly changing society. This section examines how students receive education, their substantive and procedural rights in schools.

A long list can be developed of students' substantive and procedural rights. In principle, students should have all the citizen rights except that some restrictions are justified by their immaturity. Three key points must be born in mind when reading these last few sections. One, students' substantive and procedural rights are largely bounded by citizen rights and the development of citizen rights in China are not developing at the same pace in different areas. Freedom of speech is certainly less developed than freedom of marriage. Very few legal provisions address freedom of speech other than the recognition of such a right in the Constitution; it is not a salient topic in public and scholarly discourse probably due to its political sensitivity. Two, there is a strong cultural presupposition in the traditional Confucianism about what the appropriate roles of teachers and students are in China. This cultural disposition may not be codified into law, but it does have a huge influence upon everyday human actions. For example, it had been assumed in Chinese culture that teachers have more authority and that they might check students' bags for the best interest of students. Ten years ago, few students would question this notion even though their privacy right had already been recognized in the Law on the Protection of Minors. Three, this presumption has been increasingly contested in the vocabulary of legal rights by Chinese students in recent years as a redefinition of social and legal relationships is emerging in Chinese schools.

Religious Freedom

As individual citizens, students have the constitutional right to "to believe in, or not to believe in, any religion."[108] Students cannot be discriminated against due to their religious beliefs or lack thereof.[109] Yet, it is not clear if and to what extent religious accommodations are provided in Chinese public schools, especially in those outside of the autonomous ethnic areas. Given the separation of religion and the education system[110] and the restriction of group religious activities to registered places of worship,[111] religious groups do not have equal access to public schools. Religious academies can be established if they meet certain conditions and obtain governmental approval.[112]

Traditionally, the Chinese government has been unfavorable to religion[113] and the spirit of Chinese thought has been philosophical rather than religious.[114] In the People's Republic of China, atheism is an important part of the official ideology of the Chinese Communist Party and has penetrated the curriculum. The bottom line of religious freedom in China is that the Constitution stipulates and the state protects "normal religious activities,"[115] but defining "religion" and "normal" has become crucial to the actual religious freedom of Chinese citizens and students.[116]

Student Discipline

According to the Education Law, schools are responsible for student management and discipline.[117] Students have the duty to comply with laws and regulations, abide conduct codes, study hard, and follow school rules.[118] Also, it is believed in traditional culture that a "strict" master leads to excellent disciples (*yanshi chu gaotu*). Corporal punishment was a legitimate and important part of student discipline[119] and students were supposed to totally follow any school rule and to be obedient to their teachers. However, in recent years student discipline has become a controversial topic.

Corporal punishment is explicitly prohibited by the Compulsory Education Law,[120] the Law on the Protection of Minors,[121] and the Teacher Law.[122] Tort liability under civil law also applies.[123] Teachers who disregard this prohibition may be subject to disciplinary actions, dismissals, and criminal liability if their actions constitute crimes.[124] Students can seek monetary damages from schools due to corporal punishment by teachers,[125] and while schools can later seek reimbursement of monetary damages from teachers.[126]

In practice, corporal punishment is still a substantial problem in schools and has attracted significant public attention. A 2001–2002 national survey of 6,000 students in grades five to eight revealed that 1.5 percent of students often experienced and 13.9 percent occasionally experienced corporal punishment in school.[127] In addition to corporal punishment, students are subject to the so-called "soft-violence" or "hidden harm" at schools such as sarcastic comments by teachers, coerced copying of homework on multiple occasions, and standing or running as disciplinary actions used by teachers.[128] Without direct physical contact, these disciplinary actions may constitute "transformed corporal punishment," which is also prohibited by the administrative rule issued by the Ministry of Education.[129] They may also impinge students' right of dignity under civil law[130] and rights of individual freedom and dignity under the Constitution.[131] Students usually cannot recover monetary damages for mental distress absent physical harm,[132] although some have prevailed over teachers in flagrant situations.[133]

Search and seizure by school personnel is not unusual in Chinese schools. Common instances include search of students' dorms, personal bags, as well as access to their diaries and mail. In the same national survey mentioned above, 1.8 percent of students reported frequent teachers' access to personal mail while 6.6 percent experienced it occasionally.[134] From a legal perspective, freedom from unlawful search and privacy of correspondence are fundamental rights under the Constitution.[135] Further, minors' correspondence privacy is specified in the Law on the Protection of Minors.[136]

Except for the general principle that minors cannot be expelled from school in a capricious manner under the Law on the Protection of Minors,[137] national laws have been silent with regard to the categories, conditions, and procedures relating to student discipline. In practice, disciplinary actions in school may include warnings (*jinggao*), severe warnings (*yanzhong jinggao*), documentation of violations (*jiguo*), probation (*liuxiao chakan*), involuntary withdrawal from school (*leling tuixue*), and expulsion (*kaichu xueji*).[138] The Ministry of Education prohibited the last two kinds of disciplinary actions in primary school students.[139] For senior high school students, these disciplinary actions are to be documented in their personal records and become part of their permanent dossiers unless they are later withdrawn by schools in light of the improvements that students make after being disciplined.[140]

In recent years, the system of disciplinary action has been contested by Chinese legal and educational scholars on the following grounds. First, in terms of legal hierarchy, the disciplinary actions created by educational administrative agencies or schools lack a statutory basis.[141] Since some of these disciplinary actions, such as involuntary withdrawal from school and expulsion, significantly change the status of students, their basic conditions should be prescribed by a statute passed by the legislature[142] in order to protect students' fundamental rights to education. Second, some disciplinary actions are arbitrary and unreasonable. In fact, there are instances where students received "severe warnings" in their records due only to minor altercations with teachers.[143]

Third, students generally lack due process protection in disciplinary actions. But two recent instances have shown some positive signs in due process protection. As discussed before, the revised college student management regulation requires that students' statements and defense be heard before a disciplinary action is made and that the disciplinary decision be delivered to students. It also mandates the establishment of an internal grievance committee within universities to hear students' appeals and it reserves the authority for an expulsion decision to the chancellor conference (*xiaozhang huiyi*).[144] In addition, some local educational administrative rules afford elementary and secondary students the rights to notice, hearing, delivery of disciplinary decisions, and decisions made by administrative conferences collectively.[145] Given the evolving nature of school law in China and the substantive attention that has been directed to this issue, it may be expected that these due process protections will be provided to K-12 students nationwide in the future.

Fourth, although students may file grievances[146] or administrative appeals,[147] in practice they usually cannot sucessfully bring cases of disciplinary action to court due to the nature of the judicial system in China and the nature of the school-student relationship. Unlike a tort case of students' injury that can be filed to a civil court, schools and students are not on equal footing in disciplinary actions. Insofar as school attendance is compulsory in elementary and lower secondary schools, officials prescribe the rules and make decisions about disciplinary actions. To the extent that the civil law is about the relationship between two equal parties, complaints filed under the civil law are often rejected without review. As such, the more viable approach for students is to file administrative appeals against schools.[148]

Three legal obstacles are present in the administrative approach. Unlike educational administrative agencies, schools in China are not a part of government. Instead, because schools are usually separate legal entities that must bear their own liabilities,[149] and administrative appeals are supposed to resolve concrete disputes between a citizen or legal persons and administrative agencies,[150] some administrative courts regard schools as inappropriate defendants and refuse to hear such cases.

Paradoxically, even if courts treat schools as administrative agencies, student disciplinary actions may still be excluded from judicial review because disciplinary actions for civil servants in administrative agencies are not covered by the administrative litigation laws.[151] On other occasions, student complaints are rejected on this ground. The range of cases heard by administrative courts is limited to situations wherein administrative agencies impinge on the rights of personal safety and property.[152] In fact, some courts hold that what is at stake in a disciplinary action is the right to education, which does not fall into the purview of administrative litigation. Given these legal difficulties and the reluctance of courts to hear educational cases, many Chinese students actually do not have access to judicial remedies over disciplinary actions.[153]

In short, student discipline is probably the most controversial topic dealing with the rights of students in China. While challenges continue to mount, social and legal obstacles remain.

Conclusion

It is not easy to write a chapter on the rights of students in a rapidly changing society which had a long cultural history and was strongly influenced by communist ideology. It is even more difficult to offer any conclusions. What this chapter can provide is just a description of the basic structure of educational law in China at this time, a rough configuration of relationships involved in the students' right issue, and perhaps most interestingly, some snapshots of trends in the current landscape of students' rights. However, since all of these items are undergoing significant changes, this chapter will surely be out-of-date in a relatively few years.

In order to facilitate comparisons with the other countries reviewed in this book, the following general points are listed briefly. First, Chinese educational law has primarily followed the civil law tradition even as some common law vocabulary and institutional designs are beginning to emerge with regard, for example, to the due process issue in the *Tian Yong* and *Liu Yanwen* cases. Second, as in other nations, there is a significant gap between constitutional principles and concrete student rights which the legal system can provide, between what is made possible by law and actual protection students can have in practice. Third, the rights of students are largely bounded by citizen rights and rule of law developments in China. Even so, the rising awareness of student rights, coupled with the legal and social challenges in this arena have pushed, and will continue to push, the boundary of the development of both the rights of citizens and democratization in China. Fourth, as student rights emerge, the complicated interactions between courts, legislations, administration, public opinion, and advocacy on the national and local levels will have to play themselves out.

Notes

1. A special note of thanks to David Russo, class of 2004, Georgetown University, and Second Lieutenant, Cannon Air Force Base, Clovis, New Mexico, for assisting in the editing of this chapter.

2. This Chinese saying can be translated as: Once a teacher teaches you for a single day, you need to treat him like a father for your whole life.

3. In 1979, Deng Xiaoping proposed changing the mode of state management from "rule of ruler" to "ruling the country by law" (*yi fa zhi guo*). In 1993, the Chinese Communist Party (CCP) and the State Council announced the governance of education "in accordance with the law" (*yi fa zhi jiao*). In 1997, a new wording of "rule of law" replaced "rule by law," thereby becoming the guiding principle for the CCP. In 1999, this principle of "rule of law" was incorporated into the Constitution. The significance of this change is regarded differently. Some believe that the evolution of the concepts indicated a shift from legal instrumentalism to a fundamental respect of law, while others point out that legal instrumentalism is still the dominant mode of governance. See Zhenmin Wang, "The Development of Rule of Law in China." *Harv. Asian Q.* Autumn, 2000. www.fas.harvard.edu/~asiactr/haq/200004/0004a007.htm (last visited Dec. 5, 2003); Wing-Wah Law, "Legislation, Education Reform and Social Transformation: The People's Republic of China's Experience," 22 *Int'l J. Educ. Dev.* 579 (2002).

4. See, e.g., Mo Luo, Xuesheng de quanli: Zhongguo dalu xuesheng quanli zhuangkuang baogao ["Students' Rights: Report on the Situation of Students' Rights in Mainland China"], *China Research (Century China)*, no. 3, 2001. www.usc.cuhk.edu.hk/wk_wzdetails.asp?id=1097 (last visited Sep. 3, 2005) (synthesizing, from an advocacy perspective, instances and controversies dealing with the rights of students); Tan Xiaoyu, Yanjiu quanli: xin shiqi Zhongguo jiaoyu faxue de xin fazhan ["The Right of Research: The New Development of Chinese Educational Law in the New Age"] 21 *Theory & Practice of Educ.* 16 (2001) (arguing that study of rights and duties is in the core of Education Law research, listing thirteen emerging areas on student and teacher rights); Zhang Weiping, Pingheng yu zhiyue: ershi shiji de jiaoyu fa ["Balance and Check: Educational Law in the Twentieth Century"] 93–95 (1995) (noting that one feature in the development of Educational Law is the shift of focus from duties to rights).

5. China has a written Constitution that is at the top of the legal hierarchy. An amendment to the Constitution can only be adopted by a majority vote of more than two-thirds of all the deputies to the National People's Congress. See XIAN FA [Constitution], art. 64 (1982), People's Republic of China (PRC).

6. XIAN FA [Constitution], art. 19 (1982) (PRC).

7. Constitution, art. 46 (1982) (PRC).

8. This chapter starts with the principle of "equality before the law" (Article 33). In addition to the right and duty to receive an education, other fundamental rights relevant to students' rights include freedom of speech and association (Article 34), religious freedom (Article 35), individual liberty (Article 37), human dignity (Article 38), freedom and privacy of correspondence (Article 40), and women's equal rights (Article 48).

9. Statutes are adopted by a majority vote of all deputies to the National People's Congress or its standing committee. Constitution, art. 64 (1982) (PRC).

10. These laws target educational issues in particular and are referred to as "educational law" by many Chinese scholars where it is used in a narrow sense. The Educa-

tion Law that was enacted in 1995 is supposed to be more fundamental than the other six. The other six statutes are the Regulations on Degrees (1980) (PRC), the Compulsory Education Law (1986) (PRC), the Teacher's Law (1993) (PRC), the Vocational Education Law (1996) (PRC), the Higher Education Law (1998) (PRC), and the Law on Promotion of Privately-Run Schools (2002) (PRC). It is important to note that all of these statutes were passed after the Culture Revolution (1966–1976).

11. See, e.g., General Principles of the Civil Law (1986) (PRC), Civil Litigation Procedural Law (1991) (PRC), Criminal Law (1997) (PRC), Criminal Litigation Procedural Law (1979) (PRC), Administrative Punishment Law (1996) (PRC), Administrative Review Law (2002) (PRC), State Compensation Law (1994) (PRC), Administrative Litigation Procedural Law (1989) (PRC).

12. The State Council is the executive branch of the national government in the PRC. The State Council enacts administrative regulations in accordance with the Constitution and statutes. XIAN FA [Constitution] art. 89 (1982) (PRC); LI FA FA [Legislation Law] art. 56 (2002) (PRC). Examples relevant to students' rights are the Regulation on the Prohibition against Child Labor (2002) (PRC) and Regulation on the Education of the Handicapped (1994) (PRC).

13. In light of the actual situations and needs of the jurisdiction, the People's Congress and its standing committee on the provincial levels and some major cities can enact local regulations provided that they not contravene provisions of the Constitution, national law, and administrative regulations. Constitution, art. 100 (1982) (PRC). The Legislation Law, art. 63 (2001) (PRC). The administrative unit on the provincial level includes provinces, autonomous regions, and municipalities directly under the central government (Beijing, Shanghai, Tianjin, and Chongqing). The administrative unit below the provincial level is a city; also, a county is lower than a city. A major city that has the power to enact local regulations is described as "a city where the People's Congress of the province or autonomous region is seated, the city where a specific economic zone is located, and any other major city approved by the State Council." Local legislation issued by the People's Congress in major cities must be reviewed and approved by the standing committee of the people's congress in the provisional level before taking effect.

14. Article 4 of the Constitution stipulates "Regional autonomy is practiced where people of nationalities live in compact communities; in these areas organs of self-government are established for the exercise of the right to autonomy." The autonomous regions include autonomous regions, prefectures, and counties. XIAN FA [Constitution] art. 112 (1982) (PRC). The people's congress in the autonomous region has the power to enact local regulations in light of the economic, political, and cultural characteristics of the nationalities. These local regulations can vary with respect to statutes and administrative regulations, as long as such modifications do not violate basic principles of statutes and administrative regulations. LIFA FA [Legislation Law] art. 64 (2001).

15. Before the reorganization in the executive branch of the national government in 1998, the Ministry of Education was called the Education Commission.

16. The government of PRC signed this covenant on October 5, 1998.

17. The government of PRC signed this covenant on October 27, 1997, and ratified it on March 27, 2001.

18. This convention was signed by the PRC on August 29, 1990, and ratified on March 2, 1992. The PRC signed these conventions with some reservations. In addition, international law usually does not automatically apply to domestic issues in China after the convention was signed and ratified. International law needs to be incorporated into domestic law first. For example, the Chinese government signed into the Convention on the Rights of Child in 1990 with the reservation on family planning and the age benchmark of adults. See www.ohchr.org/english/countries/ratification/11 .htm#N5. The Law on the Protection of Minors (1991) (PRC) was an effort to incorporate this international law into the domestic legal system.

19. Wing-Wah Law, "Guest Editor's Introduction," *Chinese Educ. & Soc'y*, May–June (1999), 3–8.

20. It was issued by the politburo of the CCP.

21. It was jointly issued by the Central Committee of CCP and the State Council.

22. The Several Opinions was issued by the Central Committee of CCP and the State Council jointly on February 26, 2004. The policy is referred as "No. 8 Document."

23. LI FA FA [Legislation Law] art. 56 (2001) (PRC). This is a form of delegated legislation, suggesting that with the delegation of power the State Council, the executive branch in the central government can prescribe rules in the areas that are specifically reserved to the national legislature; these are listed in Article 8 of the Legislation Law.

24. LI FA FA [The Legislation Law] art. 64 (2001) (PRC).

25. The underlying notion here and in the text accompanying the above two notes is similar to the idea of legal reservation in German Administrative Law. It suggests that some important matters can only be prescribed by the national legislature. Article 8 of the Legislation Law gives a list of reserved areas in China including national sovereignty, the establishment, organization, and power of the government, regional autonomy, crimes and penalties, deprivation of the political rights of a citizen and restriction of personal freedom, appropriation of private property, basic civil relationship, basic economic relationship, systems of litigation and arbitration, and a catch-all situation, "all other matters the regulation of which must be carried out through enactment of national laws by the National People's Congress or the Standing Committee." Education is not in the enumerated list, but in theory one cannot completely deny the possibility that education might be recognized as such a matter that necessitates statutory regulation. Insofar as the right to education is a fundamental right under the Chinese Constitution and has become a crucial topic in public discourse, it must be understood in light of the evolving features of democracy and the rule of law in China.

26. See infra note 137–140.

27. Putong gaodeng xuexiao xuesheng guiding [Regulations on Student Management in General Higher Education Institutions] (promulgated by State Education Commission, Aug. 26, 1989, effective Jan. 20, 1990, repealed Sep. 1, 2005) art. 30 (1990) (PRC) www.law-lib.com/law/law_view.asp?id=6299 (last visited Sep. 3, 2005).

28. Putong gaodeng xuexiao xuesheng guiding [Regulations on Student Management in General Higher Education Institutions] (promulgated by Ministry of Education, Feb. 4, 2005, effective Sep. 1, 2005) (2005) (PRC) www.law-lib.com/law/

law_view.asp?id=91071 (last visited Sep. 3, 2005) (Article 30 in the 1990 regulation was dropped) [Regulations on Student Management].

29. Guanyu renmin fayuan zhizuo falü wenshu ruhe yinyong falü guifanxing wenjian de pifu [A Reply on How People's Courts Cite Laws in Issuing Their Legal Documents] (promulgated by the Sup. People's Ct., Oct. 28, 1986) www.law-lib.com/law/law_view.asp?id=3936 (last visited Sep. 3, 2005) (PRC). Strictly speaking, the content of "reply" is directed to the civil and economic lawsuits, while some educational cases are administrative lawsuits. See infra note 32–36, text accompanying note 148. But the title and the issue of this judicial interpretation are framed in a general manner, and this "reply" has been used widely in judicial practices and legal research.

30. See infra note 66.

31. See infra note 145.

32. Guanyu zai xingshi panjue zhong buyi yuanyin xianfa zuo lunzuikexing de yiju de fuhan [A Reply on the Inappropriateness in Citing Constitutions in Criminal Decisions] (promulgated by the Sup. People's Ct., July 30, 1955) www.law-lib.com/law/law_view.asp?id=1012 (last visited Sep. 3, 2005) (PRC).

33. See supra note 29.

34. Written Reply to Whether Those Who Violated the Basic Constitutionally Protected Right to Education by Infringing the Right of an Individual to Select One's Own Name Should Be Held Civilly Liable (promulgated by the Sup. People's Ct., June 28, 2001, effective Aug. 13, 2001), Sup. People's Ct. Gaz. No. 5, 2001, 152, translated in Chinese *Educ. & Soc'y* (2006). The case is Qi Yuling v. Chen Xiaoqi et al. (Zaozhuang City Interm. People's Ct., May 18, 1999, aff'd in part and rev'd in part, Shangdong Province Sup. People's Ct., Aug. 23, 2001). Chinese versions are available in Wang Lei, Xuanze xianfa [*To Choose Constitutional Law*] 241–255 (2003). Qi Yuling was a junior high school student who applied for a specialized upper secondary school on graduation. Qi Yuling was admitted, but the letter mailed to her junior high school was taken by Chen Xiaoqi who entered school under the name of Qi Yuling with forged documents. In its judicial "reply," a kind of judicial interpretation to guide local courts how to apply laws in a specific case, the Supreme Court of the PRC believes that Chen Xiaoqi violated Qi Yuling's fundamental constitutional right to education. For an article discussing this case in English, see Shen Kui, Translation, "Is It the Beginning of the Era of the Rule of the Constitution? Reinterpreting China's 'First Constitutional Case,'" 12 *Pac. Rim L & Pol'y* 199 (2003).

35. See, e.g., an article by one of the Supreme People's Court's judges who drafted this reply: Songyou Huang, Xian fa sifahua jiqi yiyi ["Constitutional Justiciability and Its Significance"], in Renmin Fayuan Bao [*People's Court Daily*] (Aug. 13, 2001), available at www.gongfa.com/huangsyxianfasifahua.htm (last visited Aug. 27, 2005); an academic symposium on the significance of this case: Chongde Xu et al., Qi Yuling an dui wanshan xianfa shishi jizhi de qidi ["Symposium: Implications of the Qi Yuling Case on the Improvement of Implementation System of Constitution"], in Renmin Fayuan Bao [*People's Court Daily*] (Sep. 17, 2001), available at law-thinker.com/detail.asp?id=346 (last visited April 22, 2003).

36. Some scholars argue that this case can be resolved easily under civil liability without invoking the Constitution. See Yanan Peng, "A Sheep in Wolf's Clothing: The

PRC Constitution in Qi Yuling v. Chen Xiaoqi et al." *American-Chinese Soc'y & Culture*, vol. 5, Iss. 2, available at www.uschinasc.org/mag52/mag5205.htm (last visited Aug. 27, 2005). Liang Huixing, Zuigao fayuan guanyu qinfan shou jiaoyu quan de fashi [2001] 25 hao pifu pingxi ["An Analysis of the Supreme Court's Reply" (*Judicial Interpretation*, 2001 No. 25) on Infringement of Right to Education]. law-thinker.com/detail.asp?id=1340 (last visited April 2, 2003).

37. Shen Kui, Zhidu bianqian yu faguan de guize xuanze ["Institutional Changes and Judges' Rule Selection"], in Gaodeng jiaoyu yu xingzheng susong [*Higher Education and Judicial Litigation*] 67 (Zhan Zhongle Ed., 2003). Prior cases can be referred to but not directly cited in court opinions and are subject to the citation rule of the Supreme People's Court in 1986, supra note 29.

38. Renmin fayuan wunian gaige gangyao ["The Five-Year Reform Plan by the People's Supreme Court"], *Sup. People's Ct. Gaz.*, No. 6, 1999, 187. Available at law.chinalawinfo.com/newlaw2002/SLC/slc.asp?db=chl&gid=23701 (last visited Sep. 2, 2005).

39. *Sup. People's Ct. Gaz.*, no. 4, 1999, 139–143, translated in *Chinese Educ. & Soc'y* (2006). This case was published before the reform effort was announced.

40. Rao Yadong, Cong shenpan jiaodu tan shou jiaoyu quan de baohu yu faguan zeren ["Protection of Right to Receive an Education and Responsibilities of Judges from a Judicial Perspective"], in *Higher Education and Judicial Litigation*, 260–273, at 272, supra note 37, translated in *Chinese Educ. & Soc'y* (2006). Rao Yadong was a judge in both the Tian Yong and Liu Yanwen cases.

41. Liu Yanwen v. Beijing Univ.; Liu Yanwen v. Academic Evaluation and Granting Comm. Beijing Univ. (Haidian District People's Ct., Beijing, Dec. 17, 1999; remanded by Beijing Interm. People's Ct., Apr. 30, 2000; rev'd on other grounds, Haidian District People's Ct., Beijing, Dec. 15, 2000, appeal denied, Beijing Interm. People's Ct., Mar. 30, 2001), published in *Higher Education and Administrative Litigation*, 499–540, supra note 37, translated in *Chinese Educ. & Soc'y* (2006).

42. See text accompanying note 144.

43. This has some resemblance to developments as a result of interactions between the judicial and legislative branches in the United States such as over the rights of students with disability. See David L. Kirp, "Law, Politics, and Equal Educational Opportunity: The Limits of Judicial Involvement," 47 *Harv. Educ. R.* 117 (1977).

44. John Boli-Bennett & John W. Meyer, "The Ideology of Childhood and the State: Rules Distinguishing Children in National Constitution, 1870–1970," 43 AM. *Sociological R.* 797, 803 (1978).

45. This provision has generated some academic discussion in China centered on two major questions: Is education a right or a duty? Who has this right and who bears this duty? Some insist on a single right-based framework. Students have a pure right to receive an education, while parents, society, and state have a duty to ensure such an education by sending children to schools or by providing educational facilities and opportunities. Gong Xianghe, Shou jiaoyu quan lun [*On the Right to Receive an Education*] 9–14 (2004). In contrast, other scholars justify their position with public interest considerations and maintain that in the compulsory education stage education is a duty of students. Wen Hui, Shou jiaoyu quan de ru xian yanjiu [*A Study on the Con-*

stitutionalization of Rights to Receive an Education] 67–70 (2003). For some other general discussion about this right and duty, see Yin Li, Shou jiaoyu quanli de jiben lilun wenti tantao ["An Exploration of Some Fundamental Theoretical Questions on the Right to Receive an Education"], Zhongguo jiaoyu fazhi pinglun [*China Educational Law Review*] 345–356 (Kaisheng Lao Ed., 2002); Jiang Shaorong, Gongmin shoujiaoyuquan jiqi shixian zhong de falv guanxi ["Citizens' Right to Receive an Education and the Legal Relationship in its Actualization"], in *China Education Review* 385–398; Hu Jinguang & Ren Duanping, shoujiaoyuquan de xianfaxue si kao ["Reflections on the Rights to Education from a Constitutional Perspective"], in *China Educ. Rev.* 43–59.

46. JIAO YU FA [Education Law] art. 9 (1995) (PRC). The equal opportunity for male and female is reinstated in Article 36 of the Education Law.

47. Other rights of students include freedom of choice and access to records. See Gong Xianghe, On the Right to Receive an Education 43–49, supra note 45; Zhang Jing, Xuesheng quanli jiqi sifa baohu [*Students' Rights and Their Judicial Protection*] 152–158 (2004) [*Students' Rights*]. Note that record management is very important to students' status in Chinese educational institutions. See Rao Yudong, supra note 40, at 268–271 (interpreting schools' authority under Section Four, Article 28 of the Education Law: A student has to have a valid record in order to be granted a diploma and a degree certificate). For detailed accounts of students' record management in China, see Lao Kaisheng, Zheng Xinrong et al., Guiju Fangyuang: Jiaoyu guanli yu falü [*Educational Administration and Law*] 327–331 (1997); Chu Hongqi, Zhongxiaoxue falü wenti fenxi (lilun pian) [*An Analysis of Legal Issues in Elementary and Secondary Schools (the Theoretical Issue)*] 139–141 (2002) [*An Analysis of Legal Issues*].

48. In traditional China, the state provided but rarely required schools. So, the notion of compulsory education represents "a revolution in relations between state and society in China." Alexander Woodside, "Real and Imagined Continuities in the Chinese Struggle for Literacy," in *Education and Modernization: The Chinese Experience* 43 (Ruth Hayhoe Ed., 1992) [*Education and Modernization*]. Liu's recent empirical study indicates that schooling in China's rural areas is a result of rational choice instead of the compulsory education law. See Fengshu Liu, "Basic Education in China's Rural Areas: A Legal Obligation or an Individual Choice?" 24 *Int'l J. Educ. Dev.* 5 (2004).

49. The nine-year compulsory education is equivalent to completion of lower secondary schools. China has a basic 6-3-3-4 schooling system, with six years in elementary school, three years in lower secondary schools and upper secondary schools respectively, and four years in college.

50. JIAO YU FA [Education Law] art. 18 (1995) (PRC). YI WU JIAO YU FA [Compulsory Education Law], art. 5, 2 (1986) (PRC). This was the first educational statute enacted in People's Republic of China. It was passed to address the immediate concern of revitalizing education and reducing illiteracy after the Culture Revolution. In some areas with insufficient conditions, the school enrollment age can be postponed into seven. The enrollment age and the length of compulsory schooling can be relaxed for students with disabilities to a proper extent. Yiwu jiaoyu fa shishi xize [The Detailed Implementation Guideline on People's Republic of China's Compulsory Education Law] (promulgated by State Educ. Comm. Mar. 14, 1992, effective March 14, 1992) art.

2 www.people.com.cn/GB/jiaoyu/8216/36635/36644/2788087.html (Last visited July 31, 2005) (PRC) [The Detailed Implementation Guideline on People's Republic of China's Compulsory Education Law].

51. From the wording of Article 5 of Compulsory Education Law ("shall attend a school"), some scholar infers that home-schooling is not allowed in China. Yin Li, An Exploration, see supra note 45. But in practice, instances of home-schooling do appear in media. See Xu Xi, Wode haizi zijia shangxue ["My Child Studies at Home"], Zhongguo Jiaoyu Bao (*China Education Daily*) (Jan. 20, 2002). Available at www.jyb.com.cn/gb/jybzt/2002/jcjy/158.htm (last visited Dec. 9, 2003).

52. JIAO YU FA [Education Law] art. 18 (1995) (PRC).

53. Compulsory Education Law, art. 15 (1986) (PRC). Law on Protection of Minors, art. 28 (1991) (PRC). State Council, Regulations on Prohibition against Child Labor (2002) (PRC). Child labor is defined as minors of less than sixteen years age. This is consistent with the definition of a person with full capacity for civil conduct under the General Principles of the Civil Law, art. 11 (1986) (PRC). A person of eighteen years old is a person with full capacity for civil conduct, and a citizen of sixteen years old but not of eighteen years old whose main source of income is his labor can be regarded as a person with full capacity for civil conduct.

54. Compulsory Education Law, art. 15 (1982) (PRC); the Detailed Implementation Guideline on People's Republic of China's Compulsory Education Law, art. 13 (1992) (PRC). Woodside observed in the literacy movement in the 1980s, contracts, rather than compulsory education law, were used to achieve the policy goals. The compulsory education law did not take the place of local voluntarism. See Woodside, Real, and Imagined Continuity, supra note 48. But there were also some instances where local government or school sued the parents who fail to fulfill this responsibility. See Lao Kaisheng, Educational Administration and Law 404, supra note 47. But no statutes, administrative regulations, or administrative rules mention this judicial approach as a possible implementation mechanism, and some scholars are skeptical about it. See Zhang Jing, *Students' Rights* 207, supra note 47.

55. See text accompanying note 46.

56. Partly under the neo-liberalistic influence globally, decentralization of educational finance started in the 1980s in China. For more details about decentralization, see Kai-ming Cheng, "Education, Decentralisation and Regional Disparity in China," in *Social Change and Educational Development: Mainland China, Taiwan, and Hong Kong* 53–65 (Gerald A Postiglione & Wing On Lee Ed., 1995).

57. The Education Commission, the Detailed Implementation Guideline on People's Republic of China's Compulsory Education Law, art. 16 (1992) (PRC), supra note 50. Compulsory Education Law, art. 2 (2006) (PRC).

58. This is not a problem unique to China as charging school fees is regarded as a major obstacle for students worldwide. The paradox between free and compulsory education and charging of school fees exists in many countries. For a list of countries with school fees in public primary education, see United Nations, Economic and Social Council, Commission on Human Rights, the Right to Education: Report submitted by the Special Rapporteur, Katarina Tomasevski, U.N. Doc. E/CN.4/2004/45 (2003). For a special report on China, see United Nations, Economic and Social Coun-

cil, Commission on Human Rights; The Right to Education, Report submitted by the Special Rapporteur, Katarina Tomasevski: Mission to China, U.N. Doc. E/CN.4/2004/45/Add. 1 (2003). For a general discussion on human rights and market approach to education, see Katarina Tomasevski, Symposium, Globalization and Education: Indiana University School of Law, Bloomington, Apr. 2–3, 2004: Globalizing What: Education as a Human Right or as a Traded Service? (2005).

59. Compulsory Education Law, art. 10 (1986) (PRC); the Detailed Implementation Guideline on People's Republic of China's Compulsory Education Law, art. 16, 17, 18 (1992) (PRC); Guanyu jianquan zhongxiaoxue zhuxuejin zhidu de tongzhi [Notice on Improving the Financial Aid System for Elementary and Secondary School Students] (Education Commission & Ministry of Finance, July 7, 1995). www.law-lib.com/law/law_view.asp?id=11552 (Last visited on Aug. 28, 2005); Guanyu luoshi he wanshan zhongxiaoxue pinkun xuesheng zhuxuejin zhidu de tongzhi [Notice on Implementing and Improving the Financial Aid System for Poor Elementary and Secondary School Students] (Ministry of Education & Ministry of Finance, Sep. 24, 2001). www.law-lib.com/law/law_view.asp?id=16494 (Last visited on Aug. 28, 2005). Other efforts include a single fee system (yifeizhi) and free textbook project in poor rural areas. A single fee is to combine various fees and set up the maximum amount. See Notice on Implementation of the Single Fee System in Poor Rural Areas' Compulsory Education (State Planning Committee, Ministry of Finance & Ministry of Education, Nov. 16, 2001) www.law-lib.com/law/law_view.asp?id=16759 (last visited on Aug. 28, 2005).

60. In the United States, for example, education law was often framed in a rhetorical way in state constitutions. "With the exception of language in the declarations of rights, no other sections contained so much exhortation to virtue or justificatory prose." David Tyack, Thomas James, & Aaron Benavot, *Law and the Shaping of Public Education, 1785–1954*, 30 (1987). John Boli-Bennett & John W. Meyer, "The Ideology of Childhood and the State: Rules Distinguishing Children in National Constitution, 1870–1970," 43 *AM. Sociological R.* 803 (1978).

61. Duan Chengrong & Liang Hong, woguo liudong ertong zhuangkuang ["The Situation of Migrant Children in China"], Renkou Yanjiu [*Research on Population*], no. 1, 2004, available at www.usc.cuhk.edu.hk/wk_wzdetails.asp?id=3863 (last visited Sept 3, 2005). For a study on migrant children schools and migrant children's education in general in Beijing, see Julia Kwong, "Educating Migrant Children: Negotiations between the State and Civil Society," 180 *China Q.* 1073 (2004). See also James Irwin, "China's Migrant Children Fall through the Cracks," *The UNESCO Courrier*, Sep. 2000, 13–14.

62. In China, access to neighborhood public school is based on the household registration system (*hukou*), which does not necessarily move as the person changes her residence. Peasants and urban residents are in two distinct household registration systems and have access to different social welfare. For general residence rule in China see Basic Civil Principles, art. 15 (1986). Several Opinions of the Implementation of Basic Civil Principles (Sup. People's Ct., Jan. 26, 1988), art. 9. www.law-lib.com/law/law_view.asp?id=203 (last visited Sep. 2, 2005). Note the household registration system (*hukou*) is not defined in this basic civil law.

63. Liudong ertong shaonian jiuxue zanxing banfa [Administrative Rules on the Migrant Children's and Adolescents' Schooling (Trial)] (promulgated by the Education Commission & Ministry of Public Security, March 2, 1998). Article 11 allows public schools to collect extra fees on migrant students and Article 7 prescribes complex procedures for enrollment application.

64. Guanyu jinyibu zuohao jincheng wugong jiuye nongmin zinü yiwu jiaoyu gongzuo de yijian [Opinions on improving the compulsory education of migrant workers' children] (Promulgated by Ministry of Education, Sep. 13, 2003). www.law-lib.com/law/law_view.asp?id=82780 (last visited on Sep. 2, 2005).

65. Many migrant children are educated in migrant schools run by individuals or non-governmental organizations. 4.8 percent of school-age migrant children do not attend any school or drop out of school, while the percentage for the whole nation is 3.3 percent. See Duan Chengrong & Liang Hong, "The Situation of Migrant Children in China," supra note 61.

66. See, e.g., Zhejiang liudong renkou zinü jiuxue wenti jiben jiejue [Zhejiang Province Has Basically Solved the Problems of Migrant Children Education] (September 23, 2003). www.chinanews.com.cn/n/2003-09-23/26/349849.html (last visited Dec. 9, 2003) (More than 99 percent of migrant children in Hangzhou received compulsory education; this was regarded by Ministry of Education as an exemplar local experience).

67. XIAN FA art. 48 (1982) (PRC).

68. JIAO YU FA art. 36 (1995) (PRC).

69. Funü quanyi baozhang fa [the Law on the Protection of the Rights and Interests of Women] (promulgated by the Nat'l People's Cong. Apr. 3, 1992, amended by Standing Comm. Nat'l People's Cong. Aug. 28, 2005) art. 15–21 (PRC).

70. World Bank, China-Country Review (2002), available at www.worldbank.org.cn/English/content/gender-en.pdf (last visited Apr. 6, 2005).

71. Chunlei jihua [Spring Bud Project]. Homepage: www.chunlei.org/chunlei/ (last visited Sep. 2, 2005).

72. World Bank, supra note 70.

73. See Peking University in Discrimination Controversy, China Daily, Aug. 30, 2005, available at http://english.people.com.cn/200508/30/eng20050830_205295.html (involving preferential treatment to male students at the Foreign Language School of Peking University to balance its 4:1 female-male ratio).

74. In response to rising sexual harassment in schools, the Ministries of Education, Public Security, and Judiciary issued a joint notice to emphasize the administrative and criminal liabilities for offenders and other responsible actors such as principals, officials in local educational agencies, other related administrators, and teachers who know about, but did not report, incidents, all of whom are primarily subject to administrative disciplinary actions. The offender's actions can constitute rape or molestation under Article 236 of the criminal law (1997). This notice does not deal with civil liabilities. Guanyu Liaoning de di xiangji fasheng jiaoshi qiangjian weixie xuesheng shijian de qingkuang tongbao [A Report on Recent Teacher-Student Sexual harassment and Molestation Instances in Liaoning and other Places] (Ministry of Education, Ministry of Public Security and Ministry of Judiciary, July 28, 2003, effective,

July 28, 2003) www.law-lib.com/law/law_view.asp?id=78869 (last visited Sep. 2, 2005) (PRC). The Law on the Protection of the Rights and Interests of Women has been just amended, which gives birth to the first anti–sexual harassment statutory provision in China. Civil litigation is made available against the harasser. See Funü quanli baozhang fa [the Law on the Protection of the Rights and Interests of Women] (promulgated by the Nat'l People's Cong. Apr. 3, 1992, amended by Standing Comm. Nat'l People's Cong. Aug. 28, 2005) art. 40, 58 (PRC), supra note 69.

75. Elisabeth Croll, *Endangered Daughters* (2000).

76. Brian Stratford & Hannah Ng, "People with Disabilities in China: Aching Outlook, New Solutions, Growing Problems," 47 *Int'l J. Disability, Dev., & Educ.* 7 (2000).

77. Hanlin Yang & HongBo Wang, "Special Education in China," 28 *J. SPECIAL EDUC.* 93 (1994).

78. XIAN FA art. 45, § 3 (1982) (PRC).

79. Primarily Yiwu jiaoyu fa [Compulsory Education Law] (1986) (PRC), JIAO YU FA [Education Law] (1995) (PRC).

80. Primarily Canjiren baozhang fa [the Law on the Protection of Persons with Disabilities] (promulgated by the Standing Comm. Nat'l People's Cong., Dec. 28, 1990, effective May 15, 1991) (PRC), Canjiren jiaoyu tiaoli [Regulations on the Education of Persons with Disabilities] (promulgated by the St. Council, Aug. 23, 1994, effective Aug. 23, 1994) (PRC).

81. XIAN FA art. 45, § 3 (1982) (PRC). Compulsory Education Law art. 9 (1986) (PRC). Note the word "other" is supplied after these three disabilities in the Constitution but not in the Compulsory Education Law.

82. Canjiren baozhang fa [the Law on the Protection of Persons with Disabilities] art. 2 (1990) (PRC).

83. JIAO YU FA [Education Law] art. 10, 38 (1995) (PRC).

84. Yang & Wang, supra note 77. Compare Compulsory Education Law art. 9 (1986) (establishing special schools or classes for students with visual, hearing, and cognitive disabilities) with two disability laws—the Law on the Protection of Disability Persons art. 19, 22, 23 (1990) and the Regulations on the education of persons with disabilities art. 3, 17 (1994) (making general and special classes and institutions available, depending on the conditions of students).

85. Helen McCabe, "The Beginning of Inclusion in the People's Republic of China," 28 *Research & Practice for Persons with Severe Disabilities* 16 (2003).

86. This can be inferred from the wording of Canjiren jiaoyu tiaoli [the Regulations on the education of persons with disabilities] art. 17 (1994) (PRC).

87. Id.

88. Law on the Protection of Disability Persons, art. 22 (1990) (PRC); Guanyu yinfa putong gaodeng xuexiao zhaosheng tijian gongzuo zhidao yijian de tongzhi [A Notice on the Dissemination of the Advisory Guideline on Physical Examination in College Admission into General Higher Education Institutions] (Ministry of Education, Ministry of Pubic Health and China Disable Persons' Federation, Mar. 3, 2003) www.law-lib.com/law/law_view.asp?id=75454 (last visited Aug 31, 2005) (PRC) [Advisory Guideline on Physical Examination in College Admission].

89. Id.

90. In this case, the student who was otherwise qualified but had infant paralysis was denied admission. After the suit was filed, since the school changed its position and admitted the student, the case was withdrawn. See Wang Wei v. Pingdingshan Finance and Commerce School. For relevant information, see also Guo Zhicheng, Putong gaodeng xuexiao zhaosheng luqu quan de sifa zhiyue wenti ["On the judicial check of higher education institutions' enrollment authority"], in Lao Kaisheng, *China Educ. L. Rev.* 124–138 (2002), supra note 45.

91. See, e.g., Zhang Xianzhu v. Bureau of Personnel, Wuhu City (so-called "Song Yue Case") (Xinwu Dist. People's Ct. Apr. 2, 2004; aff'd, Wuhu Interm. People's Ct.) www.yecao.net/Html/2004432411 6-1.Html (last visited Sept. 4, 2005) (PRC) (holding that administrative decision of the Bureau of Personnel in excluding the plaintiff from the recruitment process was lack of evidence). This was regarded as the first discrimination case for hepatitis B virus carriers, even though the court's rationale was more procedurally based.

92. Advisory Guideline on Physical Examination in College Admission, art. 1, § 5 (2003) (PRC), supra note 88. Guanyu yinfa "Gongwuyuan luyong tijian tongyong biaozhun (shixing)" de tongzhi [A Notice on Dissemination of Standards for Physical Examination in Civil Servant Recruitment (in Trial)] (Ministry of Personnel and Ministry of Public Health, Jan. 17, 2005) art. 7 (PRC) www.law-lib.com/law/law_view.asp?id=88001 (last visited Sep. 4, 2005).

93. Some Chinese scholars maintain that the law does not provide a definition of "minority" and that these 55 recognized groups are "minority nationalities" rather than "minorities." Some nationalities are not recognized due to their small population. See Bai Guimei, "The International Covenant on Civil and Political Rights and the Chinese Law on the Protection of the Rights of Minority Nationalities," 3 *Chinese J. I. L.* 468 (2004).

94. Randall Peerenboom, "Assessing Human Rights in China: Why the Double Standard?" 38 *Cornell Int'l L.J.* 71, at 134 (2005).

95. XIAN FA [Constitution] art. 4 (1982) (PRC).

96. JIAOYU FA [the Education Law] art. 46 (1995) (PRC).

97. XIAN FA [Constitution] art. 4 (1982) (PRC).

98. XIAN FA [Constitution] art. 119 (1982) (PRC). Minzu quyu zizhi fa [Law on the Regional National Autonomy] (Promulgated by the Nat'l People's Cong., May 1984, amended by the Standing Comm. Nat'l People's Cong., Feb. 28, 2001) art. 36, 37 (PRC). For a historical review on the education of minorities in China, see Gerard A. Postiglione, "The Implications of Modernization for the Education of China's National Minorities," in *Education and Modernization*, supra note 48, at 307–336. For English translations of the laws and policies on minority education in China, see *Chinese Educ. & Soc'y*, issue 3 and 5, vol. 32.

99. JIAO YU FA [Education Law] art.10 (1995) (PRC); Minzu quyu zizhi fa [Law on the Regional National Autonomy] art. 37, § 2 (1984) (PRC).

100. Minzu quyu zizhi fa [Law on the Regional National Autonomy] art. 71 (1984) (PRC).

101. Rebecca Clothey, "China's Policies for Minority Nationalities in Higher Education: Negotiating National Values and Ethnic Identity," 49 *Comp. Educ. Rev.* 396 (2005).

102. Minzu quyu zizhi fa [Law on the Regional National Autonomy] art. 71 (1984) (PRC); Putong gaodeng xuexiao shaoshu minzu yukeban, minzuban guanli banfa (shi xing) [Regulations on the Management of Minority Pre-college Class, College Class within General College (in Trial)] (Promulgated by Ministry of Education, June 3, 2005). LAW-LIB (last visited Sep. 2, 2005).

103. Id.

104. Guojia tongyong yuyan fa [Law on the Nation-wide Commonly-used Languages and Characters] (promulgated by the Standing Comm., Nat'l People's Cong., Oct. 31, 2000, effective Jan. 1, 2001) art. 10. LAW-LIB (last visited Sept 2, 2005) (PRC).

105. Id., art. 8; XIAN FA [Constitution] art. 4 (1982).

106. Law on the Regional National Autonomy, art. 70 (1984) (PRC).

107. For the language policies for the college entrance exams, see Clothey, supra note 101.

108. XIAN FA [Constitution] art. 36 (1982) (PRC).

109. In addition to the Constitution, see also Law on Regional National Autonomy, art. 11 (1984) (PRC). Zongjiao shiwu tiaoli [Regulation on Religious Affairs] (Promulgated by St. Council, July 7, 2004, effective Mar. 2, 2005), art. 2. www.law-lib.com/law/law_view.asp?id=87663 (last visited Aug. 20, 2005) (PRC) [Regulations on Religious Affairs].

110. XIAN FA [Constitution] art. 36 (1982) (PRC). See also Law on Regional National Autonomy, art. 11 (1984) (PRC). Compulsory Education Law, art. 16 (1986) (PRC). See also "Opinions Concerning the Correct Handling of the Issue of Religion Interfering in School Education in Ethnic Minority Areas" (promulgated by Education Comm'n, Jan. 15, 1983), *Chinese Educ. & Soc'y*, Sep.–Oct. 1999, at 35.

111. Regulation on Religious Affairs, art. 12, supra note 109 (2004) (PRC).

112. Regulation on Religious Affairs, art. 8, 9, supra note 109 (2004) (PRC).

113. Kim-Kwong Chan, China's Socioeconomic Changes and the Implications for the Religion-State Dynamic in China, 2004 B.Y.U.L. Rev. 325, 347 (2004).

114. Youlan Feng, Zhongguo zhexue jianshi [*A Brief History of Chinese Philosophy*] (1996). The English version of this book is Youlan Feng, *A Short History of Chinese Philosophy* (1948).

115. Constitution, art. 36 (1982) (PRC).

116. Some point out that in China freedom of religion is limited to five recognized religions, Buddhism, Taoism, Islam, Catholicism, and Protestantism, and eight officially recognized national religious organizations. See Carolyn Evans, "Chinese Law and the International Protection of Religious Freedom," 44 *J. Church & St.* 749 (2002); Randall Peerenboom, "Assessing Human Rights in China," supra note 94.

117. JIAO YU FA [Education Law], art. 28, § 4 (1995) (PRC).

118. Education Law, art. 43 (1995) (PRC).

119. The most common corporal punishment in traditional Chinese schools was to strike students' palms with a ruler.

120. The Compulsory Education law, art. 16 (1986) (PRC).

121. The Law on the Protection of Minors, art. 15 (1991) (PRC).

122. The Teacher Law, art. 37 (1993).

123. Minfa tongze [General Principles of the Civil Law], art. 106, 119, 120, 121 (1986) (PRC).

124. Id.

125. Xuesheng shanghai shigu chuli banfa [Rules in Dealing with Student Injury Accidents] (promulgated by Ministry of Education, June 25, 2002, effective Sep. 1, 2002) art. 9. www.law-lib.com/law/law_view.asp?id=41297 (last visited Aug. 20, 2005) (PRC) [Rules in Dealing with Student Injury Accidents]. Other remedies under civil law include stopping illegal actions, restoration of reputation, elimination of negative influence, and apology. See General Principles of the Civil Law, art. 120, 134 (1986) (PRC).

126. Rules in Dealing with Student Injury Accidents, art. 27 (2002) (PRC).

127. Lao Kaisheng et al., Shaonian ertong renshen shanghai de xianzhuang, wenti ji yufang ["The Current Situation, Problems and Prevention of Injuries upon Adolescents and Children"], in Xin Jiaodian: Dangdai Zhongguo shaonian ertong renshen shanghai yanjiu baogao [*New Focus: A Research Report on Adolescents' and Children's Injuries in Contemporary China*] 1–78 (Kaisheng Lao & Yunxiao Sun Ed., 2002). [*New Focus*] Wang, Xiaoyuan, qingjing zhong de shaonian ertong yinxing renshen shanghai ["Hidden Harm to the Adolescents on Campus"], Jiaoyu Lilun yu Shijian [*Theory and Practice of Education*], Volume 22, issue 2, 26, at 29, 2002.

128. Id.

129. Rules in Dealing with Student Injury Accidents, art. 9 (2002).

130. The General Principles of Civil Law, art. 101, 120 (1986) (PRC).

131. Constitution, art. 37 (1982) (PRC).

132. Damages for mental distress are not made available in the General Principles of Civil Law, the lack of which has been criticized by many Chinese legal scholars. The present governing rule comes from a 2001 Supreme People's Court interpretation. See Guanyu queding minshi qinquan jingshen sunhai peichang zeren ruogan wenti de jieshi [The Interpretations of Several Issues on Mental Distress Damages in Tort Liability] (Sup. People's Ct., Feb. 26, 2005, effective Mar. 10, 2005). www.law-lib.com/law/law_view.asp?id=589 (last visited Aug. 29, 2005).

133. Beijing yi 16 sui nü zhongxuesheng zhuangao laoshi qinquan yishen shengsu ["Female Student in Beijing Wins a Tort Case in Trial against Her Teacher"], Zhongguo Jiaoyu Bao (*China Education Daily*) (Dec. 29, 2001). www.jyb.com.cn/gb/jybzt/2002/jcjy/83.htm (last visited Dec. 9, 2003).

134. Liu Wei, guanzhu xiaoyuan zhong de xinxing renshen shanghai ["Attention Needs to Be Paid on the Hidden Harms on Campus"], Zhongguo jiaoyu bao [*China Education Daily*], Mar. 30, 2003, available at www.jyb.com.cn/gb/jybzt/2002zt/zxxjy/418.htm (last visited Dec. 9, 2003).

135. Constitution, art. 37, 40 (1982) (PRC).

136. The Law on the Protection of Minors, art. 31 (1991) (PRC).

137. The Law on the Protection of Minors, art. 14 (1991) (PRC).

138. Chu Hongqi, *An Analysis of Legal Issues* 141, supra note 47. Some of the disciplinary actions can be found in administrative rules issued by the Ministry of Education for student record management in senior high schools or equivalent secondary schools. See, e.g., Guanyu gaozhong jianli xuesheng dang'an de zanxing guiding [The

Temporary Regulation on Establishing Student Dossier in Senior High Schools] (promulgated by Ministry of Education, Feb. 22, 1984) www.law-lib.com/law/law_view.asp?id=2807 (last visited July 31, 2005) (PRC).

139. Xiaoxue guanli guicheng [Regulations on Primary School Management] (promulgated by the Education Commission, Mar. 9, 1996, effective Mar. 9, 1996) art. 15 www.law-lib.com/law/law_view.asp?id=62132 (last visited Sep. 2, 2005) (PRC).

140. The general rule in China is that dossiers are established for students once they reach high school or the equivalent such as specialized upper secondary schools. Dossiers record students' test scores, physical examination records, teacher evaluation, awards, and disciplinary actions and become part of their individual record that accompanies them for life.

141. See supra note 26.

142. The commonly cited support for this argument is German administrative law theory and some judicial interpretations in Taiwan. In addition, as a fundamental right under the Chinese Constitution, education should fall into the situations prescribed by article 8 of the Legislation Law where statutory regulation is necessary for the deprivation of such a right. See supra notes 23–26.

143. Zhang Jing, Students' Rights 72, supra note 47.

144. Regulations on Student Management, supra note 27.

145. Zhongxiaoxue xuesheng chufen zanxing guiding [The Temporary Regulations on Disciplinary Actions in Elementary and Secondary Schools] (promulgated by the Educ. Agency, Qingdao, April 26, 2002, effective April 26, 2002), art. 12–18. www.qdedu.gov.cn/wenjian/13.htm (last visited on Aug. 28, 2005).

146. The Education Law, art. 42, § 4 (1995) (PRC).

147. Xingzheng fuyi fa [The Administrative Review Law] (promulgated by the Stand. Comm. Nat'l People's Cong. Apr. 29, 1999, effective Oct. 1, 1999) art. 6, § 9 www.law-lib.com/law/law_view.asp?id=478 (last visited Aug. 20, 2005) (PRC).

148. Behind this categorization of civil law and administrative law is the basic distinction between private law and public law in the civil law tradition since the Roman law.

149. The Education Law, art. 31 (1995) (PRC).

150. Xingzheng susong fa [Law on Administrative Litigation] (promulgated by the Standing Comm. Nat'l People's Cong., April 4, 1989, effective Oct. 1, 1990) art 2. LAW-LIB (last visited Aug. 28, 2005) (PRC).

151. Law on Administrative Litigation, art. 12, § 3 (1990) (PRC); Guanyu xingzheng susong fa ruogan wenti de jieshi [An Interpretation on Several Issues in Law on Administrative Litigation] (promulgated by the Sup. People's Ct. Nov. 24, 1999, effective Mar. 10, 2000) art. 4 www.law-lib.com/law/law_view.asp?id=33 (last visited on Aug. 28, 2005) (PRC).

152. Law on Administrative Litigation, art. 11, § 8 (1990) (PRC).

153. One way to get out of this loophole is to interpret schools as organizations that are delegated to fulfill governmental functions by statutes or administrative regulations. Law on Administrative Litigation, art. 25, § 4 (1990) (PRC). While this is what the judges in the Liu Yanwen case did, many more stick to the wording of the Administrative Procedure Law and are reluctant to hear student discipline cases. See supra note 41.

5

Germany

Ingo Richter

THE LEGAL FOUNDATION FOR THE RIGHTS of students in Germany is the Basic Law (GG, the *Grundgesetzr*), the constitution of the Federal Republic of Germany. The manner in which Germany's legal system is embedded in international law, in particular, in the law of the European Union (EU), and the European Convention on Human Rights, is disregarded in the present context, especially in view of the fact that it applies in equal measure for all other EU member states.

The Basic Law explicitly regulates only a small number of school-related legal issues because it has largely delegated competence for Germany's education system to the federal states (the *Länder*). However, Art. 7 (GG) states explicitly that the overall school system is subject to federal supervision; that religious instruction is a regular part of the curriculum of public schools and must be provided in accordance with the principles of Germany's religious communities, although religious instruction is not compulsory for either teachers or students; and that, certain conditions being met, private schools may be established.

Aside from the explicit provisions of the Basic Law concerning the school system, the constitution contains other directives that play a role in this connection, particularly the fundamental rights that it sets out. These basic rights include human dignity, the right to free personality development, equality before the law, freedom of religion, freedom of speech and opinion, freedom of the press and of scholarship and teaching, the rights of parents, occupational freedom, and the right of recourse to the courts.[1] The Basic Law delegates no competences whatever to the federal government concerning legislation on and administration of schools, restricting itself to optional joint federal-state educational planning.[2]

The sources of German school law must in essence be sought in Germany's sixteen federal states. Yet, since federal law has precedence over state law,[3] as in other countries such as the United States, state school laws may not be at variance with federal law. The constitutions of the federal states therefore largely reiterate the provisions of federal constitutional law, adding some specifically state-related legal provisions.

When the Federal Republic was founded in West Germany in 1949, state constitutional provisions on the denominational structure of the school system played a major role. With few exceptions, these provisions have since been abolished. Some state constitutions provide a guarantee of the rights of ethnic minorities in their school systems. Students are also commonly accorded social rights such that, for example, they are not required to pay school fees and teaching and learning materials are provided free of cost. The new federal states in particular, namely those that states created in the last phase of the former German Democratic Republic, which acceded to the Federal Republic in 1990, have provided for a right to education in their constitutions.

On the whole, state constitutional law does not play a major role in Germany's school system. Only federal states such as Bavaria and Hesse, that have highly developed levels of state jurisdiction on constitutional issues, have their own distinctive school-related state constitutional law.

The main thrust of the sources of German school law must be sought in simple state laws. This might lead one to assume that the school laws of Germany's sixteen federal states as well as the rights of students differ substantially from state to state. Yet, this is not the case. One reason for this is that there is a German national tradition of school law extending back to the late nineteenth century German *Kaiserreich*; the other reason is that the so-called conference of state education ministers is in charge of coordinating education policy and thus also school-related legislation. At the same time, it is important to understand that school-related legislation is extraordinarily intensive in Germany, far more so than in most other countries of the world.

The reason why legislation is extraordinarily intensive is because the Federal German Constitutional Court (BverfGE, *Bundesverfassungsgericht*) ruled that all essential school-related questions must be addressed in the form of laws or at least require a legal basis.[4] In this sense, the term "essential" must be understood to mean that such laws directly affect the rights of the students.

Enforcement of this principle in the 1970s led to considerable tensions between court jurisdiction and education policy. If one takes a look at the school laws of the states, it can be found that they regulate the following matters: the organization and structure of school systems, planning, organization, administration, oversight, and funding of school systems, the legal relations between school, students, and parents, and more particularly the examination system, the rights and obligations of students, the legal status of teachers, disciplinary regulations for students, and private schools. Curriculum, on the other hand, is not covered by state education laws, at least if one disregards religious instruction, a field that involves many particularities typical of the individual states.

The legal sources of student rights must be sought not only in state laws but also in regulations issued by the states on the basis of existing legislation. Aside from these regulations, there are a large number of additional rules, although these are not of a legal character. These rules serve for purposes of school administration and they are exclusively organizational in character. They generally do not affect the rights of students. Even so, they do still have a certain binding force since school administrations use these rules to bring about a certain measure of uniformity in school conduct.

One final source of school law that needs to be mentioned here is case law. The principle of the rule of law set out in the Basic Law not only guarantees that basic rights apply in school but requires the legislature to adopt laws governing student rights. The Basic Law also provides the basis for judicial review of legal decisions taken by schools. Every student has the right of recourse to the courts if he or she feels that his or her rights have been violated. This also applies for pedagogical decisions that affect the rights of students such as decisions bearing on examinations. Judicial review of such decisions is restricted in scope and concerned in particular with compliance with prescribed procedures. Still, in recent decades, this issue has served to poison the atmosphere between educators and jurists, the reason being that schools cannot see the need for any legal protection of this kind. The German administrative courts are responsible for reviewing school decisions. If constitutional questions are involved, then the state or federal constitutional courts have the last say.

The Right to Education

The Basic Law does not provide for a right to education. Pursuant to Art. 6 II of the GG, parents have the right and the obligation to educate and care for their children; the Basic Law accords no explicit right to education for children themselves. However, the right to education has nevertheless been derived from the Basic Law and recognized by the highest German courts.[5] The legal basis for this is Art. 2 I GG and Art. 12 I GG, the right to free development of one's personality and the right of free selection of one's occupation or trade. The right of free personality development also includes the right to personality formation while the right to free selection of occupation or trade includes the right to learn a freely chosen profession or trade. These legal bases are supplemented by Art. 2, sentence 1 of the First Protocol to European Convention on Human Rights. The article does not extend beyond the guarantees provided under the Basic Law and has the same status as simple federal laws. Further, most German state constitutions and school laws guarantee a right to education; but these rights too are of the same tenor of the rights set out in the Basic Law.

The legal character of the right to education has changed in the course of its history. The right to education was at first considered to be a basic social right, but basic social rights were initially seen as merely programmatic in nature, as political objectives from which citizens could derive no legal claims: they were not capable to being adjudicated. This has changed in the course of the development of the Basic Law. Today, although the right to education is a basic right like all other basic rights, since it is indeterminate in substance, it is in need of further concretization by the legislative and the judiciary. What this means above all is that relevant laws are reviewed by the courts with a view to their conformity with the basic right to education in particular in cases where citizens invoke this basic right.

The right to education does not mean that everyone has a right to demand of the state a free education that accords with his or her interests but has nothing to do with his or her abilities. In connection with the right to attend a university, the Federal Constitutional Court once noted that everyone can demand of the state only what he or she can reasonably expect of society and that, in particular, this must remain within the scope of the possible and not lose sight of the state's need to meet its other obligations.[6] The right to education has four different connotations as follow:[7]

Minimum Basic Right

According to the Basic Law, and to be more specific, Art. 20 I GG in conjunction with Art. 1 I GG (human dignity), everyone has a right to claim a minimum standard of living, meaning a right to the material and immaterial prerequisites of life in society. This includes both the right to social assistance and the right to education in the sense that everyone must be in a position to acquire the knowledge and skills needed for life in society. If private institutions are unable to ensure this, then public schools must bridge the gap. The fact that the so-called PISA studies found that one quarter of German school students had not reached median skills levels and had therefore been seen as socially endangered is in blatant contradiction to the right to education.

Right of Access

Everyone, based on his or her aptitude and motivation, has the right of access to school.[8] This right may not be restricted for religious, ethnic, or gender-specific reasons. The principle of equality of opportunity is thus respected here. However, this right can be restricted for reasons of aptitude and performance as well as for reasons of capacity, though this is subject to stringent rules. Further, financial reasons may not be allowed to restrict free access, meaning that public schools are only allowed to charge school fees if social assistance is available at the same time. Private schools, on the other hand, are allowed to charge school fees; but the Basic Law requires that they too take measures to ensure that this does not lead to any segregation based on ownership of assets.[9] Still, this state of affairs does restrict the principle of equality of opportunity.

Right to Free Personality Development

Everyone has the right to develop his or her personality in school. While it is not possible for everyone to study what he or she wants, and students and parents must accept the curricula offered by the public and private education sectors, the state is required to shape school curricula in such a way as to ensure that these curricula are in line with the aptitudes and interests of students and in accord with the wishes of their parents. It goes without saying that the state may also pursue interests of its own; indeed, it must, for it has the task of guaranteeing provision of the knowledge and skills required for life in society. However, within this framework the state must also give due consideration to the talents and interests of students. This applies, for example, to students with disabilities, who are likewise entitled to develop their personalities.[10] This applies as well for highly gifted students, who, it has been decided, should not be taught unduly long together with other students.[11] The right to free personality development also applies to the special interests and concerns of girls. While, generally speaking, the principle of equality of opportunity calls for coeducation, it is permissible in Germany to set up separate classes for girls and boys for special subjects such as the natural sciences.

Right to Participation

The state must allow students to participate in shaping the school system; in particular, it must advise them in the task of shaping their own school biography. This means that students have a right to take a hand in counseling and administration of their schools and that, aside from the compulsory targets and subjects, school curricula must contain optional elements among which students are free to choose and in the formulation of which they must be involved. State education policy does, though, provide for substantial scopes in this regard.

The right to education does not rule out compulsory school attendance. In a good number of decisions, the Federal Constitutional Court has stated that compulsory school attendance does not violate the Basic Law and that, in contrast to the Weimar Constitution, which merely required the state to provide instruction, there is no constitutional right to home-schooling.

Religious Freedom

Art. 4 I and II, 7 II and III, and 140 GG in conjunction with Art. 137 of the Weimar Constitution, which continues in effect, represent the constitutional basis for student freedom of religion. Art. 4 GG guarantees positive and negative religious freedom, that is, the freedom to believe and to profess one's belief and the freedom not to believe. This principle applies at school as well. In Germany, there is no separation of church and state.

While Article 137 of the Weimar Constitution does not create a state church in Germany, insofar as state and church are fundamentally separate entities, this principle does not rule out cooperation between church and state; on the contrary, coordination of church and state is regulated in detail in the Basic Law, in legislation, in the state constitutions, and in agreements between the state and the churches. The state is obliged to remain neutral, to assume a stance of pluralistic neutrality which means that it may not identify itself with one religious community and must give room to all religious communities. The state must also respect individual religious freedom and the freedom of worship. Coordination of church and state finds expression in the following areas:

Denominational Schools

There are denominational schools in two German federal states, in Lower Saxony and North Rhine-Westphalia. All of the other states have only interdenominational Christian schools. In the two states that permit them, denominational schools may be established on the request of parents. The Basic Law allows for both interdenominational schools and denominational schools; the interdenominational schools may also be interdenominational Christian schools.[12]

Private Schools

Schools set up by churches or their organizations are private schools. In these schools, instruction and school life may be shaped by the religion in question. Private schools are entitled to state funding, a fact which is justified with reference to the provision in the Basic Law on private schools;[13] this also applies to church-run private schools. This amounts to a guarantee for the existence of a church-run private school system.

Religious Instruction

Religious instruction is a regular subject taught in public schools as well.[14] It is taught by government-employed teachers in accordance with the principles of the religious communities in question. However, the state has a right to supervise religious instruction. No teacher may be compelled to give religious instruction. Parents are allowed to remove their children from religious instruction; students above fourteen years of age are permitted to withdraw on their own from religious instruction. Students who do not attend religious instruction must take part in alternative courses in philosophy or ethics. Due to a special provision in their state constitutions, some federal states do not treat religious instruction as a regular subject, and in such cases religious instruction is provided by churches outside of the framework of regular school lessons. These states tend to provide information on religion within the framework of general instruction. Such tendencies appear to be gaining in strength, although this is a matter of considerable controversy.

School Prayer

Whether school prayer is permissible in public schools was long a controversial matter. The Federal Constitutional Court decided the issue in favor of school prayer. Yet, prayer must not be offensive to the adherents of other denominations or religions.[15] In school practice, though, school prayer has become the exception. At best, a religious service may be held in schools at the beginning of every school year.

Religious Symbols in Schools

In the predominantly Catholic German states, crucifixes are to be found traditionally in city halls, prisons, courts, restaurants, and schools. In a sensational decision, the Federal Constitutional Court decided that crucifixes are unconstitutional if only one single student or his or her parents object to them (BVerfGE 93, 1). Insofar as such objections are made rarely, crucifixes largely continue to be used in the classrooms of the Catholic states.

In recent years, the dispute over religious symbols in school has escalated in both Germany and in other countries in connection with the controversy about the wearing of headscarves in school. Female students are allowed to wear headscarves in class if they see this practice as an expression of their religious conviction and if the school itself permits them to do so. In other words, the decision lies within local schools. Whether female teachers are likewise permitted to wear headscarves is a matter of extreme controversy, one that is likely to be resolved differently from state to state. It is as yet unclear whether this will have consequences for other religious symbols, the crucifix worn on a necklace or the *kippa* worn on the head.

The question of religious freedom for students and the relationship between church and state was settled in Germany at a time when there were, basically, only the two major Christian churches in Germany and before the new states, in which only a minority of the population is affiliated with one of the two religious communities, acceded to the Federal Republic. Issues bound up with freedom of religion have become extremely virulent due to the social and political changes that have moved Germany. The emerging tendency seems to be that in the future Muslims will lay claim to the same rights as Christians and that ethics or value-related instruction will come to play an increasingly large role in general school subjects, either beside or in the place of religious instruction.

Free Speech Rights

No provision article in German constitutional law sums up the basic political rights. Even so, individual political liberty is guaranteed in several provisions. Art. 5 I GG guarantees freedom of expression and information and freedom of the press, which is understood as including the freedom of the audio-visual and the digital media. These rights may be limited only by the provisions of "general laws." Censorship is explicitly prohibited. Art. 8 GG guarantees freedom of assembly. Art. 9 GG covers freedom of association, with Art. 9 III GG expressly referring to "the right to form associations" or the right of employers and employees to form coalitions to conduct negotiations on working conditions as well as to use the means of strike and lockout to reach their ends. However, these concretizations of the freedom of association are not found explicitly in the Basic Law; they have developed on the basis of case law. These political freedoms have both positive and negative force in that there is also a guaranteed "right to remain silent," a right not to become involved in politics.

In principle, these rights also apply in school; however, due to the special character of the school they cannot claim full validity there. This is particularly true for the freedom of association, the reason being that schools are not business enterprises and students are not employees. There is no need to go into the legal status of teachers in this connection. The fact that these rights also extend to school matters means that they apply to instruction as well. In other words, freedom of speech cannot be restricted to the schoolyard and to school recesses, and teachers must give due consideration to it in the instruction they give. Outside of school, students can, of course, invoke these freedoms without reservation, provided that they are not restricted by the rights of their parents. Unlike the situation in the past, schools are not permitted to exercise any control whatever on the non-school behavior of their students.

Public schools are obliged to maintain political neutrality. This is not to say that schools are expected to be apolitical. This cannot be in view of its tasks. Rather, this means that schools are expected to be neutral in the sense of plurality. Schools must provide information about the plurality of opinions and constitute a forum for this plurality of opinions. Schools must follow the scientific principle of weighing both sides of an argument against one another.

This principle of neutrality through plurality is eminently important for the rights of students because it gives them a right to an opinion of their own. Students may voice their own opinion, in class as well, it being only the totality of opinions that engenders plurality and neutrality. Teachers have an important control function here, though, in that one of the tasks of teachers is to ensure the freedom of expression and the plurality of opinions. Teachers are expected to be neutral and not to identify with or propagate given schools of thought. On the other hand, teachers are expected to have opinions of their own and to express them, a situation that is almost a dilemma.

Freedom of speech extends not only to political opinions but also to opinions of all kinds such as the right to pass on information, to ask questions, and to make judgments. In this connection, teachers are not permitted to distinguish stringently between valuable and worthless opinions. Teachers are not allowed to suppress an expression of opinion by asserting that it has contributed nothing to a discussion.

At the same time, student freedom of expression does not mean that every student is allowed to say whatever he or she wants wherever he or she pleases; it means rather that the use of the freedom of expression and the order required for instruction must be brought into a reasonable balance. However, teachers are also not allowed to suppress opinions by asserting that there is, at a given moment, no time to discuss them. The art is to treat the schools as institutions and instruction as a process or shape conducive to encouraging the expression of a plurality of opinions, one that is at the same time integrated within a meaningful educational process.

The question of how schools should deal with the freedom of expression of Communist students arose in West Germany in the 1970s; the question did not, understandably, arise in East Germany because the leadership there suppressed "capitalist" opinions. Today, schools are forced to come to terms with the fact that young neo-National Socialists and Islamists insist on making use of their freedom of speech at school. What should be done if a twelve-year-old enters the classroom raising his arm in the Nazi salute? What should be done when young Muslims voice the opinion that the Koran contains an injunction to slaughter apostates?

The German criminal code forbids statements of National Socialist opinion, and it contains a paragraph against what is referred to as "demagoguery" (*Volksverhetzung*) and another paragraph banning any denial or belittlement of National Socialist crimes. Yet, today the criminal law is in this regard a blunt sword, powerless against the poison of resurrected old ideologies and their radicalization. To the extent that the state refrains from using laws to restrict, in lawful ways, our freedom of speech, to that very same extent we have freedom of speech! Taking issue with such opinions is a pedagogical task, not a legal one. Indeed, this is something that is easier said than done!

Freedom of the press, guaranteed under Art. 5 I GG, also extends to newspapers that are edited and mainly read by students as well as to other media used in schools. Again and again, typical conflicts arise when students write about their teachers or, even worse, print cartoons of them in school magazines. As noted, freedom of the press extends to schools and the work done in them. As long as the bounds of the criminal code are not transgressed, schools must accept this kind of internal criticism. The freedom of assembly guaranteed under Art. 8 GG also applies for students. Generally, though, students are not able to invoke the article on freedom of assembly to take part in demonstrations during the school day.

Typical conflicts may arise in Germany when, for example, on the occasion of a controversial state visit, demonstrations are called that can take place only at a given point of time, and students are interested in participating in them. Such conflicts should be resolved pragmatically, from case to case, and generally not by legal means. The freedom of association guaranteed under Art. 9 I GG actually poses no major problems in this context; students are of course free to belong to any association they wish, outside school. In schools, too, students are free to form associations and they do so without hesitation. Even so, as a rule, such associations entail no major difficulties; they are generally permitted by law as long as they are not unconstitutional in nature.

The free speech rights of students have become increasingly less important. In open societies, young people tend more to achieve their political aims outside school or to dissociate themselves from school as an institution, and this means that, if at all, students tend to engage in political activities outside the classroom. Today, the problem facing schools is far more the political passiveness and disinterest of students than any political activism that might find expression in a free-speech movement.

Students' Rights and Discipline

If students commit criminal offenses at school, they are subject to the provisions of the criminal code. Their student status has no bearing on this. In connection with a criminal case, prosecutors and law enforcement agencies are permitted to conduct relevant investigations inside and outside schools, without requiring any approval from school administrators. The police and the prosecuting authorities are therefore permitted to carry out searches and execute arrest warrants at school, assuming that the general procedural conditions have been met. In connection with special juvenile proceedings, courts often order special measures designed to educate and correct offenders; they may, for instance, be ordered to pay compensation or engage in community work. However, schools are, as a general rule, not involved in carrying out these measures.

As far as actions of children and juveniles are concerned with regard to infractions of school regulations instead of punishable offenses, schools, and not the police or administrative authorities, are responsible for prevention and sanctions. School principals have domestic authority over their schools that can, as a rule, be exercised by caretakers or custodians. Principals or custodians will, as a rule, react immediately to minor infractions of school regulations such as filth in toilets and/or food scraps in school canteens without needing to initiate any particular procedure. Schools are expected to respond to infractions of their rules primarily by educational means. In other words, if student behavior endangers other students, teachers, or third parties, or if the behavior of students impairs educational and training work in school, teachers are expected to attempt to use pedagogical measures, in essence, dialogue, to eliminate such dangers and/or put an end to such disturbances.

Apart from dialogue, though, teachers have few other pedagogical means available to them to react to such infractions. Corporal punishment is not a pedagogical measure. In Germany, it is banned. Indeed cases of corporal punishment are prosecuted as bodily injury. Today, teachers no longer have a right to use any form of corporal punishment which might be used to justify bodily injury. Punitive writing exercises or detention, popular measures in years of old, may no longer be used to "punish" infractions of school regulations, although they may still be used for pedagogical reasons.

Discriminatory measures such as having offenders stand or go into a corner, sending them to the principal, or out of a classroom are today regarded as pedagogically unsound. In view of this lack of options to respond pedagogically to infractions of school rules, teachers are very apt not to hesitate to fall back on disciplinary measures as a means of reacting to such infractions. However, school disciplinary proceedings have been strongly formalized in recent decades with the result that the threshold to initiating such proceedings is now relatively high.

There is a type of school-specific disciplinary proceeding that is today known as an administrative proceeding. This procedure is used by schools to respond to student misconduct that cannot be dealt with by pedagogical means. The infractions involved here may include violence, drug use, truancy, disturbance of lessons, vandalism, and so forth. A school can respond by imposing the following sanctions: a reprimand, exclusion from instruction, transfer to another class, referral to another school, and dismissal from school. Such decisions are taken by faculty meetings or by school administrations with faculty participation.

The rule is that mediation is attempted before a proceeding of this kind is initiated; the mediation body is normally a committee composed equally of teachers, parents, and students. Even so, this mediation committee is not authorized to impose the sanctions referred to above. In recent years, school mediation, including mediation by students themselves, has become a very widespread practice.

Administrative proceedings are geared to the principles of administrative proceedings, not the rules governing criminal proceedings. School administrations are not authorized to carry out searches, confiscations, and arrests. These are tasks for which the police and law enforcement agencies are responsible. In cases of emergency or imminent danger, schools and teachers have the same right and duty to act as anyone else under the circumstances. Proceedings must be fair and, in particular, grant students the right to a hearing. The measures taken must be in line with the principle of reasonableness. A school principal is authorized, under certain conditions, to impose measures in the form of so-called urgent measures. Against all such measures students may both file objections in the form of administrative proceedings and file formal suit in court.

Special Populations

In Germany, some 5 percent of all students are classified as disabled. These persons are covered by rehabilitation law which today is summarized in the ninth book of the Social Security Code. According to Art. 3 GG, no one can be discriminated against due to a disability. Since, in pedagogical terms, it is impossible to determine unambiguously, and in the same way for all types of disability, whether segregation or integration is the better approach to education for disabled children, the Federal Constitutional Court declared both approaches to be constitutional. Pursuant to Art. 3 GG, there is a basic right neither to integration nor to segregation.[16]

All of the German federal states operate special schools for disabled students that distinguish between types of disabilities. Either parents or teachers may apply to have a child transferred to a school of this kind once an expert assessment has been presented. The decision can be presented to the courts for review. Although Germany has a broadly developed system of such special schools, the trend in most states is toward integration, akin to the American notion of full inclusion, meaning that the children and juveniles concerned are kept as long as possible in regular schools and are returned to regular schools from special schools if this is at all possible. Regular schools are in possession of special instruments designed to assist in integrating disabled children; these include additional and specially trained teachers.

In some of Germany's federal states, there are traditional ethnic minorities: the Danes in Schleswig-Holstein, the Serbs in Brandenburg and Saxony. The state constitutions provide for special schools for these children who have a right to instruction in their mother tongue. Despite some minor legal disputes, the problem of Germany's traditional ethnic minorities may be seen as resolved.

On the other hand, the most important problem of ethnic differentiation must be seen in migration and the schooling of children of migrants. We can distinguish five large groups of migrants: citizens of the member states of the EU; labor migrants and their children, most of whom are born in Germany; the so-called resettled persons (*Aussiedler*) who are of German descent and come to Germany from eastern Europe; asylum seekers or those who have been persecuted in other countries; and refugees whom Germany has admitted in the context of humanitarian actions and who frequently return to their home countries. Taken together, these persons account for some 10 percent of the population.

Understandably, there are substantial differences between these groups. The principle of freedom of movement applies for EU citizens living in Germany. The children of labor migrants are given German citizenship at birth and must decide at the age of eighteen between their German and their foreign citizenship. Resettled persons are automatically given German citizenship on their arrival in Germany. Asylum seekers and their children are given German citizenship as soon as they have been recognized as political refugees. The other refugees come under the humanitarian international law defined by Geneva conventions.

All migrants have a right to education such that in the school system they must, as a matter of principle, be treated like Germans even though they may not have German citizenship. All migrants are also subject to compulsory school attendance in Germany. It is not permissible to segregate students on the basis of their origins; the legal principle at work here is strict integration. In fact, though, integration or segregation has very much to do with how and where people live.

For new arrivals who have yet to master the German language and are therefore unable to follow lessons in German, there are preparatory classes for transition periods which serve to enable them to learn the German language. In some states, there have been attempts to recognize the mother tongue of migrant children as a "foreign language" instead of English, which is as a rule the first foreign language taught in German schools. Aside from assistance measures designed to improve their knowledge of German, there are otherwise no particular educational measures geared to improving the German skills of migrant children. At best, special measures may come in for consideration in connection with religion.

Emerging Issues

Germany did very badly on the PISA comparative international performance assessments with the result that this has given rise to an intensive educational-policy discussion that focused on the large percentage of German students that did poorly and on the strong correlation found between performance and parental social status. Legal arguments have also been used in the discussion. Are the 25 percent of German students who failed to reach the median skills level in reading entitled to invoke the minimum basic right to education? The German PISA Consortium regards these students as a risk group whose skills are not sufficient to cope with the challenges of day-to-day life.[17] The fact that Germany's education system branches off at a very early point of time into a number of different school types is seen by many observers as the reason for the social selection of German students referred to above. Can we derive from the principle of equality of opportunity a right to comprehensive schooling?

The settlement patterns of the German population and the migrant population have led to a marked social segregation of the overall population. In Germany's large cities there are districts inhabited predominantly by migrants. Social problems are accumulating in these districts: poverty, crime, alcoholism, prostitution.[18] This also has led to marked segregation in schools, and in some cases migrants account for 60 to 80 percent of student bodies. These are problem schools. Is there, under German constitutional law, a right to attend desegregated public schools?

Youth unemployment in Germany is not any higher than general unemployment. Yet, it still amounts to an average of 10 percent, a figure that may range as high as 25 percent in some areas. Youth unemployment is very often the beginning of what is known as a "poverty career," with all the problems this development may entail. This is why Germany has initiated a number of comprehensive programs designed to combat youth unemployment; but these programs are not producing the hoped-for results.[19] In 1997, the Lisbon European jobs summit resolved that in five years time no young person in Europe would be without training, employment, or an appropriate qualification measure for longer than six months. Although this goal was to be achieved in five years time, not much has come of it. Is there a basic social right to training for young people?

In Germany, we can observe the emergence of a violence-prone radical right-wing grouping of young people, the size of which is estimated by some to be as high as 10 to 15 percent of the total youth population. In addition, Muslim youths are coming more and more to embrace fundamentalist principles, even in public, and some of them are prepared to use violence to achieve these principles. This is seen as involving a misanthropic potential that poses a threat not only to the victims but also to German democracy.[20] Within the bounds of the law, freedom of speech affords protection for these groupings as well, and schools are largely powerless in the face of such groupings. Art. 18 of the Basic Law does offer the possibility to deprive anti-constitutional groups of their political liberties if they abuse these liberties to challenge democracy. Might there be a possibility of this kind to respond to neo-National Socialist and Islamist-fundamentalist groupings?

The German school continues to be a law-governed, bureaucratically organized state institution, with private schools closely patterned on the model of the state school system. If it is correct that the paramount goal of education in the modern world is to instill in students a personal autonomy based on individualization, then the question is whether a school of this kind is at all up to the task. Three alternatives have for this reason been sought and proposed: privatization of the overall school system; autonomization of schools within the state school system; and tertialization of the school system, i.e. transformation of schools into a kind of "mixed economy."[21]

Conclusion

In today's Germany, the rights of students are well protected. In view of the fact that West German constitutional and school law was adopted by the new federal states in connection with reunification, this can also be said for eastern

Germany. In essence, the eastern German federal states have largely adopted the school-related legal arrangements in place in western Germany.

The protection of student rights afforded by these arrangements gradually prevailed in the decades after World War II, in particular because the fundamental rights guaranteed by the Basic Law were applied to school life, the principle of the reservation of statutory powers was applied to schools, and schools were made subject to the principle of judicial review. This process of juridification has now more or less run its course. It remains to be seen whether this new established law will prove to be able to come to terms with the new problems emerging in Germany. One problem, though, remains: the distrust harbored by educators for members of the legal confraternity.

Notes

1. Art. 1–6, 12, 19, and 103 GG.
2. Art. 91 b GG.
3. Art. 31 GG.
4. BVerfGE 34, 165; 41, 251; 45, 400; 47, 46, and many others.
5. BVerfGE 58, 257.
6. BVerfGE 33, 303.
7. Richter, I. (2001). Art. 7. In: Denninger E. (et al.). Kommentarzum Grundgesetz (3rd Ed.). Neuwied: Luchterhand.
8. BVerfGE 34, 165; 33, 303.
9. Art. 7, IV GG.
10. BVerfGE 96, 288.
11. BVerfGE 34, 165.
12. BVerfGE 41, 29, 41, 88.
13. BVerfGE 75, 40.
14. Art. 7, III GG.
15. BVerfGE 52, 223.
16. BVerfGE 96, 288.
17. Deutsches & Konsortium (2001). PISA 2000. Leske und Budrick: Opladen.
18. Bruhns, K. & Mack, W. (2001). Lernen in der sozialen Stadt. Leske und Budrich: Opladen.
19. Flitner, A., Petry, C., & Richter, I. (1999). Wege aus der Ausbildungskrise. Leske und Budrick: Opladen.
20. Heitmeyer, K. (2002, 2003, 2005). Deutsche Zustände I, II, III. Suhrkamp: Frankfurt am Main.
21. Richter, I. (1999). Die sieben Todsünden der Bildungspolitik. Hanser: Munich.

6

England: Rights of Passage? School Students and the Law in England

Neville Harris

THE EDUCATIONAL SYSTEM IN ENGLAND has traditionally been viewed as a national service which is locally administered. Local education authorities (LEAs), totalling approximately 150, are responsible for ensuring that the education needs of their area are met. But, over the past twenty or so years, central government has laid down an ever-tighter framework of regulation in order to meet its national policy goals such as raised school standards, increased parental choice, and reduced local control. The power of LEAs has diminished over such matters as the secular curriculum in schools. Even so, LEAs have retained overall responsibility for ensuring that there are sufficient numbers of school places and for other aspects of school administration, such as planning, financial delegation, the enforcement of school attendance, and determining provision for students with special educational needs. At the same time, schools have gained some autonomy over financial and personnel matters whilst being tied to the curricular framework imposed by central government. For example, sex education and school discipline are now covered by detailed national legislation[1] and official guidance from the Department for Education and Skills (DfES) in London.[2]

Within the complex legal framework governing education in England, students undoubtedly have educational rights, but their derivation is problematic for two principal reasons.[3] First, legislation confers obligations and powers on the relevant education providers; it is not rights-based. Any rights that are asserted by students or their parents are derived from, and are co-relative to, the duties imposed on schools, LEAs, the Secretary of State for Education and Skills, and other agencies such as the Chief Inspector of Schools. These duties and the powers necessary to ensure their operation can be difficult for individuals to enforce. When, for instance, officials in one London LEA were unable to provide sufficient teaching staff to maintain school places for all children in its location, it was argued that it was in breach of its statutory duty to ensure that there were "sufficient" schools in the area.[4] The court held that since the duty was a mere "target" duty, not an absolute duty, it was not enforceable. The court considered that as long as LEA officials were doing all that they could to meet their duty within the LEA's available financial resources, they were performing their public law target duty. Moreover, the court did not interpret the duty as conferring any enforceable rights in private law to individual parents or students.[5]

In other cases, claims alleging negligent failures in the provision of education under statutory duties have been hindered by the courts' view that authorities' exercise of "statutory discretions" (a term which refers to the inherent discretion or capacity for choice in the way that LEAs and schools carry out their duties) is non-justiciable, thereby immunising education providers from tort liability.[6] There are oft-repeated public policy justifications for such a restriction, the principal one being that schools and LEAs might be unduly hindered in their day-to-day functions by the ongoing threat of legal liability.

The enforcement of educational rights is also hampered by the way that the legislation gives considerable scope to the authorities as to the manner in which their duties are performed. Often, statutes permit authorities' duties to be constrained by the demands of "efficiency." For example, although parents have a right to express a preference for a particular school for their child, a LEA can deny a child's admission on the ground that it would not represent an "efficient use of resources."[7]

The second problem with the notion of student rights is that most educational rights in England rest exclusively with parents.[8] Many legal commentators have highlighted the lack of independent education rights for children across areas such as school choice, the curriculum, and religious worship in schools as well as appeal and other redress procedures.[9] There is a particular concern about students in their mid- or late-teens, since the general thrust of English child law, particularly post-Children Act 1989, has been to facilitate consideration of the views of older adolescents and recognize their independent interests.[10]

Of course, rights are conferred on children by the UN Convention on the Rights of the Child, ratified by the UK. Article 12 requires states to "assure to the child who is capable of forming his or her own views the right to express those views freely in all matters affecting the child," with the child's views to be given "due weight in accordance with the age and maturity of the child." Articles 28 and 29 impose specific obligations on states as regards the provision of education,[11] although they are fairly general, easily reflected in domestic arrangements, and legally unenforceable.

Also important is the European Convention on Human Rights (ECHR), whose provisions are now enforceable in the UK courts under the Human Rights Act (HRA) 1998. They include Article 2 of Protocol 1 to the ECHR: the state must not deny the right to education. This Article is considered to confer a right directly on each child, but the Article also upholds parental rights of choice in education by requiring respect for the right of parents to ensure such education and teaching conforms to their religious or philosophical convictions. The underlying premise that parents know what is best for their child may be generally sound, but may be open to question in some cases and, moreover, presupposes a unity of interest that may sometimes be inappropriate.

The Right to Receive an Education

Enforcement of the Child's Education

In addition to its recognition by the ECHR, the child's right to education is derived from two separate duties under education law. First, there is the statutory duty of parents to ensure that their child of compulsory school age[12] receives an "efficient full-time suitable . . . to his age, ability and aptitude, and . . . to any special educational needs he may have, either by regular attendance at school or otherwise."[13] The inclusion of "or otherwise" gives parents the right to educate their child at home, regardless of the child's wishes, provided the education meets these efficiency and suitability requirements; 21,000 five- to sixteen-year-olds were home educated in 2004.[14] Second, there is the LEA's duty to ensure that there are "sufficient" schools in their area, as noted above.[15]

The parent's duty is enforceable by LEAs, initially via a school attendance order. Penalties for failure to comply with an order[16] or for breach of the parallel duty to ensure that a child who is a registered student at a school attends regularly[17] have increased in the face of evidence that on average around 50,000 children are truant on any school day and that truancy contributes to social exclusion and educational under-achievement.[18] The offences are classed as criminal and penalties would be imposed by a magistrates' court following a prosecution by the LEA. The maximum penalty for either offence is a fine of £1,000. There is a more severe penalty for cases where the parent *knows* that his or her child is not attending school regularly: in those cases, there is a separate offence punishable on conviction with a maximum fine of £2,500 and/or imprisonment for a term not exceeding three months.[19] An alternative or extra measure is a civil order, an "education supervision order" under the Children

Act 1989, providing for support, guidance, and directions to the family by an education welfare officer or social worker.

Research has shown that the overall effectiveness of prosecution in non-attendance cases is uncertain; it can improve attendance in some cases, especially where children aged under eleven are concerned, but it is ineffective where the causes of truancy are outside the direct control of parent.[20] Other measures include such as truancy sweeps (patrols of public areas such as shopping precincts/malls by police and welfare officers, who may question truancy suspects) and the issuing of penalty notices. The latter have only recently come into force[21] and their effectiveness is as yet unclear. They may be issued where an authorized officer such as a police officer or a designated officer of the LEA has reason to believe that a child's parent has committed a school attendance offence.[22] The parent has a period of forty-two days from receipt of the notice to meet their responsibility before a prosecution may be brought against them.[23] If they pay the penalty in accordance with the notice, they will not be prosecuted. The penalty is £50, if paid within twenty-eight days, or £100 if paid within forty-two days.[24]

Parents can also be asked to sign a "parenting contract" with the LEA or school governing body[25] or can have a parenting order imposed upon them by a court which convicts them of a truancy offence.[26] Under the terms of either, the parent would be expected to attend counselling or guidance sessions for a prescribed period. The idea is that parents are shown the error of their ways and learn parenting skills. The effectiveness of such measures is yet to be assessed, but their use in the area of youth justice has improved parents' confidence in coping with their misbehaving offspring.[27] One further measure is the power of an authorized police officer to remove to designated premises a truanting student who is found in a public place.[28]

In the past, the government has attempted to set targets for reduced levels of absence from school. Yet, the evidence is that levels of unauthorized absence are unchanged over the past few years despite showing an overall increase since 1996–97.[29] The government's recent proposal for reforming schools contains a promise to "clamp down on truancy."[30] Whether a real reduction in truancy is possible remains to be seen.

The Principle of Free Education

The law in England has long embodied the principle that state education should be available to all without charge. It is also a principle found in international law.[31] The Education Act 1996 includes complex rules permitting parents to be charged for extra-curricular activities, including out-of-hours school trips, or for individual music tuition; and schools are also permitted to request voluntary contributions.[32] Otherwise, education is, in principle, free.

Despite the principle of free education, there are costs associated with sending a child to school[33] such as the purchase of school uniform or other clothing and payment for optional extras such as music lessons and school trips. Indeed, parents throughout the developed world are increasingly being asked to subsidise the cost of their children's schooling.[34] Although LEAs have powers to provide clothing,[35] and a general power to pay expenses to facilitate participation in school activities,[36] school clothing grants are less readily provided than they were fifteen years ago.[37] Parents entitled to particular social security benefits are entitled to free school meals for their child,[38] although around 15 percent of those eligible fail to claim them.[39]

There are also travel costs. Recent research reveals that approximately 15 percent of five- to ten-year-olds, 36 percent of eleven- to fifteen-year-olds, and 59 percent of sixteen- to eighteen-year-olds travel more than two miles to get to their school.[40] Costs are greater where a child is accompanied to school by an adult, as is the case with 85 percent of five- to ten-year-olds.[41]

LEAs have a duty to make arrangements for the provision of free transport for a child or, in the absence of doing so, to pay reasonable travel expenses. But the child must not live within walking distance of school and the LEA must have made neither boarding provision nor "suitable arrangements" for the child to attend a nearer school.[42] A child's age and the nature of the route, or any reasonable alternative routes, are also matters that the LEA must take into account.[43] Another is the parents' wish for a child to attend a school where religious education matches their own.[44] Yet, in one case, that did not mean that Orthodox Jewish parents living in Leeds had a right to transport costs for their child to attend a Jewish school in Manchester, forty miles away.[45] The school transport duty only applies in respect of young people of compulsory school age (above), although transport provision and policies for attendance by older students must be coordinated and a "transport policy statement" prepared.[46]

Approximately 10 percent of all pupils in England currently receive free home to school transport on a daily basis,[47] at an annual cost of £662 million in 2002–03.[48] Of this sum, 70 percent is expended on transport for children with special educational needs:[49] if a student has a formal statement of special educational needs that specifies transport arrangements, the LEA will be under a duty to meet the transport costs.[50] New legislation on school travel schemes is planned to reduce the proportion of children being driven to school by car each day, thereby hopefully avoiding problems associated with traffic congestion and lack of exercise.[51]

Participation in Post-compulsory Education

The UK government wants to increase the proportion of students who continue their education beyond compulsory school age, whether in secondary or further education.[52] Currently, the UK is ranked twenty-seventh out of the wealthiest thirty countries for participation in education by young people aged seventeen, and this "feeds into our historic legacy of low adult skills, and contributes to the dramatic gap between those who do best in our system and those who do least well."[53] Measures to improve participation include curriculum reform, to increase the vocational aspects of courses and thereby their attractiveness to the less academically orientated. Yet, they also include financial incentives, in the form of weekly educational maintenance allowances, entitlement to which is subject to strict conditions concerning attendance and completion of tasks.[54]

Choice of Schools

As noted above, parents in England have a right to express a preference for a school; and the child or young person must be granted a place at the selected school unless to do so would not be compatible with "efficient education and the efficient use of resources" or with any approved arrangements for the selection of pupils on the basis of their high ability or aptitude.[55] Parents have a right of appeal if unsuccessful. In 2003–04, 59,420 appeals were heard.[56] The courts have confirmed that school admission rights, including those concerned with appeals, reside with parents but not their children.[57] A committee of MPs has proposed that children should be involved in the secondary school admission process, because they tend to identify "reasonable and rational factors on which to base decisions on school preference."[58]

Discrimination against persons on the grounds of their sex (or transgender) or marital status; their colour, race, ethnic or national origin or nationality; or their disability; is unlawful where it occurs in the school admission process.[59]

Religious Freedom of Students

Currently, around two-thirds of schools in England are not affiliated to any particular religion.[60] Nonetheless, because religious education is part of the required basic curriculum in *all* state schools and the law requires each student to participate in a daily act of collective worship,[61] religion retains a place within the life of even the most secular of schools. Each locally determined religious education syllabus for non-denominational schools (the agreed syllabus) must "reflect the fact that the religious traditions in Great Britain are in the main Christian whilst taking account of the teaching and practices of the other principal religions represented in Great Britain."[62] Similarly, the separate duty concerning collective worship specifically requires that most acts of worship at such schools should be "wholly or mainly of a broadly Christian character" although not distinctive of any particular Christian denomination.[63] However, England has a multi-ethnic and religiously diverse population, and in an attempt to recognise that, a multi-cultural and/or multi-faith approach has been taken within many LEAs, both in the framing of the agreed syllabus for religious education and in the nature of the collective worship that takes place.

There is, in fact, some degree of flexibility under the legislation such that, for example, a school can apply for a dis-application of the requirement for broadly Christian collective worship.[64] Further, a court has accepted that worship does not have to venerate Christ to be "broadly Christian" and that "the tenor of the legislation is against a doctrinal and divisive approach."[65] Despite this element of flexibility, there have been calls to end this emphasis on Christianity within the law on religious education and collective worship applicable to non-denominational schools, either because formal participation in Christian religious obsevance is diminishing (church attendances have declined steadily over the past fifty years) and so the requirement is out of date,[66] or due to the fact that the law is discriminatory within the terms of the ECHR.[67] It is, however, arguable that, in the light of relevant Strasbourg jurisprudence,[68] the statutory right of parents to withdraw their children from collective worship and/or from religious education at school while being permitted to have their children receive religious education elsewhere meets the requirements of Article 2 of Protocol 1 and Article 9 (freedom of religion).

Denominational schools can basically determine the kind of religious education that they want: in the majority of denominational schools religious education will follow the trust deed, the tenets of the religion or religious denomination or, if the parents prefer it, the agreed syllabus.[69] Although it might be assumed that, by sending their child to a school with a religious character, the parents would want their child to receive its denominational religious education, they do nevertheless have the right to withdraw their child from it. This right is not enjoyed by the student him/herself. In that sense, the student, even if aged sixteen or over, does not enjoy freedom of religion other than vicariously via his or her parents' right but might do under the ECHR, Article 9, discussed below. As already noted, the young person also has no right of choice over the school itself.

The wearing of religious dress has generated the occasional dispute over the years, including a 1983 case in which a school's refusal to admit a Sikh boy wearing a turban was held to constitute unlawful race discrimination.[70] The HRA 1998 has now made it potentially a matter of fundamental right. An important case has concerned a complaint brought by a sixteen-year-old Muslim girl with the assistance of her elder brother.[71] The girl's school's policy on dress had been formulated in consultation with local Muslim community representatives. The wearing of the *shalwar kameeze* (headscarf) was permitted but not the *jilbab* (long cloak). The girl had been aware of the rule when she joined the school but she had subsequently become more devout and held a more strict view on religious dress. The girl claimed that she was excluded from school by virtue of the application of the policy and that her free expression of religion under Article 9 of the European Convention on Human Rights was being denied.

The Court of Appeal concluded that she had been excluded, unlawfully, by virtue of the school's refusal to permit her to attend wearing the jilbab. As regards interference with her freedom to manifest her religion, the court said that as the school had not approached this matter correctly when formulating its policy, it had acted unlawfully. The wider effect of the decision was not that it would necessarily be unlawful for any school to ban the wearing of the jilbab or any other particular form of dress, but rather that schools would need to recognize the importance of individual students' freedom of religion and would have to consider the relevant questions carefully in deciding upon their policy. Although the House of Lords upheld the appeal by the school and found that the girl's right to manifest her religion was not infringed and that if there was an interference with that right here it was legally justified under Article 9, schools will still need to be mindful of their duty under this article in formulating their policy.

Free Speech Rights of Students

Freedom of expression, including freedom of speech, is protected by Article 10 of the ECHR, although interference with it is possible on various grounds such as the protection of health or morals or the reputation or rights of others.[72] Article 10 is considered to be of more relevance to the rights of teachers than those of students.[73] For example, it was suggested that the (now-abolished) prohibition of the promotion by teachers of "the acceptability of homosexuality as a pretended family relationship" might conflict with free expression rights.[74]

Students whose verbal or other forms of expression are considered to be offensive or disruptive to the educational process are liable to disciplinary action by teachers, particularly where racist or homophobic utterances are made and certainly where their intent or effect is the harassment or bullying of others. On the whole, the courts will leave to teachers' and governing bodies' judgment as to whether a particular sanction amounts to a justifiable response to students' statements, as in a case when the court upheld a decision not to reinstate a student who had been excluded for failing to apologise after he had sworn in school in the presence of a teacher.[75]

On the other hand, official guidance advises against exclusion for breaches of school rules on appearance, including jewelry and hairstyle,[76] presumably on the basis that they do not present a sufficient threat to the running of the school. Otherwise, freedom of expression by students would be subject to the same restrictions that apply across society. For example, threatening or abusive language or statements that are intended to incite racial hatred would be punishable under the criminal law as might the daubing or spray-painting of slogans and other graffiti defacing property.

Discipline and Students' Rights

Introduction and General Duties

School discipline is the subject of a range of legislative provisions and official guidance.[77] It will be extended, as set out in proposals published toward the end of 2005, by legislation that will "introduce a clear and unambiguous legal right for teachers to discipline pupils."[78] However, the law and guidance pay little attention to the independent rights of the student, although the guidance now pays some regard to students' right to express views and attend some of the disciplinary processes.

General responsibility for discipline within schools rests with the school's governing body and the head teacher.[79] The head teacher must publicize the school's disciplinary measures and code of behavior by making them known within the school and to parents of registered students. At least once every school year the head teacher must bring the measures to the attention of all students, parents, and persons employed or providing services at the school.

Home-School Agreements

Parents are being asked to take responsibility for the conduct of their children, both generally and in relation to the completion of schoolwork. Parents must be invited, but may not be compelled as a condition of the entry or continued enrolment of their children, to sign a declaration committing them to the terms of a home-school agreement. A home-school agreement is a document outlining a school's aims and values, its responsibilities as regards the education of children, parental responsibilities concerning the education of their children at the school, and the expectations of schools as regards the conduct of their students.[80]

The law does not make students parties to these agreements, which seems odd given that their principal purpose is to help to secure good behavior. Nonetheless, if a student is considered to have "sufficient understanding of the home-school agreement," he or she may be invited to sign the parental declaration "as an indication that he acknowledges and accepts the school's expectations of its [students]."[81] It would be somewhat charitable to regard this power as recognizing the child's right of participation as enshrined in Article 12 of the UN Convention on the Rights of the Child (above), not least because the student's signature is directed toward an acknowledgment by the student of his or her responsibilities rather than rights. An official survey has revealed that students are enthusiastic signatories to these agreements.[82]

Detention and the Use of Force

School detention was first covered by legislation in 1997.[83] The power may only be used where a head teacher has expressly included it within a school's disciplinary measures and publicized it. Parents must be given at least twenty-four hours' notice in writing of a student's detention, but there is no provision for a parental veto. Detention may only be given where it is "reasonable," which means, among other things, that it must constitute a "proportionate punishment in the circumstances of the case." A school must also give consideration to factors such as the student's age, special educational needs (if any), religion, and travel arrangements.

The operation of this statutory provision has yet to be subjected to systematic research. On paper, at least, it provides a framework in which rationality and proportionality should be the guiding principles in any decision. However, in many respects, it seems a rather outdated and pointless form of punishment. Whether it is sanctioned by Article 5 of the ECHR, which provides for everyone to have "the right to liberty and security of person," is also yet to be tested. Art 5.1(d) permits "the detention of a minor by lawful order for the purpose of educational provision," but when used as a punishment, detention is not directly for the purposes of educational provision.

Also introduced in 1997 is a statutory power for teachers to use "reasonable force" in certain circumstances. It represents an attempt to balance the rights of students with the need to protect teachers from unwarranted litigation alleging abuse when bodily contact occurs. The power may be exercised where there is a risk to pupil safety or of damage to property, or in order to prevent a pupil from "engaging in any behaviour prejudicial to the maintenance of good order and discipline at the school or among any of its pupils, whether that behaviour occurs during a teaching session or otherwise."[84]

While threats to the "good order" might be perceived as fairly commonplace in schools, the stated intention is that the power should be used only as a last resort and not for dealing with "trivial misdemeanours" by students.[85] That power is distinguishable from corporal punishment by teachers.[86] In *Campbell and Cosans v. UK*,[87] the European Court of Human Rights held that parents could hold a philosophical conviction against the use of corporal punishment that required respect for the purposes of ECHR, Article 2 of Protocol 1.

In *Costello-Roberts v. UK*,[88] the court confirmed that corporal punishment was not intrinsically a form of torture or inhuman or degrading treatment proscribed by Article 3 of the ECHR, but might be in particular circumstances. By this time, however, teachers' "reasonable chastisement" defense under domestic law had already been abolished in relation to state schools.[89] Under 1998 legislation, it was also removed in relation to independent schools.[90] Teachers would therefore be liable to tort actions if they used corporal punishment.

A small number of schools founded on strict Christian beliefs have asserted that corporal punishment cannot be proscribed in this way without infringing various rights of teachers and parents under the ECHR, including the right to manifest one's religion or beliefs under Article 9. They believed in the biblical saying: "spare the rod and spoil the child." In 2004, the House of Lords held that while the administration of corporal punishment could amount to a manifestation of a belief, interference with it was justified under the permitted limitations within Article 9(2) in that it was "prescribed by law" and "necessary in a democratic society" for the protection of "the rights and freedoms of others."[91] Baroness Hale said that "if a child has a right to be brought up without institutional violence, as he does, that right should be respected whether or not his parents and teachers believe otherwise."[92] The parents' claim of breach of Article 2 of Protocol 1 also failed.

Searches

There is, at present, no specific legislation on school searches, but that is set to change. Proposed legislation, the Violent Crime Reduction Bill, which is likely to be voted through and become law some time in 2006 or 2007, will introduce a new, unprecedented, statutory power for members of school staff to search students or their possessions for knives, blades and, more generally, items classed as "offensive weapons," and to seize and retain any items found. The searches will be able to be carried out on school premises or elsewhere, if a student is under the lawful control or charge of a school, such as when on a school trip.

Intimate searches will not be allowed, in that a student may only be required to remove outer clothing (which "includes an outer coat, a jacket, gloves, and a hat"). A searcher will need to be of the same sex as the student, and more than one other adult person of the same sex as the student will have to be present when the search is carried out. Under the present law, if a student is suspected of carrying a weapon but will not agree to be searched by staff, the school would need to summon the police, who have the necessary powers under the general law to search suspected offenders. That would still be the position in relation to searches for drugs after the new Bill, which does not apply to them, becomes law. In either case, the government's current guidance suggests that the school staff probably have the power to search school property such as lockers if the student refuses authorization.[93]

Exclusion from School

In the course of a school year a student may be excluded on disciplinary grounds for a fixed period of up to forty-five days or fixed periods totalling up to forty-five school days; or he or she may be excluded permanently.[94] If a student is excluded for more than forty-five school days in total but not permanently, it is unlawful and violates the student's right to education under the ECHR, Article 2 of Protocol 1.[95]

There were over 300,000 fixed period exclusions from schools in England in 2003–04, relating to 201,000 students or 2.6 percent of the school population.[96] Permanent exclusions peaked at 12,665 in 1996/97, but there have been over 9,000 permanent exclusions in each of past four years and the 2003–04 total was just under 10,000, the highest total since 1998–99.[97] In 2003–04, almost 30 percent of exclusions in England were for persistent disruptive behavior; over 20 percent for verbal abuse or threatening behavior toward an adult; and 20 percent for physical assault on another student.[98]

Permanent exclusion is the most severe sanction that can be imposed by a school for indiscipline, as acknowledged by the right of appeal attached to it. Notwithstanding the duty of LEAs to make alternative arrangements for those excluded from school, there will undoubtedly be disruption to the young person's education and a significant blot on his/her academic record. Exclusion is associated with educational under-achievement, social alienation, and criminality.[99]

On taking a decision to exclude, a head teacher must have regard to official guidance.[100] Exclusion is referred to as a "serious" step which should normally be used only when other measures have been tried and failed and generally not as a first step, apart from cases of "serious actual or threatened violence against another pupil or a member of staff," sexual abuse or assault, supply of an illegal drug, or the carrying of an offensive weapon.[101]

Due process has been an important issue, whether in relation to the investigation of the facts, the decision to exclude, or the appeal process. Various principles have been established. For instance, arrangements for the students' continuing education must be made and the exclusion of students with special educational needs should be avoided. The case law indicates that the evidence put before an appeal panel must be balanced[102] and should refer to any positive as well as negative factors within the student's record;[103] a student's previous record will be relevant to the reasonableness of exclusion;[104] there should be a proper investigation, with the student being entitled to give his or her version of events before the decision to exclude is taken; and witness evidence should be put before the appeal panel, although written rather than oral evidence might be sufficient.[105] There is also considerable case law on the standard of proof required in exclusion cases.[106]

Various procedural requirements are prescribed, such as the head teacher's duty to inform the parents or, if aged eighteen or over, a student, of the reasons for the exclusion and their right to make representations.[107] The guidance indicates that although only the parent or a student aged eighteen or over has a right to attend and address the governing body, a younger student should be permitted to do so "if the parent requests this."[108]

If, as is usually the case, a permanent exclusion is upheld by the governing body, the parent, or the student aged eighteen or over, has a right of appeal to an independent appeal panel.[109] In 2003–04, 1,100 appeals were made, of which 21 percent succeeded. The success rate has fallen markedly since the period 1999–2001; a factor could well be changes to the composition of appeal panels in 2002, with the appointment of more ex-teachers to them.[110] Students, unless aged eighteen, have no right to attend and make representations to the panel although their parents do.[111] Yet, the guidance states that students should normally be allowed to do so if they wish and the parents agree. It also states that students may appear as witnesses, with their parents' consent.[112]

Even the small number whose exclusion was found by an appeal panel to have been wrong, for example, because the student was not shown to have been the culprit or the exclusion was unreasonable in relation to the wrong committed and/or the student's previous record, are not guaranteed reinstatement. The guidance says that the panel must "balance the interests of the excluded pupil against the interests of all other members of the school community" and may still decide that reinstatement is "not in the best interests of all concerned."[113] Even where the panel orders a reinstatement, the school has a degree of managerial discretion and can avoid returning the student to his previous class; the head teacher is entitled to take account of teachers' refusal to accept him back into their class and, through their unions, to threaten strike action if their wishes are ignored.[114]

None of the above statute law or guidance will apply if a student is excluded from an independent school. Instead, the student's parent would need to seek a remedy through a private law claim for breach of contract.[115]

English statutory law prohibits discrimination on the grounds of sex, race, colour, ethnicity, national origins, and nationality in relation to exclusion or "any other detriment."[116] The official guidance on exclusions stresses the importance of avoiding racial or gendered stereotyping of pupils which might lead to inequality in treatment. There have, nevertheless, been complaints that the much higher incidence of permanent exclusion among African Caribbean boys suggests that race discrimination may be occurring.[117]

Students with statements of special educational needs are much more likely to be permanently excluded from school than other students.[118] Many children with special needs are disabled physically and/or mentally disabled. It is now "unlawful for the body responsible for a school to discriminate against a disabled pupil by excluding him from the school, whether temporarily or permanently."[119] Discrimination means less favourable treatment than others receive, for a reason related to the child's disability, being treatment which is not "justifiable."[120]

Alternative Education for Excluded Students

LEAs have a duty to make arrangements for the provision of "suitable full-time or part-time education at school or otherwise" for children of compulsory school age who, by reason of exclusion, or other reasons, may not otherwise receive suitable provisions.[121] In a recent case, Lord Justice Sedley confirmed that "it is the LEA's obligation to ensure that no child falls out of the education system, even if excluded from school."[122] Around 50 percent of excluded students are later placed at a "pupil referral unit."[123] While the education provided at these units is often not full-time, the courts have held that it does not necessarily matter, if the student is being provided with "stepping stone back to mainstream school education."[124] Further, the House of Lords has also held that since the statutory duty is mandatory, a LEA cannot abrogate its responsibilities by asserting a lack of funds.[125]

Special Populations

Anti-discrimination law, outlined earlier, also applies to the education provided at a school.[126] Additionally, there is a new emphasis on the promotion of equality. For example, schools must take reasonable steps to ensure that a disabled student is not substantially disadvantaged as a result of his or her disability, in relation to the services provided by the school;[127] LEAs must prepare accessibility strategies and plans concerning disabled students' access to education;[128] and school governing bodies and LEAs must promote racial equality.[129] In addition, there are numerous programmes and initiatives concerned with those facing particular social and other barriers to learning, including immigrants and Gypsies.[130]

So far as the children of asylum seekers are concerned, the government initially took the view that it would be preferable, while the family's claim was being determined, that the children should be educated within accommodation centres rather than in school. The Nationality, Immigration, and Asylum Act 2002 empowers the Secretary of State to make such arrangements,[131] but the government has not yet brought these controversial statutory provisions into effect. Indeed, now that it has abolished plans for these centres, the provisions seem certain to be shelved permanently. Meanwhile, even though there is evidence that LEAs and schools can respond positively to the challenge of including asylum seeker and refugee children,[132] research in England has found that in the process of dispersing asylum seeker families, which is national policy, their education tends to be marginalized and this can result in their placement in schools which do not have adequate resources to meet their educational needs.[133]

Around one in five students has special educational needs, meaning a learning difficulty which is significantly greater than that of others in their age group or which arises from a physical and/or mental disability which hinders their capacity to make use of standard educational facilities. Under complex legislation,[134] LEAs and schools have a wide range of duties to identify and support these students. Those with the greatest needs will undergo a formal assessment process that can lead to the preparation of a "statement" setting out the child's needs and required provision.

Parents may request that a particular school is named in the statement as a child's placement, but their LEA can refuse if it is unsuitable for the child or if his/her attendance would prejudice other students' education or the efficient use of resources.[135] There is a statutory presumption that a child with special needs should be educated in a mainstream school as opposed to one catering specifically for students with learning difficulties.[136] The parents (but not the child, regardless of his or her age) have a right of appeal to the Special Educational Needs and Disability Tribunal against various decisions taken in the course of these processes. Although the students themselves have few independent rights, the authorities are expected to take account of their views when making decisions about their education.[137]

The courts have failed to accord giftedness the status of a learning difficulty for the purposes of the above law.[138] Even so, in the past few years the government has promised support for particularly gifted students as a separate area of national policy.[139]

Emerging Issues

Gradually, students' participation rights are being extended. Important in this area is a new duty on LEAs and governing bodies of maintained schools to have regard to official guidance "about consultation with pupils in connection with the taking of decisions affecting them," which must "provide for a pupil's views to be considered in the light of his age and understanding."[140] The published guidance stresses that student participation is beneficial not only for the young people themselves but also schools, conveying the message that young people are "major stakeholders in society with important contributions to make to the design and delivery of services they receive, including education"[141] and that students should have equal opportunities to be heard regardless of factors such as their ethnicity, gender, or disability.[142]

Another new duty requires the views of parents and those of students to be taken into account when a school is inspected.[143] This emphasis on collective rights is carried through into recent government proposals "to engage young people in positive activities and empower them to shape the services they receive."[144] "Empowerment" is a current buzzword in government education policy but its realization is problematic.[145] One might assume that education would be one of the services that young people would like to play a role in shaping. There is also to be an "opportunity fund" in each local authority "to be spent on projects that young people want—for example, providing a youth café or running a sports league."[146] This could indirectly extend rights to education in its broadest sense, but does not seem to contemplate any rights specifically concerned with schooling, even if many schools now have an extended community role[147] that might encompass some of the opportunity fund projects.[148]

In the light of the government's aim of "balancing greater opportunities and support with promoting young people's responsibilities,"[149] further calls by children's rights campaigners for individual young people, especially ones aged fourteen or over, to be given more effective rights to participate in the various decision making processes that affect their own education are likely.

Proposals for "personalised learning" to engage all children, including those likely to lack enthusiasm or to feel excluded by reason of their social background, have recently been published.[150] The kind of flexibility and variety within the curriculum that is promised could raise achievement levels but will be difficult to deliver.

Conclusion

The government continues to promote the idea of education as a lifelong activity for every citizen. Even so, education clearly remains at its most potent during the formative period of childhood and adolescence. Indeed, in recent years, the government has developed important policies on early-years educational provisions, as illustrated by measures to extend "nursery" education and to provide a statutory curricular framework for children aged three or four.[151] As yet, there is no duty on parents to ensure their very young child's participation in these forms of education, but it may be introduced in the future.

Either way, there is a compulsory period of education from age five to sixteen, leaving aside problems of truancy and exclusion. There is also voluntary participation by many students who are aged seventeen or eighteen. The latter age group comprises young people who are attaining, or on the threshold of, adulthood. However, as yet, student rights largely fail to reflect the evolving capacities of young people and this gives rise to anomalies. For example, sixteen- or seventeen-year-olds who leave school and take jobs would acquire employment rights as individuals, including rights to pursue claims against their employers in employment tribunals if dismissed. Yet if such individuals were permanently excluded from school, only their parents could appeal. That almost all education rights for those aged under eighteen should, in effect, be "owned" and enforceable by parents or care-givers of students rather than students themselves is inappropriate, particularly in the case of sixteen- or seventeen-year-olds.

Leaving aside the issue of self-determination, it could be argued that while educational rights are highly contingent and arise out of duties on schools and LEAs that are mostly far from absolute, and although factors such as social class and ethnicity affect the individual's capacity to utilize them,[152] these rights are on the whole reasonably well protected. Few claims for infringements of human rights due to aspects of educational practice in England have succeeded, although the ECHR rights that are incorporated into the HRA 1998 provide, in themselves, a very loose framework for the recognition of students' rights.

Notes

1. Legislation here refers to either Acts of Parliament/statutes (primary legislation made by the UK Parliament) or regulations or orders, known as statutory instruments (secondary legislation, made by government ministers).

2. See N. Harris, "The Regulation and Control of Sex Education in Schools," in N. Harris Ed. *Children, Sex Education and the Law* (London: National Children's Bureau, 1996), 1–23; P. Meredith, "Some Shortcomings in the Provision of Sex Education in England," in N. Harris and P. Meredith Ed., *Children, Education and Health. International Perspectives on Law and Policy* (Aldershot: Ashgate, 2005), 105–128; N. Harris and K. Eden with A. Blair, *Challenges to School Exclusion* (London: Routledge Falmer, 2000).

3. The term "students" is used in place of the standard UK terminology, "pupils," which is in fact starting to come under pressure from the term "learners."

4. Education Act 1944, s 8, since replaced by the Education Act 1996, s 14.

5. R v. Inner London Education Authority ex p Ali and Murshid (1990) 2 Admin LR 822.

6. See in particular X (Minors) v. Bedfordshire County Council [1995] ELR 404; 2 AC 633; [1995] 3 WLR 153; [1995] 3 All ER 353; [1995] 2 FLR 276 (House of Lords); and Phelps v. London Borough of Hillingdon [2000] ELR 499; [2000] 3 WLR 776; [2000] 4 All ER 504 (House of Lords).

7. School Standards and Framework Act 1998, s 86(3); Education Act 1996, Sched 27 para 3.

8. As observed by UN Commission on Human Rights, Report submitted by Katarina Tomaševski, Special Rapporteur on the right to education, Addendum. Mission to the United Kingdom 18–22 October 1999, E/CN.4/2000/6/Add 2 (www.unhcr.ch/Huridcoda) (Centre for Human Rights, Geneva, 2000), paragraph 90.

9. For example, C. Hamilton, "Rights of the Child: A Right to Education and a Right in Education," in C. Bridge Ed., *Family Law Towards the Millennium: Essay for M. Bromley* (London, Butterworths, 1997) 201–233; P. Meredith, "Children's Rights in Education," in J. Fionda Ed., *Legal Concepts of Childhood* (Oxford, Hart, 2001); N. Harris, "Education Law: Excluding the Child" (2000) 12(1) *Ed. and the Law* 31–46; and J. Fortin, *Children's Rights and the Developing Law* (London, Lexis Nexis Butterworths, 2003).

10. See L. Cannon, "Special Educational Needs and the Case for Children's Rights" (2005) 6(2) *Ed. Law Jnl* 108–122.

11. Article 28 provides, inter alia, for a right to education, which should be on the basis of equality of opportunity; primary education compulsory and free to all; and measures should be taken to encourage regular attendance at schools and the reduction of drop-out rates. Article 29 indicates the matters toward which education should be directed, such as the development of the child's personality, talents, and mental abilities to their fullest potential and "the preparation of the child for responsible life in a free society, in the spirit of understanding, peace, tolerance, equality of sexes, and friendship among all peoples, ethnic, national and religious groups and persons of indigenous origin."

12. Broadly, ages five to sixteen: Education Act 1996, s. 8.

13. Education Act 1996, s 7.

14. Figures cited in L. Rogers, "Number of Children Taught at Home Soars," *The Sunday Times*, June 26, 2005.

15. Education Act 1996, s 14(1).

16. Ibid., s 437.

17. Ibid., s 444.

18. See, for example, Social Exclusion Unit, Truancy and School Exclusion (London: The Stationery Office, 1998). As regards measures to be taken at school level, see Office for Standards in Education (Ofsted), Improving Attendance and Behaviour in Secondary Schools (London: Ofsted, 2001).

19. Education Act 1996, s 444(1A) and (8A), inserted by the Criminal Justice and Court Services Act 2000, s 72. The power to imprison in non-attendance cases had previously been removed by Children Act 1989.

20. National Audit Office, Improving School Attendance in England, HC 212 (London: The Stationery Office, 2005); S. Kendall and others: School Attendance and the Prosecution of Parents: Effects and Effectiveness (Slough: NFER/LGA, 2004).

21. Under the Anti-social Behaviour Act 2003.

22. Education Act 1996, ss 444A and 444B, inserted by the Anti-social Behaviour Act 2003, s 23.

23. The Education (Penalty Notices) (England) Regulations 2004 (SI 2004/181).

24. Ibid.

25. Typically, a board comprising ten to fifteen individuals, including representatives of local businesses and professions, parents, the religious foundation (in the case of a denominational school) and teachers, plus LEA nominees. The head teacher is usually also a member.

26. Crime and Disorder Act 1998, s 8; Education (Parenting Orders) (England) Regulations 2004 (SI 2004/182); Anti-social Behaviour Act 2003, s 19.

27. Youth Justice Board for England and Wales, Positive Parenting—the National Evaluation of the Youth Justice Board's Parenting Programme (London: Youth Justice Board, 2002).

28. Crime and Disorder Act 1998, s 16.

29. Comptroller and Auditor General, Improving school attendance in England, HC 212 (The Stationery Office, 2005).

30. HM Government, Higher Standards, Better Schools for All. More choice for parents and pupils, Cm 6677 (London: The Stationery Office, 2005), para 7.33.

31. The principle of free education in international law tends to be expressed in relation to primary or elementary education only, as in Article 28 of the UN Convention on the Rights of the Child.

32. See the Education Act 1996, ss 450–457.

33. E. Tanner, et al., *The Costs of Education. A Local Study* (London: Child Poverty Action Group, 2003), 1. For a useful historical summary, see also A. Riley, "The role of school meals in tackling child poverty," in C. Hurley and A. Riley, *Recipe for Change* (London: Child Poverty Action Group, 2004), 13–21.

34. N. Vandycke, Access to Education for the Poor in Europe and Central Asia. Preliminary Evidence and Policy Implications (Washington DC: World Bank, 2001), 13; see also House of Commons Work and Pensions Committee, First Report Session 2003–04, Child Poverty in the UK Vol I HC 85-I (London: The Stationery Office, 2004), para 95.

35. Education Act 1996, ss 510 and 511.

36. Ibid., s 518.

37. House of Commons Work and Pensions Committee, First Report, Session 2003–04, Child Poverty in the UK, Vol. I, HC 85-I (London: The Stationery Office, 2004).

38. Education Act 1996, ss 512(3) and 512ZB (substituted and added by the Education Act 2002, s 201); and the Education (Free School Lunches) (Prescribed Tax Credits) (England) Order 2003 (SI 200/383).

39. Note 37 above, para 100.

40. M. Barnes et al., Families and Children in Britain. Findings from the 2002 Families and Children Study (FACS), DWP Research Report 206 (Leeds: Corporate Document Services, 2004), table 4.2.

41. Ibid., table 4.5.

42. Education Act 1996, ss 509. As regards the meaning of "suitable arrangements," see Re S (Minors) [1995] ELR 98; Re C (A Minor) [1994] ELR 273; R v. Kent CC ex p C [1998] ELR 108; R v. Vale of Glamorgan County Council ex p J [2001] ELR 223; R (on the application of T) v. Leeds City Council [2002] ELR 91; R (Jones) v. Ceredigon County Council [2004] EWHC 1376 (Admin). On the way this duty has been applied, see also R v. Carmarthenshire CC ex p White [2001] ELR 172 and R v. Vale of Glamorgan County Council ex parte J, op. cit. "Walking distance" is defined, with regard to a child aged under eight, as two miles, and for an older child as three miles: Education Act 1996, s 444(5). This distance is to be measured by the "nearest available route"; see further Rogers v. Essex CC [1985] 1 WLR 700 and R v. Devon CC ex p George [1989] AC 573 (route does not cease to be available merely because a child cannot travel it unaccompanied without risk of danger).

43. Education Act 1996, s 509(4)(a).

44. Ibid., s 509(4)(b).

45. The Queen on the application of T v. Leeds City Council [2003] ELR 91 at 97E–F.

46. Education Act 1996, ss 509AA-509AC, inserted by the Education Act 2002, Sched 19 paras 3–5.

47. House of Commons Education and Skills Committee, Third Report Session 2003–04, Draft School Transport Bill Report HC 509 (London: The Stationery Office, 2004), para 19.

48. Ibid., para 10.

49. Ibid., paras 10 and 14.

50. But "transport should only be recorded in the statement in Part 6 [non-educational provision] in exceptional cases where the child has particular transport needs": DfES, Special Educational Needs Code of Practice (London: DfES, 2001), para 8.89.

51. Education and Inspections Bill 2006, Part 6.

52. Secondary education includes "full-time education suitable to the requirements of pupils who are over compulsory school age but under the age of nineteen which is provided at a school." Education provided at a "sixth form college" (colleges which cater primarily for seventeen- and eighteen-year-olds and generally operate in areas where secondary schools cater only for ages eleven to sixteen) is classed as further education, as is most education at a college of further education: Education Act 1996, s 2, as amended.

53. DfES, Five Year Strategy for Children and Learners, Cm 6272 (London: The Stationery Office, 2004), ch 6 para 8.

54. Education Act 2002, ss 14 and 181.

55. School Standards and Framework Act 1998, s 86.

56. DfES, Admission Appeals for Maintained Primary and Secondary Schools in England 2003/04 (Provisional) (SFR 21/2005) (London: DfES, 2005), table 1. The success rate was one in three of the appeals.

57. R v. London Borough of Richmond ex p JC [2001] ELR 21; The Queen on the application of B v. Head Teacher of Alperton Community School and Others; The Queen v. Head Teacher of Wembley High School and Others ex p T; The Queen v.

Governing Body of Cardinal Newman High School and Others ex p C [2001] ELR 359, per Newman J at para 16.

58. House of Commons Education and Skills Committee, Fourth Report Session 2003–04, Secondary Education: School Admissions, Vol. 1, Report HC 58-1 (London: TSO, 2004), paras 118–120, referring to J Templeton and S Hood, Changing Schools: The Impact of the School Admission Process on Children (London: Office of the Children's Rights Commissioner for London, 2002).

59. Sex Discrimination Act 1975, s 22; Race Relations Act 1976, s 17; Disability Discrimination Act 1995, s 28A.

60. Department for Education and Skills, Statistics of Education. Schools in England. 2004 Ed. (London: DfES, 2004), tables 22a and 22b. Just over 14,000 schools were non-denominational and approximately 7,000 were denominational, of which 4,700 were Church of England, 2,000 were Roman Catholic, 26 were Methodist, 80 were "other Christian," 33 were Jewish, 4 were Muslim, 2 were Sikh, and 2 were "other."

61. School Standards and Framework Act 1998, s 70; Education Act 2002, s 80.

62. Education Act 1996, s 375(3).

63. School Standards and Framework Act 1998, Sched 20, para 3.

64. Education Act 1996, s 394.

65. R v. Secretary of State for Education ex parte R and D [1994] ELR 495, per McCullough J. at 502D.

66. D. Bell (Chief Inspector of Schools in England), Change and Continuity: Reflections on the Butler Act. Speech to Commemorate the 60th Anniversary of the 1944 Education Act: London, House of Commons, 21 April 2004.

67. Article 14, read with Article 2 of Protocol 1.

68. E.g. Valsamis v. Greece (1997) 24 EHRR 294; Kjeldsen, Busk, Madsen and Pedersen v. Denmark (1978–89) 1 EHRR 711.

69. School Standards and Framework Act 1998, Sched 20, para 4.

70. Mandla v. Dowell Lee [1983] 1 All ER 1062.

71. R (SB) v. Head Teacher and Governors of Denbigh High School [2005] ELR 198; *sub nom* R (Begum) (etc.) [2006] UKHL 15.

72. Article 10(2).

73. See e.g. X v. UK (1979) 16 DR 101.

74. H. Mountfield, "The Implications of the Human Rights Act 1998 for the Law of Education" (2000) 1(3) *Ed. Law Jnl* 146–158, at 157.

75. R v. Governors of St Gregory's RC Aided High School and Appeal Committee ex M [1995] ELR 290. See also R v. Governors of Bacon's City Technology College ex part W [1998] ELR 488.

76. Department for Education and Skills, Improving Behaviour and Attendance: Guidance on Exclusion from Schools and Pupil Referral Units (London: DfES, 2004) (www.teachernet.gov.uk/management/).

77. DfES, Bullying: Don't Suffer in Silence (London: DfES, 2002); Idem, Social Inclusion: Pupil Support (www.dfes.gov.uk/publications/guidanceonthelaw/10-99/) (updated, 2004); Idem, note 76 above. For a review of the law, see N. Harris, "The legislative response to indiscipline in schools in England and Wales" (2002) 14(2) *Ed. & the Law* 57–76; and O. Hyams, *Law of Education* (Bristol: Jordans, 2004), ch 10.

78. HM Government, Higher Standards, Better Schools for All. More Choice for Parents and Pupils, Cm 6677 (London: The Stationery Office, 2005), para 7.8. See the Education and Inspections Bill 2006, Part 7.

79. School Standards and Framework Act (SSFA) 1998, s 61.

80. Ibid., ss 110 and 111. The agreements give rise to no liability in contract or tort: s 111(6).

81. Ibid., s 110(5).

82. DfES, "Home School Agreements" (www.dfes.gov.uk).

83. Education Act 1996 s 550B, added by the Education Act 1997 s 5.

84. Education Act 1996 s 550A, added by the Education Act 1997 s 4.

85. Hansard, House of Commons, Vol. 289, cols 84–87, 27 January 1997, per Mr E. Forth MP.

86. The power to use "reasonable force" (above) is expressed not to authorize "anything to be done in relation to a pupil which constitutes the giving of corporal punishment": Education Act 1996, s 550A(2).

87. (1982) 4 EHRR 293.

88. [1994] ELR 1.

89. Education (No 2) Act 1986, s 47.

90. SSFA 1998, s 131, substituting a new s 548 in the Education Act 1996. Note that action taken in order to avert an immediate danger of injury to a person or to property is excluded from the definition of corporal punishment (1996 Act, s 548[5]).

91. R (Williamson) v. Secretary of State for Education and Employment [2005] ELR 291 (House of Lords).

92. Ibid., para 86.

93. DfES, Drugs: Guidance for Schools, DfES 0092/2004 (London: DfES, 2004), para 4.10; DfES/Home Office, School Security: Dealing with Troublemakers www .dfes.gov.uk/schoolsecurity/dwthome.shtml (July 20, 2005), paras 6.2.3–6.2.4.

94. Education Act 2002, s 52 and the Education (Pupil Exclusions and Appeals) (Maintained Schools) (England) Regulations 2002 (SI 2002/3178) Exclusion on "precautionary" grounds may also be permissable: see Ali v Headteacher and Governors of Lord Grey School [2006] UKHL 14.

95. A v. Head Teacher and Governors of The Lord Grey School [2004] ELR 169.

96. DfES, Permanent and Fixed Period Exclusions from Schools and Exclusion Appeals in England, 2003–04 (London: DfES, 2005).

97. Ibid.

98. Ibid.

99. Audit Commission, Misspent Youth (Audit Commission, 1996).

100. Above n 94 (regulations), reg. 7; the guidance is in DfES, n 76 above.

101. DfES, n 76 above, para 12.

102. R v. Governors of Bacon's City Technology College ex part W, above n 75.

103. R v. Board of Governors and Appeal Committee of Bryn Elian High School ex parte Whippe [1999] ELR 380.

104. R v. Staffordshire County Council Education Appeals Committee ex parte Ashworth (1997) 9 Admin. L.R. 373.

105. See, e.g., R v. Governors of St Gregory's RC Aided High School and Appeals Committee ex parte M, above n 75; R v. Roman Catholic Schools ex parte S [1998] E.L.R. 304; R v. Headteacher and Independent Appeal Committee of Dunraven School ex p B [2000] ELR 156; The Queen on the application of C v. Sefton MBC IAP and Governors of Hillside High School [2001] ELR 393; S, T and P v. London Borough of Brent Etc [2002] ELR 556; R (J) v. Head Teacher and Governing Body [2003] ELR 743; R (T) v. Head Teacher of Elliott School [2003] ELR 160.

106. See, e.g., The Queen on the application of B (etc), above n 55; The Queen on the application of K v. Governors of the W School and West Sussex County Council [2001] ELR 311; The Queen on the application of S v. Head Teacher of C School and Others [2002] ELR 73; The Queen on the application of S v. Governing Body of YP School [2004] ELR 37.

107. Education (Pupil Exclusions and Appeals) (Maintained Schools) (England) Regulations 2002, above n 94, reg 4.

108. Guidance, above n 76, para 80.

109. Education (Pupil Exclusions and Appeals) (Maintained Schools) (England) Regulations 2002, above n 94, reg 6.

110. In both 1999–2000 and 2000–01, over 30 percent of appeals succeeded.

111. Education (Pupil Exclusions and Appeals) (Maintained Schools) (England) Regulations 2002, above n 94, Schedule, para 10.

112. Guidance, above n 76, para 103.

113. Ibid., paras 120 and 123.

114. Re L [2003] UKHL 9, [2003] ELR 309; P v. NASUWT [2003] UKHL 8 [2003] ELR 357; The Queen on the application of MB v. IAP of SMBC [2002] ELR 676; R v. Governors of W School and T LEA ex p H [2001] ELR 192; R v. South Tyneside Education Dept and Governors of Hebburn Comprehensive School ex p Cram [1998] ELR 508.

115. R v. Fernhill Manor School ex parte A [1994] ELR 67; R v. Muntham House School ex p R [2000] ELR 287; R v. Cobham Hall School ex p S [1998] ELR 389; R v. Governors of Haberdashers' Aske's Hatcham College Trust ex p T [1995] ELR 350.

116. Sex Discrimination Act 1975 s 22, Race Relations Act 1976, s 17.

117. E.g., L. Bourne et al., *Outcast England: How Schools Exclude Black Children* (London: Institute of Race Relations, 1994); Commission for Racial Equality, *Exclusions from School and Racial Equality* (London: CRE, 1997).

118. Above n 94.

119. Disability Discrimination Act (DDA) 1995, s 28A(4), added by the Special Educational Needs and Disability Act (SENDA) 2001 Act, s 11.

120. DDA 1995, s 28B, added by SENDA 2001, s 12.

121. Education Act 1996, s 19. LEAs also have a power under section 19 to provide full-time or part-time education otherwise than at school for young people who are above compulsory school age.

122. A v. Head Teacher and Governors of Lord Grey School, above n 95, para 6; see also Ali, above n 94.

123. DfES, Press Notice, 24 January 2002.

124. The Queen on the application of S v. Head Teacher of C High School and Others, above n 105, per Richards J at para 49.

125. R v. East Sussex County Council ex p T [1998] AC 714, [1998] 2 WLR 818.

126. Sex Discrimination Act 1975, s 22; Race Relations Act 1976, s 17; DDA 1995, ss 28A–28C.

127. DDA 1995, s 28C.

128. DDA 1995, s 28D.

129. See the Race Relations (Amendment) Act 2000.

130. See N. Harris, *Education, Law and Diversity* (Oxford: Hart, forthcoming).

131. Nationality, Immigration, and Asylum Act 2002, s 29(1)(f).

132. A. Reakes and R. Powell, *The Education of Asylum Seekers in Wales: Implications for LEAs and Schools* (Slough: NFER, 2004).

133. M. Arnot and H. Pinson, *The Education of Asylum Seeker and Refugee Children* (Cambridge: University of Cambridge, 2005).

134. Education Act 1996, Part IV, and various sets of regulations made thereunder. There is a Special Educational Needs Code of Practice (DfES, 2001) to which LEAs, schools, and the appeal tribunal are to have regard in exercising their functions: ibid., s 313.

135. Education Act 1996, Schedule 27 para 3.

136. Ibid., ss 316 and 316A.

137. See the Code of Practice, above n 134, part 3. See also Harris, n 9 above.

138. See R (CES)(A Minor) v. Oxfordshire County Council [2004] ELR 489; R v. Secretary of State for Education ex p C [1996] ELR 93; R v. Portsmouth City Council ex p F [1998] ELR 619.

139. See DfES, above n 53, ch 5, para 15.

140. Education Act 2002, s 176(1) and (2).

141. DfES, Working Together: Giving Children and Young People a Say, DfES guidance 0134/2004 (London: DfES, 2004), para 2.1.

142. Ibid., para 3.1.

143. Education Act 2005, s 7.

144. Department for Education and Skills, Youth Matters, Cm 6629 (London: The Stationery Office, 2005), para 12.

145. See N. Harris, "Empowerment and State Education: Rights of Choice and Participation" (2005) *Modern Law Review*, 68(6), 925–957.

146. Note 144 above, para 16.

147. See N. Harris, "'Extended Schools': A legal Framework for Childcare Provision in Schools" (2001) *Ed. Law Journal*, 2(4), 194–201.

148. Note 144 above, para 19.

149. Ibid., para 13.

150. HM Government, Higher Standards, Better Schools for All. More Choice for Parents and Pupils, Cm 6677 (London: The Stationery Office, 2005), chapter 4.

151. School Standards and Framework Act 1998 Part V; Education Act 2002, Part 6.

152. See S. Tomlinson, *Education in a Post-welfare Society* (Buckingham: Open University Press, 2001).

7

Malaysia

Tie Fatt Hee

The main source of law governing the educational system in Malaysia is the Federal Constitution.[1] Legislation enacted in Parliament, namely the Education Act 1996,[2] constitutes another source of law that regulates the system of education in Malaysia. There is also a set of subsidiary or delegated legislations made by persons such as the Minister of Education whose powers are conferred on them by Acts of Parliament.[3] In addition, the Ministry of Education has the authority, from time to time, to issue procedural and administrative guidelines related to school management and governance that are sent to schools in the form of administrative circulars. These circulars contain provisions concerning such issues as corporal punishment, proper school attire, students' attendance, and procedure to be followed when school discipline is enforced. Further, the common law exerts a significant influence on the law governing education in Malaysia.

Some of the fundamental liberties guaranteed by the Federal Constitution are equality before the law and equal protection from the law, the right to receive an education, freedom to profess, practice, and propagate religion, freedom of speech and expression, and the right not to be unlawfully deprived of property and in any case not to be deprived of it without adequate compensation. Thus, this chapter reviews these and other issues pertaining to the educational rights of students in Malaysia.

The Right to Receive an Education

The right of students to receive an education in Malaysia encompasses the constitutional right to receive an education; the right of parents to decide how their children are to be educated; the right to receive instruction using one's own mother tongue; the right to receive primary education; and, the right of students to receive educational support from their parents.

Students have a fundamental right to receive an education that is guaranteed by the Federal Constitution.[4] Every religious group has the right to establish and maintain institutions for the education of children in its own religion. The fundamental constitutional right to receive an education is an absolute right and it cannot be compromised. The government is responsible to ensure that the right is protected.

The Education Act 1996 also ensures that students have a right to receive an education. The preamble to the Education Act 1996 expressed that the system of education in Malaysia subscribed to the general principle that pupils are to be educated in accordance with the wishes of their parents.[5] The phrase "wishes of their parents" is interpreted as to allow parents a right to decide on the type of school, language, and medium of instruction that their child would be educated. This provision is vital with regard to the right to learn one's own mother tongue, an issue that is close to the heart of every parent.

Students from different races are allowed to learn one's own mother tongue or language if parents make a request for the teaching of languages such as Chinese, Tamil, or indigenous languages in school.[6] Educational legislation mandates the Ministry of Education to provide facilities for the teaching of these languages. These facilities are made available only if the parents of at least fifteen students in the school made a request. This provision shows that the government is committed toward promoting the development of the language of the other races.

The Minister of Education is responsible to provide primary education to all students in government and government-aided primary schools.[7] Primary education is compulsory. Another responsibility of the Minister is the duty to establish and maintain the national and national-type schools.[8] The Minister of Education is also under a duty to provide secondary education in the national secondary schools.[9] There is a legal obligation to establish and maintain these schools.[10]

The right of students to receive an education extends to tertiary education. Parents owe a duty to provide an education to their children until they have obtained a first degree. The legal obligation continues even when the parents are separated. The court reiterated this principle in two cases.

In the first case, a marriage was dissolved by mutual consent.[11] The wife prayed for a dissolution of the marriage, a half share in the matrimonial home, a lump sum payment, monthly maintenance, and a sum of money for the daughters until they complete their university degree. The judge directed that the husband pay a sum of money for the daughters including the medical bills and their education up to tertiary first degree. The husband appealed and claimed that the court should not have ordered any maintenance for the two daughters beyond their eighteenth birthday. In dismissing the appeal, the court held that the appellant was under a legal obligation to support his daughters until they received their first degrees and were educationally equipped to find their rightful place on the job market. Further, the appellant is not allowed to reprobate what he has approbated.

In the second case, the petitioner obtained consent orders for the respondent to pay the petitioner maintenance for the three children of their marriage.[12] Later, the respondent stated that he would stop maintenance payment for the eldest child as she had attained the age of eighteen years. The petitioner contended that maintenance of the child did not stop at eighteen years but continued until the child obtained a first degree. The argument was based on the provisions in s 95 of the Law Reform (Marriage and Divorce) Act 1976. The respondent further alleged that an involuntary financial dependence constitutes a form of physical disability which was within one of the exceptions to s 95. The High Court agreed and extended the consent order beyond the age of eighteen years in the event that the eldest child and/or other children of the marriage gained a place in any educational institution of higher learning to obtain their first degree respectively. Nevertheless, the Federal court reversed this decision. It stated that s 95 only encompasses physical and mental disability. It excludes financial dependence for the purpose of pursuing tertiary education on attainment of eighteen years of age.[13]

Both of the courts in the above two cases examined the combined effect of some of the provisions in the Law Reform (Marriage and Divorce) Act 1976. [14] These provisions reinforced the general principle that a child of a marriage was not to be denied or deprived of maintenance for the purpose of realizing the right of access to education. The right to receive an education continues until tertiary level and attainment of a first degree. This right extends beyond the age of eighteen years. This was based on the argument that a child's involuntary financial dependence for purposes of pursuing and completing their tertiary education was deemed to be a form of physical disability, a condition that is within one of the exceptions under the Act.

Religious Freedom of Students

All individuals have a right to practice and propagate one's religion.[15] Although the Federal Constitution states that Islam shall be the religion of the country,[16] there is freedom of religion.[17] However, the Federal Constitution indicates that individuals under the age of eighteen years do not have the right to profess a religion. The religion of persons under the age of eighteen shall be decided by their parents or guardians.[18] The provision is significant as almost all students in Malaysia would be in school and are at the eleventh year of the school years when they are under eighteen years of age. [19]

Under the civil law, students are considered to be minors when they are below eighteen years old. In one case, the appellant, who was a Buddhist, discovered that his daughter, who was almost eighteen years old, was missing and converted to become a Muslim. The father brought an action seeking a declaration that as a lawful father and guardian, he had the right to decide the religion, education, and upbringing of his infant daughter. The High Court dismissed the application and an appeal was made to the Supreme Court, which allowed the appeal.

The judge held that in normal circumstances, a non-Muslim parent or guardian has the right to decide the choice of various issues that affects the infant's life until the age of majority, which is eighteen years under the civil law.[20] The Court ruled that national interests override the freedom of religion vested to infants. Parental permission must be obtained before an infant is allowed to receive instruction related to a religion other than his own. Thus, infants do not have an automatic right to receive such instruction. Parents or guardians possess the right to decide on a minor's religion until the child reaches the age of majority. In the case of non-Muslims, it is the parent or guardian who ultimately has the choice to decide on the religion of the minor.

In a subsequent case, the judge did not concur with the view of the Supreme Court. The Court seemed to be more flexible in its interpretation of the provision in the Federal Constitution. The plaintiff's daughter aged seventeen years converted to Islam without his knowledge and consent.[21] The father applied to the High Court seeking a declaration that as the lawful father and guardian, he had the right to decide her religion and education; that the infant shall be brought up in the Buddhist faith according to his wishes; that the infant's conversion without his consent, was null and void; and, that an order that the registration of conversion of the infant into the Muslim faith in the records be expunged.

Interestingly, the Court decided that the girl above eighteen years old had the right to choose her own religion provided that she did so of her own free will according to the Federal Constitution,[22] reiterating that every person has the right to profess and practice his religion and, subject to certain conditions, to propagate it.[23] The Court also stated that no person shall be required to receive instruction in or take part in any ceremony, act, or worship of a religion other than his own.[24] The Court examined the words "be required to" and concluded that a person has the choice of doing either or all these things on his own free will where he is not "required" to do so by some other person.

Conversely, the Federal Constitution also expressed that the religion of a person under the age of eighteen years shall be decided by his parent or guardian.[25] In this case, the learned judge opined that the provisions in the Federal Constitution were not applicable to the case as there was no evidence to support the fact that the infant had been "required" to receive instruction in or to take part in any ceremony or act of worship of a religion other than her own.[26] The Court dismissed the plaintiff's allegation that he has the right to decide on the daughter's religion.[27]

Religious freedom also encompasses the right and freedom to wear attire which is synonymous with one's belief and religion. It includes the freedom to wear a headgear, scarf, or a veil. Muslims in Malaysia sometimes wear a headgear that is known in local terminology as a *serban* that is similar to a turban. One critical issue that becomes contentious is whether students have the right to wear this type of headgear to school based on the argument that the attire is encouraged by one's own religious belief.

In a landmark case, the court addressed three important issues related to religious freedom of students, namely students' freedom of religion with respect to wearing of religious attire in school; the type of authority that is vested in a school principal; and, the doctrine of natural justice.[28] The plaintiffs were male Muslim pupils who wore turbans to school. When the plaintiffs refused to accede to the request by the principal to refrain from doing so, he dismissed them from school. The plaintiffs applied for a court order to declare the expulsion null and void. They also sought reinstatement back to school.

The plaintiffs argued that there was a serious infringement of their fundamental right of freedom of religion. In particular, the students argued that the defendants acted contrary to the constitutional provisions that prohibit discrimination based on religion, race, creed, and place of birth. It was alleged that the expulsion was made without an opportunity to be heard, contrary to the rules of natural justice and inconsistent with the provisions in the Federal Constitution. On the other hand, the defendants argued that the plaintiffs had breached one of the rules that were established according to the school regulations.[29] In response, the defendants argued that the principal had set up the rules according to the guidelines that have been established by the Ministry of Education. [30]

The High Court allowed the plaintiff's application and granted an order to allow the students to return to school. The court held that the principal had acted in an unreasonable manner as he had no jurisdiction to prohibit pupils from wearing the headgear and thus acted ultra vires. The court maintained that the Ministry of Education was the only organization with the authority to determine policies concerning school uniform. Further, the court pointed out that the Ministry of Education did not set up the rule related to the wearing of a turban since such attire was not mentioned in the Ministry's own set of guidelines and rules concerning school uniform.[31] As such, the court concluded that the rule which disallowed wearing of turbans was null and void.

The court also examined the issue of whether there has been a breach of the principle of natural justice. The court observed that the principal failed to provide notice to the plaintiffs to show cause or give an opportunity to the plaintiffs to be heard. The court treated the principal's action as a denial of justice since there was no opportunity given for the students or their parents to be heard. The court decided that there was a breach of the rules of natural justice and allowed the plaintiffs to return to school.

The Federal Constitution affirmed that every Muslim has a right to follow and practice his religion. The court stated that the prohibition to wear the headgear was inconsistent with the Federal Constitution and thus, is null and void. The court also distinguished a situation where one is wearing a *purdah*, a veil that covers the entire face, from that of wearing a turban. It recognized the fact that one who wears a purdah cannot be recognized or identified unlike a person who wears a turban. There is a risk that a person who wears a purdah with the face concealed could disrupt public peace. *Syariah* law permits a turban to be worn and is deemed to be acceptable in the local community. Further, it is not void under the civil law for both Muslims and non-Muslims. Accordingly, the court found that since wearing a turban was valid under the Federal Constitution the defendants were not entitled to expel the plaintiffs based on the prohibitions contained in the school regulation.

The Court of Appeal did not concur with the decision of the lower court. It allowed the appeal, explaining that the principal acted properly in expelling the students.[32] The court dealt with the critical issue of whether the wearing of a serban forms an integral part of the religion of Islam. It considered the role of evidential issues and the burden was placed on the respondents to adduce sufficient relevant admissible material to prove that the wearing of a serban was mandatory in Islam. However, the respondents failed to do so. Evidence revealed that it was permissible but not mandatory for a male Muslim to wear a serban.

The court further reiterated that at common law, educational institutions are entitled to determine the appropriate uniform that is to be worn by its pupils and to maintain discipline. Generally, the courts are reluctant to interfere in the management of the institutions except where there has been a breach of the duty to act fairly. The court affirmed that the Department of Education and the principal should have been responsible to evaluate the appropriate uniform to be worn at school and the way in which school discipline is maintained.

The judges distinguished between religious observances that are related to dress, food, ceremonies, and the mode of religious worship. These practices are regarded as integral parts of a religion. The court expressed its readiness to intervene and examine legitimate complaints under the Federal Constitution if the authorities act to deny such practices.[32] In this instance, the court did not consider the relevancy of Article 11(4) Federal Constitution. Instead, it examined the issue of whether there was a violation of the students' right to profess and practice the Islamic faith. Subsequently, the plaintiffs appealed. However, it was rejected by the Federal Court as it opined that the school authorities had acted according to the law when it prohibited students from wearing turbans to school.

The issue of whether the wearing of certain attire constitutes an integral part of a religion had, in fact, been examined by the court in an earlier case.[34] The case concerned the dismissal of a public civil servant who refused to comply with a governmental administrative circular that prohibited public servants from wearing veils while on duty.[35] The circular had been issued due to security reasons since veils concealed the whole face. In particular, the circular was issued based on one of the provisions of the Federal Constitution which declares that the provision did not authorize any act contrary to any general law relating to public order, public health, or public morality.

The court thought that a veil, unlike a turban, makes it difficult to identify the staff on duty and poses a serious threat to public security. The judge also referred to an earlier court's attempt to distinguish between religious practices and religious faith.[36] Although the State has the authority to protect an individual's religious faith and belief, it is pertinent to note that when religious practices subvert public order, morality, or health, the court was ready to place less priority to religious practices and more emphasis on the need to protect the public interest and safety.

The plaintiff appealed to the Supreme Court which concurred with the decision of the High Court in rejecting the plaintiff's appeal. The Court held that the wearing of the purdah by a female Muslim is not an integral part of the religion of Islam. Although the Federal Constitution guarantees every individual the right to profess and practice his religion, the Court did not treat it as an absolute right, reasoning that any act that is contrary to the general law related to public order, public health, or morality is prohibited. The Court acknowledged that the government has prescribed the mode of dress and prohibited the wearing of attire that covers the face by a female officer in the public services during office hours. The Court determined that the regulation did not affect the officer's constitutional right to practice her religion. In addition, the Court was of the view that Islam as a religion does not prohibit a Muslim woman from wearing and neither does it require her to wear a purdah.[37]

Free Speech Rights of Students

Students are entitled to the right to freedom of speech by virtue of the provisions stipulated in the Federal Constitution. They enjoy the same rights and privileges as other citizens. However, free speech by students is limited to the condition that it does not create a threat to national security, public order, or morality. A speech that is defamatory or one that incites racial hatred is deemed to be one that is a threat to public order. A student can be punished if the speech undermined school authority and adversely affects the function of the school. The school bears the burden of proof to show that a legitimate interest has been affected by the student's expression or freedom of speech. Students who speak on matters that are personal in nature do not receive constitutional protection.

Student Rights and Discipline

The law related to student discipline and due process in Malaysia was established in a case that was eventually resolved by the highest court of appeal at that time, the Privy Council in the United Kingdom.[38] The court addressed the issue of whether a school headmaster who chose to expel a student was under a duty to comply with the procedure and rules of natural justice. The student was expelled from school due to misconduct committed on a number of occasions.[39] The headmaster had called the student to his office to investigate some complaints on misconduct and warned him that he might have been dismissed. The headmaster exercised his authority according to the provisions contained in one of the school regulations.[40]

The plaintiff argued that there had been a breach of the rules of natural justice since the defendants, the headmaster and school, did not provide adequate notice about the dismissal and an opportunity to be heard. Nevertheless, the High Court held that the headmaster acted in good faith and had good reason to expel the student.

The court then examined the issue of whether the headmaster followed proper procedures in arriving at the decision to expel the appellant. It expressed its opinion that the defendant's issuance of a mere warning to the plaintiff that he might possibly have been expelled did not meet the requirements of natural justice. The court added that since the defendant did not give adequate notice to the plaintiff to appreciate the exact nature and purpose of the interview, he was deprived of the opportunity to be heard because the headmaster did not inform him specifically that he would be expelled if he did not provide a satisfactory explanation. The court held that the order of expulsion was null and void. It ordered the school to reinstate the plaintiff. The defendant appealed.

The Federal Court reversed the decision of the High Court, holding that the procedure adopted by the headmaster complied with the rules of natural justice.[41] The court noted succinctly that the school regulation vested the defendant with a quasi-judicial function that allowed him to determine the prescribed form of procedure to be followed. This court interpreted this as subject to some form of inquiry that must be held according to the rules of natural justice. On the other hand, the court conceded that a head teacher was required to maintain discipline and order. The court asserted that an elaborate inquiry was not needed before the defendant dismissed the student. The court recognized that a school comes under the category of the vast area of the law where the principle of *audi alteram partem*—literally, hear the other side—can only be applied on a general consideration. The Federal Court stated that there was sufficient evidence to prove that the defendant acted fairly before making the order of expulsion. An appeal was made to the Privy Council.[42]

The Privy Council affirmed the decision of the Federal Court. It decided that the headmaster acted in a fair manner in dismissing the student since he informed him about his misconduct and gave him an opportunity to explain his behavior. The Council further reiterated that the procedure used in a criminal trial is not applicable in school administration and matters related to the expulsion of a pupil.

Generally, the rules of natural justice require that a person charged with making the decision should act fairly. This means that a headmaster is under a duty to act in a fair manner before enforcing a disciplinary policy.

Corporal Punishment

In Malaysia, corporal punishment is permitted in school. The enforcement of corporal punishment is governed by the rules and regulations set out in the administrative circular and guidelines issued by the Ministry of Education.[43] Corporal punishment is educational and deterrent in nature. Even so, a school principal is responsible to ensure that it is not abused when it is meted out to deter students from repeating the offence. The task may be delegated to a teacher who is appointed in an official manner. Corporal punishment on female students is prohibited. Further, it is not allowed in public or during the school assembly. When used, corporal punishment consists of caning with a light cane restricted to the palm or on the covered buttocks area. The use of excessive force is prohibited. A confidential record of all corporal punishment must be kept.

Students have the right to resort to litigation where the school breached the rules and regulations related to corporal punishment. An action may be taken for breach of the rules of natural justice such as when a school failed to conduct an investigation of misconduct prior to punishment or not allowing a student an opportunity to be heard. The use of excessive force is tantamount to assault and it is a criminal offence.[44]

School Searches

School searches are normally carried out when there is a theft, a suspicion that a student has brought materials to school that are prohibited, or when a student is suspected of being a gang member. In Malaysia, the courts have yet to resolve a case related to school searches. Nevertheless, students have the constitutional right to protection from potential abuse of the process. [45] The court is likely to refer to the provisions in the criminal law when such a case arises.

Special Populations

Malaysian courts consider the best interests of students with disabilities when dealing with matters related to their educational needs. There is one reported case involving the education and rehabilitation of students with disabilities. A pupil suffered from a mild form of spastic dipelgia, a physical disability that affects his motor ability.[46] Even so, the student was intellectually normal and studied at an elementary school for six years. He used a wheelchair to move about and a walking frame to walk. On completion of elementary education, he applied to transfer to a middle school but was rejected due to his physical handicap. The middle school taught the American school curriculum and received an annual grant from the United States government.

At the initial stage, there was no intimation that the plaintiff would not have been allowed to transfer to the new school. However, the first intimation was a letter that requested that his parents provide documents on his medical suitability to attend the new campus. The pupil's application was rejected, as he required extensive and expensive compensatory education.[47] The amount of the expenditure involved in establishing an expensive disabled friendly environment was the main reason for the decision to reject the plaintiff. A subsequent appeal to the secondary school was rejected.

The plaintiff then made an application for an interlocutory injunction to restrain the defendant from prohibiting him from continuing his education. The plaintiff contended that there was a serious question to be tried as it was based on his legitimate expectation to continue his education. The court allowed the application with costs.

The court reiterated that in terms of the law and justice, disabled children's basic rights to education overrides financial considerations. The court was prepared to ensure that the educational needs of disabled children were met even when there is an obstacle.[48] The presence of the plaintiff does not make a material difference for teaching purposes since his normal cognitive functions did not require any special teaching facilities.

In its analysis, the court referred to various judicial principles under the common law where injunctions were issued to prohibit actions which precluded a class of children from attending school. The court also reviewed the development of the law in the United Kingdom, the United States, and Canada where the cases tend to be more disabled-friendly even if it meant schools had to incur extra expenditures. In the United Kingdom, the court granted an injunction to restrain a local education authority from implementing a policy that conflicts with children's statutory right to free education.[49] An injunction was granted to allow admission to be open for grammar schools based on the reason that children's educational need should be accorded paramount consideration.[50] Similarly, an injunction was also issued to prevent the local education authority from implementing a policy that prohibits schools from providing secular education in primary school.[51]

In England, the courts tend to place greater emphasis on the educational needs of a dyslexic child rather than the financial resources of the local education authority.[52] This was similar to that of the United States where the Supreme Court agreed that a school board had to bear the expenses of keeping a student with a disability in school.[53] In Canada, an interlocutory injunction was also granted to prevent the implementation of a policy that abolished uni-denominational schools and created inter-denominational schools. It was vital to prevent irreparable damage to students who are denied their right to uni-denominational education.[54]

The court granted an injunction to prevent irreparable harm to the plaintiff's education and his rehabilitation. As a general rule, the courts in Malaysia are inclined to safeguard the legal rights of students with disabilities. The educational needs and rehabilitation of the students is given priority despite the argument that it may be a financial burden to the other party. The judicial tendency is to provide greater protection to students with disabilities and to ensure that their education can continue.[55]

Emerging Issues

The law related to education is developing at an early stage. The right to receive education is a fundamental right that is enshrined in the Federal Constitution. There is an obligation to ensure that parents are able to send their children to schools of their choice. An issue that has become a perennial problem in the urban area is the increase in demand for children to be educated in primary schools, in particular, Chinese primary schools. Proposals to increase the number of these schools in densely populated urban areas evoked less encouragement and support from the other political parties.[56] The unequivocal opposition arises due to the fear that increasing the number of these schools would contradict steps to foster national integration in the multi-ethnic, multicultural, and multi-religious society. This argument may not be acceptable to others who perceived the restriction as being biased and discriminative.

The Federal Constitution provides that special privileges be given to the Malay and native populations.[57] The privileges include special positions in the public service, scholarships, educational, and training privileges. Places are reserved in educational institutions, the university, and colleges for Malays and natives. The social contract that was agreed by the various political parties before the country achieved independence has been viewed less favorably. As a consequence, scholarships provided by the government and opportunities to pursue further study at higher levels has always been a source of dissatisfaction among the minority races.

Conclusion

Generally, students enjoy limited educational rights in respect of religious freedom, free speech, and in terms of the enforcement of discipline in school. Education law is at present, relatively new and is at the initial stage of development. Litigation that involves allegations of infringement of the right of students is rare and limited. Even so, as society evolves into one that is becoming more litigious as a result of the advent of globalization and development in information technology, the scene may change completely in the near future. These influences may lead to a more active and vocal demand for the rights of students to be protected and further enhanced in Malaysian schools.

Notes

1. The Federal Constitution is a written constitution modeled along the Indian Constitution, which in turn, is based on basic principles of the British government and constitutional conventions. It has been described as based upon the "Westminster" model.
2. Education Act 1996 (Act 550). International Law Book Services: Kuala Lumpur.
3. Section 3 of the Interpretation Acts defines subsidiary legislation as "any proclamation, rule, regulation, order, notification, by-law, or other instrument made under

any Act, Enactment, Ordinance, or other lawful authority and having legislative effect." Examples include Educational Regulations (Special Education) 1997; Educational Regulations (National Curriculum) 1997; and, Educational Regulations (Parent-Teacher Association) 1998.

4. Article 12 Federal Constitution states that there shall be no discrimination against any citizen with respect to rights in education in terms of religion, race, descent, or place of birth.

5. See generally Education Act 1996.

6. s. 2 Education Act 1996.

7. s. 27 Education Act 1996.

8. s. 28 Education Act 1996.

9. s. 30 Education Act 1996. The categories of national secondary schools are academic secondary schools, technical secondary schools, and secondary schools of such other descriptions as the Minister of Education may determine from time to time.

10. s. 31 Education Act 1996.

11. Ching Seng Woah v. Lim Shook Lin [1997] 1 MLJ 109.

12. Punithambigai a/p Poniah v. Karunairajah a/l Rasiah & Anor [1999] 6 MLJ 729.

13. Karunairajah a/l Rasiah v Punithambigai a/p Poniah [2004] 2 MW 401.

14. s. 52, s. 92 and s. 95 Law reform (Marriage and Divorce) Act 1976.

15. Article 11 (1) Federal Constitution is expressed in the following "Every person has the right to profess and practice his religion and, subject to clause 4, to propagate it."

16. Article 3 (1) Federal Constitution states that "Islam is the religion of the Federation; but other religions may be practiced in peace and harmony in any part of the Federation."

17. Article 3 (1) Federal Constitution guarantees the freedom of religion. An affirmation of Article 3 was specifically stated in paragraph 15 of the Malaysian Report of the Inter-Governmental Committee 1962.

18. Article 12 (3) Federal Constitution states that "no person shall be required to receive instruction in or to take part in any ceremony or act of worship of a religion other than his own." However, Article 12 (4) Federal Constitution expressed that for the purposes of Article 12 (3), the religion of a person under the age of eighteen years shall be decided by his parent or guardian.

19. All students commenced formal schooling at the age of six. Primary school education is six years whereas secondary education is five years.

20. In Re Susie: Teoh Eng Huat v Kahdi of Pasir Mas Kelantan & Majlis Ugama Islam dan Adat Istiadat Melayu, Kelantan [1986] 2 MW 228.

21. Teoh Eng Huat v. Kadhi, Pasir Mas, Kelantan & Anor. [1990] 2 MLJ 300.

22. Article 11 Federal Constitution states that every person has the right to profess and practice his religion. However, an exception is in Article 11 (4) as State law and Federal law may control or restrict the propagation of any religious doctrine or belief among persons professing the religion of Islam. Article 12 Federal Constitution states that there shall be no discrimination against any citizen on the grounds only of religion, race, descent, or place of birth in respect of the right to education.

23. Supra note 11.

24. Article 12 (3) Federal Constitution.

25. Article 12 (4) Federal Constitution.

26. Supra note 16.

27. The court acknowledged that the Guardianship of Infants Act 1961 was applicable to the case in so far as the provisions do not contradict the Muslim religion. The Guardianship of Infants Act 1961 enables the father as the guardian to have custody of the infant and is responsible for her support, health, and education. It allowed the plaintiff's application with regard to the right to decide on the education and upbringing of the infant until majority. Nevertheless, this is subject to the condition that it does not conflict with the infant's choice of religion as guaranteed under the Federal Constitution.

28. Meor Atiqulrahman bin Ishak dan lain-lain lwn Fatimah bte Sihi dan lain-lain [2000] 5 MLJ 375.

29. Art 3 (5)(v) of the School Rules 1997.

30. Ministry of Education Circular Letter No. 9/1975.

31. See generally the Ministry of Education Rules of School Uniform No. 3/1983.

32. Fatimah bte Sihi & Ors v. Meor Atiqulrahman bin Ishak & Ors (Minors, suing through Syed Ahmad Johari bin Syed Mohd) [2005] 2 MLJ 25.

33. Supra note 11.

34. Hajjah Halimatussaadiah bte Hj Kamaruddin v. Public Services Commission Malaysia & Anor [1994] 3 MLJ 61.

35. Halimatussaadiah bte Hj Kamaruddin v. Public Services Commission Malaysia & Anor [1992] 1 MLJ 513.

36. State of Bombay v. Narsu Appa Mali AIR [1953] Bom. 84.

37. Ibid.

38. The Judicial Committee of the Privy Council in London was the highest court of appeal before 1985. Final appeals were made to His Majesty the King which was actually heard and disposed of by the Privy Council. In 1985, appeals to the King were abolished. This means the function of the Privy Council was abolished. A new court of final appeal known as the Supreme Court was set up. Following some changes the present final court of appeal is called the Federal Court.

39. Mahadevan v. Anandarajan & Ors. [1970] 1 MLJ 50.

40. Regulation 8 of the Education (School Discipline) Regulations 1959 provides that whenever "it appears to the satisfaction of the head teacher of any school—(a) to be necessary or desirable for the purpose of maintaining discipline or order in any school that any pupil should be suspended or expelled . . . he may by order expel him from such school." This regulation empowers a head teacher to expel a pupil whenever it appears to his satisfaction to be necessary or desirable for the purpose of maintaining discipline or order in the school that the pupil should be expelled.

41. Anandarajan & Ors. v. Mahadevan [1971] 2 MLJ 8.

42. Mahadevan v. Anandarajan & Ors. [1974] 1 MLJ 1.

43. School Regulations (School Discipline) 1959.

44. See generally the provisions related to assault under the Penal Code, in particular s. 320 which define what amount to serious injuries; s. 321 intention to cause in-

jury; s. 322 intention to cause serious injuries; s. 350 criminal use of force; and, s. 351 assault.

45. Article 5 Federal Constitution states that no one shall be deprived of his life or personal liberty except according to the law. It is pertinent to note that students are prohibited from having any tattoo on their body as it is the normal practice for members of certain gangs to use this as a symbol of affiliation. Interestingly, Article 8 expressed that all persons are equal before the law and entitled to the equal protection of the law.

46. Jakob Renner (An infant suing through his father and next friend, Gilbert Renner) & Ors v. Scott King, Chairman of Board of Directors of the International School of Kuala Lumpur & Ors. [2000] 5 MLJ 254.

47. Ibid.

48. Ibid.

49. Guardians of the Poor of Gateshead Union v. Durham County Council [1918] 1 Ch D 146.

50. In Bradbury v. London Borough of Enfield [1967] 3 All ER 434 (CA).

51. Wilford v. County Council of the West Riding of Yorkshire [1908] 1 KB 685.

52. R v. East Sussex County Council ex p Tandy [1998] 2 All ER.

53. See Cedar Rapids Community School District v. Garret F., 526 U.S. 66 (1999).

54. Re Hogan et al. and School Boards for ten Districts et al., Newfoundland (1997) 149 DLR (4th) 468.

55. Supra note 42.

56. See Malaysian Chinese Association. (2005). MCA memo on ninth plan for PM. Retrieved March 13, 2005, from www.mca.org.my/.

57. Article 153 Federal Constitution states that quotas are reserved for Malays and natives of the States of Sabah and Sarawak in respect of services, permits, and other aspects.

8

Netherlands

Ben P. Vermeulen and C. (Niels) W. Noorlander

THIS CHAPTER PROVIDES A BRIEF DESCRIPTION of the legal position of students in the Dutch educational system. In concentrating on the rights of young students in primary and secondary education, the chapter primarily speaks of them as *pupils* (and their parents representing them). Until the 1960s, the legal status of pupils within the Dutch school system was weak. Since then, pupils have increasingly been seen as legal subjects who have certain claims and rights with respect to their school boards.[1]

The legal status of the Dutch pupil is, to a large extent, determined by the basic norms regulating the school system. The basic structure of this system, as laid down in Article 23 of the Constitution, is a binary one. This binary structure is linked to the dichotomy that Dutch law makes between public law, regulating the vertical-hierarchical relation between state and citizen, and civil law that concerns the horizontal relation between individuals, including civil law corporations. It consists of two types of schools, public-authority schools and private, non-state schools, which like Yin and Yang complement and supplement each other.[2]

Public-authority schools (public schools) are generally governed by local authorities, often by the municipal executive. They do not enjoy autonomy in terms of a freedom to ground the educational principles of the school in a specific religion or belief, although they are free to choose a specific pedagogical approach such as Montessori or Dalton. Education provided by these schools is regulated by law; it must be non-denominational, based on the principle of neutrality. Due to this principle, public schools are not allowed to select pupils and teachers on the basis of denominational criteria. The status of the pupils is determined by public law.

Public schools, which are freely accessible to all pupils, have a certain primacy, since the government has to guarantee that within a small distance from home there should be a public school available for every pupil. Aside from that, both subsystems, public-authority schools and private schools, have equal status. Public and non-state (private) schools receive funding according to identical or equivalent criteria. It is evident that the strict church-state separation that characterizes the US school system is absent here.

Non-state schools (also called independent or private schools) are run by corporate bodies under civil law; they are also known as foundations or associations. Although these schools are, in general, fully governmentally funded, they enjoy a level of autonomy safeguarded by the Constitution: the freedom of education. This freedom consists of three rights: the right to shape a school according to a religious or philosophical worldview, and to provide education of a distinctive religious or philosophical character, *vrijheid van richting*; pedagogical and organizational autonomy which overlaps the prior right, *vrijheid van inrichting*; and the right to establish a school in order to provide the type of education covered by the two previously named rights, *vrijheid van stichting*.

The right to give non-state, government-funded schools a distinctive religious or philosophical character, the *vrijheid van richting*, may be regarded as the core of the freedom of education. It is this aspect of the *vrijheid van inrichting*, the pedagogical and organizational autonomy, which is guaranteed best when it concerns schools founded on distinct religious grounds. The freedom to organize a school and provide education on the basis of a specific religious or philosophical view is explicitly safeguarded in Article 23 which declares that when the government issues quality standards (funding conditions for private schools), this freedom must be respected, especially, *but not only*, in relation to the choice of teaching materials and the right to appoint teachers. For instance, this freedom also includes the right to select pupils on the basis of denominational criteria.

The *vrijheid van inrichting*, the pedagogical-organizational autonomy, is less protected when school policies are based on non-denominational considerations. For example, a school board's discretion to decide which pupils to admit is much wider when it is based on religious adherence than when its decisions are based on "secular" standards, such as purely pedagogical criteria. The right to establish a non-state school, *vrijheid van stichting*, is also strongly linked to the *vrijheid van inrichting*, the freedom to give such a school a distinctive religious or philosophical character.

The majority of non-state primary and secondary schools, consisting of two-thirds of all schools, at least formally have a Christian character. However, it has to be stressed that most of the Catholic and Protestant schools do not, in fact, nowadays retain a strongly distinctive religious character and present themselves as "open" and pluralistic.

As has become clear, non-state, or independent, schools have a right to select teachers and pupils on the basis of criteria derived from their denominational or pedagogical ethos. Even so, this right may not be exercised arbitrarily since it is limited by specific provisions in the Education Acts and by general legislation. The legal relation between a school board and pupils may be characterized as a civil law contract, although its material content, the substantive norms regulating it, are to a large extent derived from the aforementioned public law provisions and principles.

The Right to Receive Education

Pupils have a right to (receive) primary and secondary education. This right is guaranteed in Article 2 of the First Protocol of the European Convention on Human Rights (ECHR), which is a self-executing treaty provision, as such applicable within the Dutch legal system.[3] According to the first sentence of this article, "No person shall be denied the right to education." It primarily protects the right of equal access to *public* primary and secondary schools. In Dutch education law, it is assumed that Article 2 Protocol 1 ECHR requires that children of illegal immigrants in their school age cannot be denied the right to education, and should be admitted to primary and secondary education.

The courts have denied Article 2 Protocol 1 ECHR so-called "*horizontal* effect," to the effect that it is not equally applicable to the relation between pupils and non-state schools. The Supreme Court, for instance, ruled in a case in which a Catholic school expelled pupils because their parents for religious reasons did not allow them to take certain classes, "that one cannot derive from this provision [Article 2 Protocol 1 ECHR] the obligation for non-state schools to admit pupils who in conformity with their parents' wishes refuse to attend specific lessons."[4]

For the age range of four to sixteen years, education is provided free of cost; school fees are voluntary. In primary schools, the books and materials are also free; in secondary schools, they are not. Parents have to pay a school fee for pupils who are sixteen or older (in the near future it will be for those who are eighteen or above) when a school year starts.

The right to education is supplemented with an obligation to be educated: the right to education in Article 2 Protocol 1 ECHR does not imply the right *not* to receive education. Primary and secondary education is obligatory up to the age of sixteen. The Compulsory Education Act nevertheless contains a provision for exemption from mandatory schooling when parents, for reasons of conscience, object to all available schools in a neighborhood; only then home-schooling is allowed. Yet, this option is actively discouraged by the authorities. Only a few hundred families attempt to acquire this exceptional status.

The right to education is further protected by what is called the "guarantee function" of the public school (Article 23 section 4 of the Constitution). In principle, every pupil must have access to a public school in the neighborhood. This does not entail an unrestricted right to be admitted to a *specific* public school of one's choice: although a public school is not allowed to refuse pupils on denominational grounds, which would violate the principle of neutrality of public schools, Article 23 section 3 of the Constitution, it may restrict admittance on practical grounds (for instance lack of space).

The right to equal access to schools is also inherent in the constitutional principle of equality. According to the first sentence of Article 1 of the Dutch Constitution, all persons have to be treated equally in equal cases. The second sentence of this provision prohibits discrimination. In 1994, the General Equal Treatment Act (*Algemene Wet Gelijke Behandeling*, AWGB) came into force.[5] This Act endeavors to give "more substance," more precision, and more effectiveness to the general, broad principle of equality as laid down in Article 1 of the Dutch Constitution. The AWGB is not only applicable to "vertical" relations between public authorities and individuals in public schools, but is to a certain extent also applicable to "horizontal" relations, those between individuals and private organizations such as private denominational schools.

The structure of the AWGB is determined by the principle that differentiations on (suspect) grounds such as race, sex, and religion are prohibited in certain specific areas including work, commercial transactions, and education. The AWGB distinguishes between so-called direct and indirect differential treatment. Direct differential treatment explicitly refers to a suspect criterion like race, etc., and is always prohibited. Indirect differential treatment is a form of differential treatment in which a criterion is applied that seems to be neutral, but in practice disproportionately targets persons sharing a common characteristic such as race. As to education, indirect differential treatment is prohibited, unless a school board is able to give strong arguments due to such concerns as safety, order, and/or educational purposes in favor of it.

Within certain legal limits, non-state denominational schools are not as fully bound by the equality principle and the AWGB as public schools and have the right to refuse to admit pupils on the basis of religious standards. When a refusal is grounded on denominational criteria, this right is protected by the *vrijheid van richting*, the freedom of education guaranteed by Article 23 of the Constitution. In the famous 1988 *Maimonides* judgment, the Supreme Court ruled that an orthodox Jewish school could exclude a boy from a liberal Jewish family because its action was based on a consistent policy and since this policy was directly related to the school's religious foundation, the school therefore could rely on its freedom of education.[6] Due to legal technicalities, the Court did not decide the other core issue, whether the application of religion-based criteria that were linked to ethnicity, in this case, the criterion that a nonbeliever nevertheless was regarded as Jewish when he or she had a Jewish mother, should have been regarded as racial discrimination.

In line with *Maimonides*, the AWGB leaves denominational, non-state, schools the freedom to use criteria derived from their religious "mission" to decide which pupils they admit on the basis of such criteria as long as they do so in a consistent manner. This means that *Maimonides* would probably be decided in the same way under the regime of the AWGB as it was in 1988. It also indicates that if a denominational school selects among pupils on denominational grounds on a case-by-case basis rather than in a consistent manner, it cannot appeal to the exemption of the AWGB (Article 7, Section 2 of the AWGB) since this would be a breach of Article 7, Section 1 AWGB. In practice, this means that the majority of non-orthodox schools cannot invoke the exemption.

Private denominational schools also have the authority, guaranteed by the *vrijheid van inrichting*, to apply admission criteria that are not linked to their religious identities. For instance, these schools can refuse pupils on practical grounds such as "the school is full"; due to pedagogical motives such as "we do not have the specialized teachers that meet the needs of this handicapped pupil"; or for "public order" reasons such as "students who wear clothing that suggests Nazi sympathies will be refused because of possible conflicts with students from ethnic minorities."[7] While this freedom, which also can be claimed to a certain extent by public schools, is less well protected than the freedom to select on denominational grounds. If the selection process leads to a refusal on the basis of a criterion that mostly affects religious or ethnic-minority pupils, a school board has to show a compelling legitimate interest to apply this criterion; otherwise its application amounts to indirect differential treatment prohibited by the AWGB.

In our opinion, this last notion has been wrongly applied in a judgment concerning the expulsion from a Catholic school of two Muslim girls who refused to attend swimming lessons because of their religious beliefs. The Court of Appeal ruled this expulsion lawful based on freedom of education: "The school has referred to their constitutional guaranteed freedom of education. This freedom comprises in any case the freedom to regard swimming-lessons as a necessary part of the curriculum; in this regard the board is also free to teach this in 'mixed' classes, and to appoint male teachers."[8] The Court allowed the school board a margin of discretion that is too wide; the board's decision was not based on a religious view, *vrijheid van richting*, and was not grounded on the Catholic identity of the school, but merely on its general pedagogical freedom, *vrijheid van inrichting*, which is less well protected than its religious autonomy.

In another case, a Court of Appeal correctly rejected the admission policy of a school for hotel management that admitted an equal number of male and female students, thereby rejecting proportionally more female than male candidates.[9] The school's educational philosophy was not based on denominational principles but on the aim to prepare students adequately for management positions within the hotel sector. Requiring an equal male-to-female ratio was not regarded as a sufficient reason for this differential treatment.

Religious Freedom in Schools

Article 6, section 1 of the Dutch Constitution provides, "Everyone shall have the right to manifest freely his religion or belief, either individually or in community with others, without prejudice to his responsibility under the law." This freedom of religion comprises not only the freedom to establish and have a religion, including the right to change one's religion or not to have a religion, but also the freedom *to behave* in accordance with a specific religion or to profess or propagate a religion in ritual, cult, and/or clothing.[10] Article 9 of the European Convention on Human Rights likewise protects religious freedom.

The direct relevance of these provisions in education law cases until now has been limited. One reason for this is that the space reserved for religious expression is subject to limitations that are inherent to the fact that students are part of a collective pedagogical process, in which certain restrictions as to place, time, and mode are unavoidable. For instance, an appeal to religious freedom in order to claim a right to perform a ritual during class will probably be dismissed as frivolous. Further, an appeal to religious freedom by a pupil against a denominational school that relies on its own religious basis will generally fail: the school's freedom of education will prevail.[11]

Religious freedom is often more effectively protected through the prohibition of discrimination on the basis of religion in the aforementioned General Equal Treatment Act (AWGB). In the application of the AWGB, the Equal Treatment Commission (*Commissie Gelijke Behandeling*, Cgb) plays a dominant role. The Commission is a public authority that examines, at the request of private persons or organizations or on its own accord, the AWGB conformity of acts of the government or specific private organizations (like school boards) in equal treatment cases. The Commission is not a judge. It offers opinions which are not legally binding. The decisions are, nevertheless, considered important because they are often regarded as authoritative interpretations of the AWGB; in general, these are to be followed by the courts. Since its foundation, the Commission has presented several important views concerning religious issues in education.

One of the issues addressed by the Commission concerned whether freedom of religion bestows a positive obligation on the board of a public school to provide students with the means to exercise their religious freedom at school effectively. Do they, for example, have a right to be provided an unoccupied classroom in order to pray there? Since the Dutch Education Acts do not contain specific provisions on other religious activities than religious instruction, the Commission decided that a public school board may place a classroom at the disposal of its students for praying. However, since there is no obligation for the board to do this, by refusing their students that facility due to the principle of neutrality, the board did not violate the AWGB.[12]

Most Commission cases involving religion deal with dress codes. Dress codes that mainly affect pupils of a certain persuasion often amount to prohibited differential treatment on the basis of religion. The reasons behind dress codes are crucial in order to answer whether there has been direct or indirect differential treatment in a concrete case. The Commission has, for instance, decided that if a headscarf is forbidden because of its religious connotations only, then religion is the ground for differential treatment of Muslim girls and the code must be regarded as a form of *direct* differential treatment, prohibited by the AWGB.[13]

If, on the other hand, a dress code does not forbid an article of clothing as a religious expression but for other reasons such as safety during gymnastics or pedagogical concerns, there is no direct differential treatment. Such a measure can nevertheless result in forbidden indirect differential treatment, when the neutral criterion in effect leads to a prohibition on wearing for example a Muslim headscarf. In order to be legally admissible, such indirect differential treatment must be justified by an objective justification. Whether a chosen instrument, a dress code, is necessary is therefore crucial.

In judging the necessity of a dress code, several matters must be taken into account such as safety, hygiene, and pedagogical arguments. In 2000, the Commission had to deal with the question of the legitimacy of a prohibition placed by a school board on wearing a chador, a veil that covers the whole face except for the eyes, and applied a very strict necessity test.[14] It decided that although the objective sought by the dress code, to create a pedagogical environment for open communication and preparing students for future jobs that demanded such communication, was not discriminatory, it did not fulfill a real need and therefore was not strictly necessary. Not all teachers had problems with teaching someone whose face they could not see and the school could not put forward authoritative didactic arguments that substantiated the claim that a student's wearing a chador had caused troubles in the past. According to the view of the Commission, the didactic arguments put forward by the school board were insufficient to necessitate the dress code in question. Further, only few persons wore a chador, and there were sufficient ways of communication left. Therefore, the indirect differential treatment could not be objectively justified.

We believe the Commission's view was wrong. It attached too much weight to the fact that some teachers apparently had no difficulties with the chador. Yet, in cases like this, a margin of appreciation should be left to school boards and not to a few individual teachers. The Commission attached too little weight to the pedagogic freedom of the school board. Within limits, school boards should have the right to establish rules in view of the educational process. From this point of view, the standard of proof that a dress code always has to be justified by authoritative didactic arguments is too high.[15]

In a case in 2003, the facts were essentially the same as in the dispute from 2000, but the Commission reached a different conclusion. In the 2003 case, the Commission ruled that the school had given plausible arguments that wearing a chador frustrated the necessary communication between teachers and students as well as between students themselves. The fact that some teachers thought otherwise did not undermine the competence of the school board, which was responsible for the pedagogic climate as a whole, to enforce the dress code. The school board sufficiently had demonstrated that the chador hindered the educational process and was not compatible with the requirements of the types of jobs for which the students were educated.[16]

It has to be stressed that non-state denominational schools not only have the right to select pupils on the basis of their religious views, but also have a larger degree of discretion than public schools in prohibiting religious manifestations that are not in conformity with these views. A public school is not allowed to refuse or expel a Muslim girl due to her headscarf as that would be contrary to the principle of state neutrality and with the AWGB. Yet, a denominational school may do so, provided that this is based on a coherent and consistent policy. For instance, the Commission ruled that a Roman Catholic school could expel Muslim students because they began wearing headscarves; this school could rely on a strict policy forbidding, on denominational grounds, clothing with non-Christian connotations.[17]

Freedom of Speech in Schools

The freedom of speech is laid down in Article 7 of the Dutch Constitution. Article 7, section 1, of the Dutch Constitution states: "No one shall require prior permission to publish thoughts or opinions through the press, without prejudice to the responsibility of every person under the law." Further, Article 7, section 3, provides, "No one shall be required to submit thoughts or opinions for prior approval in order to disseminate them by means other than those mentioned in the preceding paragraphs, without prejudice to the responsibility of every person under the law."

Freedom of speech primarily functions in "vertical relations" between public authorities and individuals. At the same time, this freedom may also have a certain relevance within "horizontal relations," such as those between the board of a private school and a student. Until recently, few cases have addressed the issue of the freedom of speech of pupils.

One case has dealt with the question of whether one could prohibit a group of pupils from wearing so-called "bomberjacks" and black sweaters from a brand called "Lonsdale," clothing that is associated with neo-Nazism. A school board demanded that a group of youngsters who caused trouble and fought with pupils from ethnic minorities signed a document in which they promised to stop wearing these provocative clothes. One boy refused to do so, and was suspended. The president of the court ruled that in the light of Article 7, section 3, of the Constitution, restrictions on the content of expressions could only be based on a specific Act of Parliament.[18] In addition, he ruled that restrictions of the freedom of expression in public and private education are justified if they intend to avoid situations endangering the order in school or the educational process, provided that they are necessary to avert this danger. In view of the association of the prohibited clothing with neo-Nazism and the incitement it caused, the court ruled that the prohibition was acceptable because it was directed at a content-neutral goal: re-establishing the order at school. The court also took notice of the effectiveness of the prohibition: peace within the institution was restored after the other pupils signed the document and stopped wearing these clothes at school. The suspension order nevertheless was quashed, though not for substantive reasons, but due to procedural inadequacies.

Student Rights and Discipline

Schools have an inherent right to take measures to ensure internal order. The authority to take disciplinary actions can be seen as a feature inherent to an educational institution, flowing from its pedagogical autonomy: this type of institution has the task to educate pupils, which implies the authority to lay down and enforce basic rules. Dutch education law explicitly mentions only two disciplinary measures: suspension and expulsion. This does not exclude the possibility of inflicting other less severe disciplinary measures; the authority to apply these punishments flows from the pedagogical task and autonomy of the school.

Suspension is an order measure whereby a pupil is temporarily denied the right to participate in the educational process of the school. Suspension is considered a disciplinary measure only when it comprises at least a full day. Denying the right to take part in the education of a school for less than one day is regarded as a (merely) pedagogical measure. The Primary Education Act does not contain any rules with respect to suspension. The suspension measure in secondary education is regulated in the *Inrichtingsbesluit WVO.* Article 13, section 1, of this decree provides that suspending a pupil is only allowed for the duration of one week.

The decision of a school board has to be communicated to the parents in writing. In light of the fairness principle, pupils and their parents should, in principle, be allowed a hearing by the school board before this measure could be inflicted. As to secondary education, the decision should contain a valid motive, and has to specify the start and duration of the suspension and of any other measures taken (Article 13 lid 1 Inrichtingsbesluit WVO). In our opinion, boards of primary schools have the same obligations in this matter as those of secondary schools.

While suspension does not terminate the legal relationships between school boards and students, in the case of expulsion this relationship comes to a definite end. Expulsion is a measure that can only be taken when a pupil is a danger to the integrity of school or endangers the order or safety in school. The decision to expel pupils from school is partly regulated by the same norms that apply to suspension. Moreover, students and their parents have to be allowed a hearing beforehand; decisions must be communicated in writing to students and their parents before they can be implemented (Article 63 sections 1, 2, and 3 Primary Education Act; Article 14 en 15 Inrichtingsbesluit WVO).

Decisions to expel pupils must also mention that they or their parents can object to such an action within six weeks. Article 40(1) of the Primary Education Act stipulates that the school board has the obligation to help find another school for the pupil. If, after eight weeks, no other school is prepared to admit the pupil, he can be expelled definitely. Article 26(1) of the Secondary Education Act provides that the final expulsion of a pupil who is subject to the Compulsory Education Act cannot take place until after the school board has ensured that another school is prepared to admit the pupil.

Dutch education law does not contain provisions regarding corporal punishment. In the past, corporal punishment was a widely accepted instrument for disciplining pupils and was regarded as an inherent right of teachers. However, we believe that according to the current *communis opinio* this "right" can be considered as being abolished. This is confirmed by the fact that there is substantial support in politics and in society to create a legal prohibition on the application of any form of physical and psychological violence within the family. *A fortiori* corporal punishment in the school is therefore also forbidden.[19] This is in line with developments in international law. For instance, the Committee on the Rights of the Child is very clear about the unacceptability of corporal punishment within school: "Education must also be provided in a way that respects the strict limits on discipline reflected in article 28(2) [of the Convention of the Rights of the Child] and promotes non-violence in school. The Committee has repeatedly made it clear in its concluding observations that the use of corporal punishment does not respect the inherent dignity of the child nor the strict limits on school discipline."[20]

Special Populations

One of the main tenets of the Dutch education system is the equality principle. This principle is enshrined in Article 1 of the Constitution and is developed further in, among others, the General Equal Treatment Act (*Algemene Wet Gelijke Behandeling*, AWGB, already discussed in other paragraphs). To a large extent, the AWGB only protects formal equality, in that certain differentiations are forbidden. At the same time, Dutch education law also strives for material equality, through positive action that compensates existing inequalities within society; this is especially so with regard to primary schools with large numbers of disadvantaged pupils that receive substantially more government funding than other schools. Broadly, two types of funding schemes can be distinguished.

There are schools that have a large number of pupils who, due to their socio-economic background, probably need extra assistance. Schools with such a student body receive extra funding to attract more teaching staff to meet the needs of such pupils. The largest two groups in need of extra attention each contain around 200,000 pupils. One of these groups consists of the children from Dutch parents who both have only received lower education. Above a certain minimum number of such pupils, the school gets 25 percent extra funding for every extra pupil belonging to this category. The other category can be roughly defined as children (a) with at least one parent from Southern Europe, Turkey, Morocco, Tunisia, Surinam, the Netherlands Antilles, or another non-European non-English-speaking country, (b) who have at least one parent with only lower education. Above a certain minimum number of these pupils, a school gets 90 percent extra funding for every extra pupil belonging to this category.

There is a striking discrepancy here in that schools with many pupils of the second category, often called "black schools," receive much more money than schools with many pupils of the first category, that have a large number of Dutch pupils from the lower socio-economic strata, formerly often called "laborers' schools." The government has proposed to remove this discrepancy by making the funding scheme largely independent from the ethnic factor. This will result in lesser funding of black schools and more funds for the laborers' schools.

The other funding scheme is concerned with children whose *onderwijsachterstand* or underachievement, has been established through individualized tests. Here we also must distinguish between two types of pupils. One type consists of pupils with learning or behavioral problems. In order to help these children, a number of primary schools must cooperate to establish a *special* primary school that receives more funding than the "normal," average primary school. Pupils who are diagnosed as having specific learning or behavioral problems may attend this special school. Even so, there is a budgetary limit on the amount of extra funding to be spent on such a special school. This measure is meant to avoid hasty referrals of pupils by the primary schools to the special school and to stimulate them to integrate these pupils as much as possible in a "normal" primary school.

The other category of pupils mainly consists of handicapped children. Depending on the extent of their handicap, to be assessed in an elaborate testing procedure, the parents of these children receive something like a voucher, with which they can "buy" a place with extra facilities for their child at a regular primary school, a special primary school, or an institution specialized in taking care of pupils with that particular handicap.

Emerging Issues

The main issues in current debates and policies have to do with so-called "black" schools and also with Islamic schools which, by the way, are always "black" schools. In the last forty years, the ethnic and cultural composition of the Dutch population has changed considerably. The number of so-called "ethnic minorities," persons coming from countries other than those in Western Europe and North America, as well as their children, has risen continuously. The four largest ethnic-minority groups, Turkish, Moroccan, Surinamese, Antillean, together comprise some one million persons out of sixteen million Dutch residents. In recent years, there has also been a substantial growth of the number of asylum seekers' children from Afghanistan, Iran, Iraq, Somalia, and Sri Lanka.

These demographic changes obviously have their impact on the composition of the school population. The percentage of ethnic-minority children in primary and secondary schools has risen, and the number of so-called black schools has grown considerably. At present, some 600 out of 7,100 schools are black schools, those with more than 50 percent of ethnic-minority pupils that may be presumed to have learning disadvantages and therefore receive additional funding. A further consequence has been a moderate growth in the number of denominational schools based on a minority religion, especially Islamic schools. At the moment, there are approximately forty Islamic primary schools and two Islamic secondary schools in the Netherlands.

These developments have created a lively political debate about whether the trend toward further segregation between white schools and black schools, as well as the growth of the number of Islamic schools, should be countered by legal measures. One argument in favor of such measures is that it is surely more difficult to realize a minimum of communication and social integration between black and white children in ethnically segregated schools than when the school population consists of an adequate ethnic mixture. In that last instance, it is more probable that Dutch would be the main language in the playground and that friendships between black and white children would develop. In addition, there is some empirical evidence that pupils with learning disadvantages benefit from the presence of pupils without such disadvantages.

One way to counter the trend toward further segregation is a government policy requiring schools to achieve an adequate mix of black and white pupils. Yet, such a policy must, to a large extent, be voluntary to be compatible with human rights provisions.[21] One must keep in mind that the existence of white schools and black schools is, to a large extent, brought about by the ethnic composition of the district in which a school is located. Countering segregating tendencies by imposing ethnic quotas and the like, a solution that would certainly lead to the refusal of pupils merely because they would disturb the required "mix," will probably be regarded as a breach of the principle of parental choice as guaranteed in Article 2 Protocol 1 ECHR. Further, a compulsory desegregation scheme would be incompatible with the constitutional requirement that the public school system has to admit every child. Finally, such a policy, when based on ethnic quotas, would be in contravention with the AWGB[22] and international instruments; a quota-system, however well intentioned, would amount to prohibited direct differentiation based on racial or ethnic origin.

Another option put forward is to strengthen the position of pupils and their parents. Quite often it is assumed that non-state denominational schools (ab)use their right to select in order to refuse minority children, which leads to a disproportionate number of these children in public-authority schools which do not have this right. By giving parents a legal claim to have their children admitted to the school of their choice, a desirable mix will be brought about, or so it is presupposed. We have serious doubts about such a policy. First, an unconditional freedom of choice would be inconsistent with the freedom of education, the right to select on denominational grounds, as enshrined in Article 23 of the Constitution. It is true that this right may be restricted. Yet, a legal measure that denies that right even to the small number of denominational schools that consistently apply their religious criteria when admitting and refusing pupils would surely be unconstitutional as it would be incompatible with the freedom of education as understood in the Netherlands.

The proponents of this option also seem to believe that strengthening parental choice would result in an adequate "ethnic mix." This belief is incorrect. The existence of segregation between white and black schools is largely the result of housing patterns and not of frustration by school boards of parental choices; it is in part the *result* of parental choice, the so-called "white flight" and the preference of large numbers of Moroccan and Turkish parents for public and Islamic schools as well as for schools in the neighbourhood, that has led to segregation.[23]

Perhaps a more effective and acceptable course of action would be to allow local authorities to develop "mild" desegregation policies. Recently, the Dutch Education Council suggested that particularly in the larger cities there might be sufficient reason to spread pupils across all schools within the municipality.[24] The Council stipulated that legally binding arrangements should have an explicit basis in an Act of Parliament, be justified by cogent interests, not be based on ethnic criteria but on educational criteria related to learning advantages and disadvantages of the pupils (determined for instance by home language or the level of parental education),[25] leave intact the freedom of the "strict" confessional schools to refuse pupils on denominational grounds, and be decided upon by local authorities. The Minister of Education reacted in a broadly positive vein, but is not willing to give local authorities the final say in developing legally binding desegregation policies. In her view, it is up to the authorities *together* with the private schools to make desegregation plans.

Another issue is the growth of the number of Islamic schools. This is related to the segregation issue because all Islamic schools recruit their pupils primarily from immigrant children with learning disadvantages and therefore also are black schools, but is nevertheless a different one. The main concern here has to do with fears in government and society of Islamic fundamentalism. It has to be stressed that it would be unconstitutional to close down or hinder the setting up of Islamic schools as such. In addition, it may be that such schools are instilling in their students values that are not fully in line with the basic principles of Western society such as individualistic humanism and the separation of church and state; but, even if this last allegation were true, which to date has not been proven, as long as these schools fulfill the legal criteria, they have the constitutional right to be funded.

The growth of the number of Islamic schools could be stopped by changing the rules concerning the foundation of schools. The Minister of Education has suggested that all newly founded schools that have too many pupils with learning disadvantages should not receive government funding. This proposal, although not prima facie unconstitutional, nevertheless is problematic. First, there is the practical problem that it, in fact, prohibits the foundation of (all) new schools in urban areas that mainly consist of ethnic and cultural minority groups and thus a concentration of pupils with learning disadvantages. Another problem is the result that no new Islamic schools can be established which, of course, is probably one of the main reasons behind the proposal. As indicated before, all Islamic schools are black schools. Thus, an ostensibly neutral criterion in fact amounts to differential treatment of Islamic schools compared to others. Such differential treatment is not always prohibited. It should then be justified by strong arguments. The question is, then, whether a restriction of the freedom to establish one's own schools, which primarily affects religious minorities, can be justified. Until now, in our opinion such a justification has not been shown.

Conclusion

The Dutch system is a binary one, consisting of public schools run by local authorities and non-state, private schools. Both types of schools are funded on an equal basis and have to fulfill similar quality standards. Public schools must be open for every pupil while private schools may select on the basis of denominational criteria and, in general, enjoy a freedom of education. This system has worked fairly well in the twentieth century but is now under attack. One trend is the juridification of the relation between schools and pupils/parents. There is a tendency to regard pupils/parents as critical consumers who have a contract with schools and have certain claims and fundamental rights; the necessary corollary is that schools are something like enterprises operating on the educational market. To some extent, this trend is linked up with the ongoing process of secularization, resulting in endeavours to limit the autonomy and distinctive ethos of denominational schools, by strengthening the legal position of pupils, by introducing desegregation schemes, and by limiting the possibilities of minority religions, especially Islam, to establish new schools.

On the other hand, there is a sense of urgency, a feeling that the educational system somehow must make up for such problematic trends in society as segregation, individualization, and lack of social cohesion, among others. This suggests that the schools should have a distinctive ethos and must strive to be a strong community, integrating pupils while instilling in them certain social values. It is evident that these two perspectives, schools as neutral businesses trying to satisfy their customers, and schools as value-based communities trying to create social cohesion are not easily reconciled.

Notes

1. A comprehensive description and analysis of the legal status of pupils in Dutch education law is given in C.W. Noorlander, *Recht doen aan leerlingen en ouders*, Nijmegen: Wolf Legal Publishers 2005.
2. Cf. also Henk J.M. Hoefnagel & Ben Vermeulen, "Recent Developments in Dutch Legislation on Education," *European Journal for Education Law and Policy* 1997, nr. 1, 155ff.
3. See on this provision J. De Groof, G. Lauwers Ed., *No Person Shall Be Denied the Right to Education*, Nijmegen: Wolf Legal Publishers 2004; and in particular B.P. Vermeulen et al., "The European Convention on Human Rights and the Dutch Education System" (ibid., 369–386).
4. Hoge Raad (Supreme Court) April 9, 1976, Nederlandse Jurisprudentie 1976, 409 (Terheijden).
5. Staatsblad 1994, 230.
6. Hoge Raad January 22, 1988, Administratiefrechtelijke Beslissingen 1988, 96.
7. Voorzieningenrechter Rb. Haarlem March 21, 2003, Administratiefrechtelijke Beslissingen 2003, 234 (with note by Vermeulen).
8. Hof Den Bosch September 5, 1989, Rechtspraak Vreemdelingenrecht 1989, 96.
9. Hof Den Haag October 27, 1992, Nederlandse Jurisprudentie 1993, 680.
10. Kamerstukken II 1990/91, 22014, nr. 6, 39–40.
11. Hoge Raad (Supreme Court) April 9, 1976, Nederlandse Jurisprudentie 1976, 409 (Terheijden).
12. Cgb August 3, 2000, decision 2000-51, Rechtspraak onderwijsrecht 2000–2002, 47 (with note by Noorlander).

13. Cgb February 3, 1997, decision 97-14.

14. Cgb September 6, 2000, decision 2000-63, Rechtspraak onderwijsrecht 2000–2002, 49 (with note by Noorlander).

15. B.P. Vermeulen, "*Islamitische kledingperikelen in het onderwijs*", School en Wet 2003, nr. 2, 48.

16. Cgb March 20, 2003, decision 2003-40, Administratiefrechtelijke Beslissingen 2003, 233 (with note by Vermeulen).

17. Cgb August 5, 2003, decision 2003-112, Administratiefrechtelijke Beslissingen 2003, 375 (with note by Vermeulen).

18. Voorzieningenrechter Rechtbank Haarlem March 21, 2003, Administratiefrechtelijke Beslissingen 2003, 234 (with note by Vermeulen).

19. Noorlander 2005, 603ff.

20. Committee on the Rights of the Child, *The Aims of Education*, March 17, 2001, CRC/GC/2001/1 (General Comments), § 8.

21. B.P. Vermeulen, *Witte en zwarte scholen*, Den Haag 2001.

22. As decided in Cgb November 6, 2001, decision 2001-99, Administratiefrechtelijke Beslissingen 2002, 48 (with note by Vermeulen); Cgb July 29, 2003, decision 2003-105, Administratiefrechtelijke Beslissingen 2003, 376 (with note by Vermeulen).

23. S. Karsten et al., *Schoolkeuze in een multi-etnische samenleving*, Amsterdam 2002; Onderwijsraad (Education Council), *Vaste grond onder de voeten. Een verkenning inzake artikel 23 Grondwet*, Den Haag 2002.

24. Onderwijsraad (Education Council), *Bakens voor spreiding en integratie*, Den Haag 2005.

25. Maybe a change of the AWGB will be necessary. The Cgb has ruled that an integration policy of "mixing," developed by a Christian school board for its fourteen schools, according to which on every school no more than 15 percent of the population should consist of pupils with a non-Dutch home language, was not justified by compelling reasons, therefore amounted to (indirect) differentiation on the basis of race and thus was in breach of the AWGB (Cgb 29 July 2003, decision 2003-105, Administratiefrechtelijke Beslissingen 2003, 376 [with note by Vermeulen]).

9

New Zealand

Paul Rishworth

The New Zealand Constitution

New Zealand's constitution is "unwritten," in the sense that there is no single written document that creates and empowers the three branches of government. For historical reasons, New Zealand's Parliament enjoys a legislative power without any of the formal restraints that a constitutional bill of rights might supply. As a result, no New Zealand court may declare a legislative enactment to be ultra vires or invalid. That state of affairs is known in New Zealand, as in the United Kingdom, as "parliamentary supremacy."

It would be wrong to conclude that civil liberties are precarious as a result, or that Parliament routinely enacts laws that would be unconstitutional if there were a written constitution with a bill of rights. As a small country with a three-year election cycle, the ballot box has traditionally been seen as the bulwark against oppressive laws. Further, New Zealand's own proclaimed commitment to human rights, to various international instruments as well as to the domestic human rights statutes that Parliament has enacted, serves to ensure that the "rights implications" of proposed legislation and policies are generally well debated. Generally, civil liberties and equality are as well protected in New Zealand as they are in countries with constitutional rights.

In 1990, a statutory Bill of Rights was enacted by the New Zealand Parliament. This enactment, the New Zealand Bill of Rights Act 1990, affirms a set of rights and freedoms derived from the International Covenant on Civil and Political Rights. Importantly, s 4 of the New Zealand Bill of Rights explicitly preserves Parliament's supremacy: it provides that no enactment is to be invalid by reason of inconsistency with the Bill of Rights. Despite that major limitation, the New Zealand Bill of Rights has proved to be quite significant in New Zealand law.

First, the Bill of Rights assuredly controls administrative action, except in the rare case where an infringing action is positively authorised by legislation. Second, s 6 of the Bill of Rights requires that all legislation be interpreted consistently with the rights and freedoms it contains. As in the United Kingdom under its similarly worded Human Rights Act 1998 (UK), this is a significant practical restraint on Parliament's legislative power. It means that rights-infringing meanings of enactments are avoided by the judiciary unless Parliament has made a rights-infringing intention very clear. This is significant in the education context, for much that occurs in state schools rests ultimately on the exercise of the broad statutory powers of management conferred by the Education Act 1989. Those powers can readily be interpreted consistently with the Bill of Rights. In other words, nothing that is actually done in a school ought to infringe the right of a student as affirmed in the Bill of Rights. If it does, then it is unlawful unless clearly authorised by legislation, and that would be rare.

Responsibility for Education Law and Policy

New Zealand is a unitary state and education is a matter for national legislation. Education is funded from general taxation revenue, not property taxes. Major aspects of educational policy are determined by the Cabinet, on the advice of the Minister of Education. The Ministry of Education provides policy advice and general oversight of the public school network. Since a major reform accomplished by the Education Act 1989, the operation of each state school has rested with a locally elected board of trustees. Each board comprises at least three and up to seven elected parent representatives, the electorate being the parent community of a school, together with the principal, a representative of the school's teaching staff, a student representative (for secondary schools), and, if a Board desires, co-opted members. A school's board of trustees has full responsibility for the operation of the school. In practice, a board discharges that function through the principal who manages the school on a day-to-day basis.

The Treaty of Waitangi and the Maori Dimension to New Zealand

This brief account of the country's constitutional arrangements, and the place of education within them, would be incomplete without reference to the

Treaty of Waitangi. The Treaty of Waitangi is generally regarded as New Zealand's founding document. Signed in 1840 by Maori chiefs and a representative of Queen Victoria, it comprises three clauses which, in the English language version, are straightforward. Article 1 records the transfer of sovereignty from the Maori tribes to the English Crown; article 2 is a promise by the Crown to respect and protect Maori property rights; and article 3 provides that Maori and British subjects will be treated equally.

The Treaty was also written and signed in Maori, and the Maori version records the promises and obligations rather differently. For example, article 1 of the Maori version confers on the Crown only a right to "govern" and not the complete "sovereignty" of the English version. This fits with the Maori version of article 2, wherein the Crown promises to protect not just Maori property but also Maori political authority and self-government. The Maori version is argued to contemplate a state in which the Crown and Maori govern in partnership. In New Zealand, the expression "Crown" is, in this context, synonymous with "the state."

Largely through the power and force of numbers, New Zealand's history has proceeded along the lines of the English rather than the Maori version of the Treaty. Yet, in recent decades, the ideas in the Maori version of the Treaty have had significant political traction. By way of a sort of "blending" of the two Treaty translations, it is now generally accepted by New Zealand governments of all persuasions that Maori must be separately considered, and Maori themselves consulted, in any significant policy development affecting their interests. Indeed, since the move in 1993 to proportional representation in Parliament, Maori have had increasing influence in national politics.

In education, this translates into ready acceptance by policy makers and legislators of Maori aspirations for an education system that values and perpetuates the Maori language and cultural understandings. However, the Treaty is not itself a source of law: it cannot be relied upon directly in a court. It is "constitutionally important," but is not a Constitution. As will be seen below, the Treaty influences policy development and thus the content of enacted law.

The Right to Receive an Education

The Education Act 1989 entitles every New Zealand citizen, and every legal resident, to a free education in a state school from the date of his or her fifth birthday until 31 January in the year after he or she reaches the age of nineteen years (section 3). The Act also makes it compulsory to attend school from the age of six to sixteen (section 20). The state maintains a network of schools, but parents may elect private education for their children. All private schools must be "registered" under s 35A of the Education Act 1989, which sets out a list of criteria for registration, one of which is that the school must "[provide] suitably for the inculcation in the minds of students of sentiments of patriotism and loyalty."

A state school is required to enrol any eligible student who presents himself or herself for enrolment, unless the school is "overcrowded." This is a term of art, signifying acceptance by the Ministry of Education that, because of space constraints, the school needs an "enrolment scheme" to limit numbers by defining a geographical "home zone." Students outside of a home zone may apply for any places left unfilled by in-zone students. Insofar as successful schools are popular with students and their families, they all have enrolment schemes and zones. This drives up property values within the school's zone.

The subject of school zoning has become politically contentious over the past decade, the previous National party Government, in power from 1990 to 1999, having introduced a system of "choice" in which overcrowded schools were entitled to determine their own criteria for accepting students. There was criticism that successful schools selected only students that would enhance the school's reputation for academic or sporting prowess. In 2000, the criterion for school selection reverted to geographical zones, as described above.

Educational quality is regulated and monitored by a number of state agencies. First, all teachers are required to be registered and certified by the New Zealand Teachers Council as meeting the required standard. Second, an Education Review Office has statutory responsibility for periodic inspection and reporting on every state school. These reports are publicly available and are an influential commentary on school attainment and quality. Third, the New Zealand Qualifications Authority is charged with the function of setting national standards for qualifications in secondary education, as well as in post-school education and training.

The role of courts in assessing educational quality is very limited. This was the subject of significant litigation in 2003, when a coalition of parents of children with disabilities sued the Minister of Education, contending that their children received an education of lesser quality than that of normal children. The parents' argument hinged on the fact that section 8 of the Education Act explicitly conferred, on disabled students, the "same rights" as all other students. That focused attention directly on what the "right to an education" actually comprised for all students. The Court was invited to find that it envisaged an education that reached a certain, judicially enforceable, standard. This argument succeeded in the trial court but, on appeal, the New Zealand Court of Appeal ruled that the "right" to an education was a right of *access* only.[1]

Educational quality was, in the Court's view, not justiciable. It was to be monitored through the operation of the various statutory bodies created by the Education Act, along with political oversight by the Ministry of Education and the input of parents through school boards. The Court left room for allegations of negligence in the delivery of education. Even so, cases of this type would necessarily involve individualized inquiries in relation to particular students, and not the systemic complaint about educational quality made by the plaintiffs in the case before the Court.

Freedom of Expression

All persons in New Zealand enjoy the rights to freedom of thought and expression conferred by section 14 of the New Zealand Bill of Rights Act 1990. The fact that the Bill of Rights is not a superior law does not, however, explain the rarity of litigation over freedom of expression in schools. After all, most limits on student expression arise out of school rules and associated disciplinary action rather than legislation. The right to freedom of expression in the Bill of Rights is, in principle, quite capable of vitiating school rules that impose unreasonable restrictions. Even so, there has been no post-1990 litigation on freedom of expression.

The leading reported case remains one from the 1970s about hair length.[2] A high school suspended a pupil indefinitely for his continual disobedience in refusing to have his hair cut. The appeal to the courts was based, in those pre-Bill of Rights days, on the claim that the school rule was unreasonable and hence amenable to judicial review and nullification as if it were a municipal bylaw. The Court rejected that argument, holding that the student had not demonstrated that restrictions on hair length were unrelated to control and management of the school. It followed that the school's board had acted within its powers. This result was consistent with the general tenor of United States litigation over hair length in the 1970s.

For many years both prior to and since the advent of the Bill of Rights there have been debates over whether school uniforms are consistent with freedom of expression. The issue typically arises when a uniform is advanced as a means of turning around a poorly performing school. The legality of school uniforms has never reached a courtroom but most agree that a school policy prescribing uniforms is a lawful exercise of a school board's power of governance, and not inconsistent with the freedom of expression in the Bill of Rights.

Disputes about uniforms, haircuts, and other forms of personal adornment are now invariably taken to the Human Rights Commission rather than the courts. The Human Rights Commission is a statutory body created under the Human Rights Act 1993. Its main function is the general promotion of human rights, but it has also the specific function of receiving and seeking to mediate complaints about discrimination. Unresolved complaints are referred to an Office of Human Rights Proceedings which may take action on an individual's behalf before the Human Rights Review Tribunal. This service is free to complainants so there is obvious incentive to complain to the Commission rather than a court. School disputes involving religion and expression therefore tend to be cast as discrimination complaints but, even if they are not, the Commission tends to receive them.

One fertile source of disputation has been school rules about jewelry and adornments such as crosses, pendants, tongue studs, and hairstyle. An important consequence of successful mediation is that complaints do not lead to precedent-setting appellate litigation. Nevertheless, some of the mediated outcomes are well known in the community: the Commission ruled in one matter that a male Muslim student must be granted an exemption from a "short pants" rule, and in another case ruled that girls be allowed the opportunity to wear "culottes" rather than skirts for reasons of modesty when playing on gymnastic equipment.

There has been no litigation over pure expression such as student speeches. When, in 2002, a student was disciplined for an evocative essay there was much controversy in newspapers but no litigation ensued; the assigned topic was "How my body lets me down" and the essay described a male student having an erection.

In general terms, it has to be said that New Zealanders do not tend to litigate matters involving civil rights, save, of course, where it is the litigant's *liberty* that is at stake, as in the criminal arena. Certainly, there is no culture of litigation over school disputes. The incentives that might produce one, such as fee-shifting statutes and a tradition of large exemplary damages awards do not exist in New Zealand. Political solutions are usually found, and are seen as speedier and cheaper. It should also be said that schools are, in the main, relatively tolerant in such matters. Where they are not, students live with it or move to another school. There are some signs of change, discussed below under "emerging issues."

Religious Freedom of Students

Since the first comprehensive legislation on education in 1877, there has been a requirement that primary education be "entirely of a secular character"; the phrase is now found in section 77 of the Education Act 1964. The intention was to avoid sectarian strife in education. However, right from the earliest days, there was a ready means of circumvention available to schools contemplating religious instruction.

The so-called "secular clause" appeared in the Act alongside a requirement that schools be open for two hours in the morning and two hours in the afternoon. Insofar as schools operated for longer than four hours each day, they felt able to introduce religious instruction into the notional "extra" time that they taught. Eventually, in 1962, this stratagem was formally legitimated: legislation was passed positively to authorise primary schools to "close" for up to one hour per week for the purpose of religious exercises and instruction (this is now section 78 of the Education Act 1964). Today, many primary schools avail themselves of this opportunity; it is a decision for each school's board of trustees and principal to make.

The Education Act specifically allows an opt-out, whilst also making it clear that school facilities may be used for it. Nothing in the legislation requires that the instruction be in the Christian religion, but the predominantly Christian background to New Zealand's citizenry has meant that virtually all such instruction is, in fact, Christian. The Churches Education Commission, representing the principal Christian denominations, organises what is commonly called the "Bible in Schools" programme and offers this service to schools through trained volunteers using an approved curriculum. Overall, it is said that about 5 percent of children exercise the opt-out provision. The "take up" by schools varies throughout the country, being low in the liberal capital city and higher in the more conservative south of the country.

There have been, as yet, no legal challenges to this religious instruction. Given that it is specifically authorised by the Education Act, a successful challenge would be difficult if not impossible, provided that the school follows the appropriate procedures. The prevailing view seems to be that the non-discriminatory character of the legislation, being neutral as between religions, and the availability of the "opt out," makes the status quo consistent with students' and parents' religious freedom. The lawfulness of any particular example of religious instruction would turn on how the legislation is applied.

As to secondary schools, the Education Act is silent on whether they be secular or not, and there is no positive authorisation of religious instruction. But the general understanding is that there ought to be no religious instruction, as such. A more general "values" education is more likely. Still, there has been a lengthy tradition in the older public schools of Bible readings and prayers at assemblies. These are sometimes mixed with readings from other religious texts as well. There has been no litigation about such practices, save for one case where the legality of religious exercises arose incidentally.

In *Rich v. Christchurch High School Board of Governors*, a student challenged her expulsion on procedural grounds.[3] The underlying disciplinary offence was that she had orchestrated a boycott of a school assembly on the grounds that hymns were sung and prayers were said. The New Zealand Court of Appeal ruled that, in view of the school's practice of granting exemptions to students who requested, it had acted lawfully in holding religious exercises at assembly and, therefore, in disciplining a student who challenged its authority to do so.

In 2003, a Christchurch secondary school constructed, with approval of the Ministry of Education, a prayer room for its Muslim students. While there was some political controversy about this, such expenditure could be justified for educational reasons. It facilitated the attendance of the school's large Muslim community, who might otherwise have had to travel off the campus for daily prayer. It can be seen, therefore, that the principle of religious freedom in New Zealand is not seen as precluding accommodation of religious belief, even if it involves the expenditure of public funds. The important point is that there was an educational reason for the expenditure.

Religious parents may secure for their children a publicly funded education in a religious school if they opt to send them to an "integrated" religious school. These schools are described below in the section dealing with "special populations."

The religious freedom of students themselves is protected through the New Zealand Bill of Rights provisions and through the prohibition of religious discrimination contained in s 21 of the Human Rights Act 1993. In that regard, the Human Rights Commission has in the past ruled that a Muslim student was entitled to special accommodation under a school's uniform rules, and that students wishing to wear ornaments such as crosses and Maori pendants must be allowed to do so, subject to reasonable requirements about size and shape. Save for the case mentioned above, the courts have not considered religious freedom issues in schools.

Student Rights and Discipline

Corporal punishment of students was abolished by legislation in 1990, by which time most schools had abandoned the practice in any event.

Apart from various in-school disciplinary measures such as detentions, the main disciplinary measures available to schools are to "stand down," "suspend," "exclude," or "expel." The availability of these four responses depends on the student's conduct having reached the level defined in section 14 of the Education Act 1989: "gross misconduct or continual disobedience [that] is a harmful or dangerous example to others," or behaviour such that the student or others will be "seriously harmed."

A "stand down" is ordered by the principal and may be for up to ten days per year. A "suspension" is first imposed by the principal but must be considered by the school's Board of Trustees, who may lift or extend the suspension, and in sufficiently serious cases may extend it indefinitely. An indefinite suspension of a student under sixteen years is "exclusion": the student is required to attend another school. Students over sixteen years old may be "expelled," with no requirement to enrol elsewhere.

The Education Act 1989 and the rules of natural justice ensure that a student facing disciplinary measures receives adequate notice of the "charges." He or she has a right to attend the Board of Trustees hearing with family and legal representation. Most school litigation in New Zealand arises out of suspensions and expulsions. Courts will rigorously scrutinise the procedures employed, since the student's right to education is at stake. In the leading case, a school was held to have acted unlawfully when the principal applied a so-called "zero tolerance" policy about consuming alcohol. The student had sipped beer from a can on a school trip. The High Court held that it was legal error to apply the policy slavishly. The principal failed to exercise the statutory discretion properly insofar as he did not ask whether what this student had done, on this occasion, amounted to gross misconduct.[4]

The question of school power to conduct searches has been a vexed one in New Zealand. There is no statutory authority for teachers to search students, and nor is there any decided case on the legality of school searches. But school searches do occur, mostly without incident or complaint. The prevailing view amongst New Zealand commentators has been that the Education Act 1989 implicitly empowers such reasonable searches as may be necessary to maintain a safe and orderly educational environment. The Supreme Court of Canada so ruled on broadly comparable legislation in 1998[5] and supports the general view in New Zealand. Of course, it is well understood that the implied power is constrained by section 21 of the New Zealand Bill of Rights which confers a right against unreasonable search and seizure.

Advisors to schools on searches generally take the lead from the criminal jurisprudence under the New Zealand Bill of Rights where, to be reasonable, searches must be justified at their inception and executed in a reasonable manner. It is likely that courts would countenance a lower level of suspicion for a school search than that required for police searches. One school search case was commenced but settled before trial; the search was seen as indefensible since it was a dragnet "strip search" of two entire classes for a missing fifteen dollars.

Some schools in New Zealand have brought drug sniffer dogs on to school premises. No legal challenge has been brought to this practice. It is argued that the sniffing of air space around student lockers and bags is not a search.

From time to time, schools have sought to introduce drug-testing regimes for students. It is generally taken for granted that refusal to participate in a drug test programme could not be a proper basis for school discipline. Routine drug testing is not employed—not, at least, with disciplinary sanctions.

One area in which drug testing has been introduced by some schools, and probably lawfully, is into the suspension process. As noted above, school boards may extend a suspension that was ordered by the principal. The Education Act allows a board to set conditions for a student's return to school, and the provision of a positive drug test result may well be a lawful condition when it is attached to a student whose suspension was for a drug-related matter.

Special Populations

All New Zealand schools, both public and private, are prohibited from discriminating on the grounds set out in the Human Rights Act 1993. These grounds include the usual ones, along with some that are less usual such as family status, political opinion, sexual orientation, and "presence in the body of organisms capable of causing illness" (section 21[1][h][vii]). However, it is a truism that different treatment of certain groups is sometimes required in order to ensure an overall equality. The Human Rights Act 1993 permits, therefore, some forms of different treatment. Indeed, it permits schools that are maintained wholly or principally for students of one sex, race, religious belief, or for students with a particular disability.

Many private schools are single-sex schools, and so are some of the nation's oldest and most successful public schools. There is no public sentiment against single sex schools, especially in an age when they are said to be especially good for girls' education.

The protection for schools for separate races seems at first sight to be odd. But invidious use of this exemption is unlikely, for no government would establish a school along racial lines unless its intention was benign, and no private school would receive the necessary certification to operate unless the intended purpose and effect would be beneficial to the race concerned. Of course, some might say that schools employing racial classifications can never be benign or beneficial. But these issues have not been explored in New Zealand because there has been no attempt to introduce racially selective schools in modern times. Why, then, have the specific provision to allow them? The reason is that there are a number of schools for Maori pupils which have a long and venerable history reaching back to early days of the New Zealand colony. No one wished to frustrate the operation of those schools through ruthless adhesion to a principle of equality. This is part of a broader philosophy in New Zealand; whereunder special treatment for the Maori race is not necessarily seen as invidious, especially if it has a long history. It might be different if the schools were to be created now.

In public schools, the Maori dimension of New Zealand life is currently reflected in a variety of ways. First, every school is required to have a charter, and its charter is required to contain the following aspirations (s 62 of the Education Act 1989):

(i) [T]he aim of developing, for the school, policies and practices that reflect New Zealand's cultural diversity and the unique position of the Maori culture; and
(ii) the aim of ensuring that all reasonable steps are taken to provide instruction in *tikanga Maori* (Maori culture) and *te reo Maori* (the Maori language) for full-time students whose parents ask for it.

It will be noted that these aspirations are expressed for the benefit of *all* students, not just Maori. This is one aspect of New Zealand's commitment to biculturalism based on the Treaty of Waitangi.

Another way in which the Maori dimension of New Zealand is reflected in the Education Act is in the power conferred on the Minister to establish *kura kaupapa Maori*. These are Maori language immersion schools, and are to be operated in accordance with an approved Maori philosophy known as *Te Ahu Matua* (sections 155 and 155A of the Education Act 1993). Entry is not restricted by race, but parents must accept that the school operates with that philosophy.

For students with disabilities the governing principle is that they have the same rights to education as other students. In recent years this has been taken to mean that disabled students should be "mainstreamed" so far as possible, with special assistance if that is required. But there are also special schools for those with particular disabilities, such as deaf and blind students and those whose disability precludes mainstreaming.

Another way the Education Act caters for special populations is by empowering the Minister to establish "designated character" schools, these being schools with a particular educational philosophy or approach. It would be possible, under this provision, to establish a school for, say, gifted children. The pre-requisite is that the parents of at least twenty one potential students request the establishment of such a school. The Minister is not compelled to establish a school upon such request, merely empowered to do so.

For parents who seek a religious dimension to their child's education, there is the option of private schools, and also "integrated" schools. Integrated schools were made possible under the Private Schools (Conditional Integration) Act 1975. The catalyst was the funding crisis in Catholic education, and the pressure that would be placed on public schools if the Catholic schools failed. The Act allowed *any* private school to elect to "integrate" into the state system, while retaining its "special character"—which may be a religious or philosophical character. All Catholic schools have subsequently integrated, as have other religious schools including some operated by evangelical Christians, Hare Krishna, Jews, and Muslims. Montessori and Rudolph Steiner schools are also eligible, and some have integrated. After integration a school's salaries and operating expenses are paid by the state and the schools are treated as state schools in every respect, save that they may maintain their special character and hire staff who are sympathetic to that character. The school's proprietors retain ownership of and must maintain the school's assets.

Emerging Issues

Student rights, in the sense of freedom of expression and religious rights, have not loomed large in New Zealand. However, it is likely that they will do so in the future, especially in relation to religion. In the last two decades, New Zealand has moved inexorably toward a "rights" culture, under the influence of international developments and the high profile that the United Nations human rights treaties have enjoyed. The enactment of the Bill of Rights in 1990, for example, was expressed to be affirmation of the rights in the International Covenant on Civil and Political Rights. Over the past decade, there has been a sea change in the way the judiciary in Commonwealth countries deals with human rights issues, and this has filtered into legal education. The sensibilities of judges and lawyers on human rights issues are different from what they once were, and recourse to the courts is more likely in an age when the cry of "human rights" is on nearly everyone's lips.

At the same time, there has been huge growth in immigration and refugee claims, especially from countries that have not, historically, been providers of migrants to New Zealand. The result is a much more multi-cultural society in which principles of equality and dignity are becoming all the more important. In short, the stage is set for more, rather than less, disputation about rights. Religious issues will probably be the first reef over which the rights wave breaks. The ability of primary schools to have religious exercises is especially likely to be debated. While the general idea might survive, more thought will have to be given to the way that religious exercises and instruction are implemented in practice.

A related issue concerns the place of Maori spirituality in New Zealand. Many Maori hold Christian beliefs as a result of early missionary activity. The successful Maori claim to recognition as a distinct culture has led to space being made for the Maori world-view to be incorporated into schools at all levels. This leads to some dilemmas for schools about the role that religion plays in Maori meeting protocol. Meetings and meals generally commence with a prayer or invocation. This can lead to criticism and resentment from parents of conservative religious persuasion who say, probably rightly, that their own religious practices would not be similarly accommodated. This issue arises in New Zealand society generally, beyond the education sphere: national and local government similarly accedes to Maori prayers in circumstances where they would probably not tolerate prayers from other groups.

To date, some complaints have been made to the Human Rights Commission about these matters but they have not been successful. Partly this is because the issues have not been well articulated. But another relevant factor is the generally secular character of New Zealand society. Profession of religious belief is very much lower in New Zealand than in the United States, and one consequence, ironic, perhaps, is that religion is seen as relatively unimportant such that its incorporation in the public sphere does not shock civil liberties groups into bringing law suits. Religious issues are seen as relatively trivial. But all it takes is a sufficiently motivated plaintiff, much more likely in the multi-cultural climate of 2007 than in the past, and these matters may well be tested in court.

Conclusion

As has been seen, student rights in New Zealand have not been the subject of extensive litigation in the courts. Political solutions are generally sought, and the reality is that student rights are none the worse for that. New Zealand is a small country, where the actions of a school board in relation to a student can easily become national news. This produces a moderating influence, for public opinion can be an exacting judge. But increasing rights-consciousness and the influx of migrants with different religious beliefs are likely to test this state of affairs over the next decade.

Notes

1. Attorney-General v. Daniels [2003] 2 NZLR 742.
2. Edwards v. Onehunga High Sch. Bd. [1974] 2 NZLR 238.
3. Rich v. Christchurch High Sch. Bd. of Governors (No 1) [1974] 1 NZLR 1.
4. M and R v. Palmerston North Boys High School Bd. of Trustees [2003] NZAR 705.
5. R v. MRM [1998] 3 SCR 393.

10
Northern Ireland

Laura Lundy

The United Kingdom (UK) is comprised of Great Britain and Northern Ireland. Although Northern Ireland is a separate legal jurisdiction with its own court system, it is currently governed through an arrangement known as "direct rule" by the Westminster Parliament in London.[1] This has been the case on and off for the past thirty years, during which Northern Ireland has been embroiled in a violent conflict between its Protestant and Catholic communities. In 1974, in response to escalating violence, and in the context of allegations of widespread discrimination against the minority Catholic community, the Northern Ireland Parliament was abolished and legislative authority was transferred to Westminster.[2] In 1998, the main political parties agreed upon a peace settlement ("the Belfast Agreement") which provided, inter alia, for the devolution of executive and legislative responsibility to a new power-sharing Northern Ireland Assembly. This was established in 1999 but was suspended twice before being dissolved in October 2002 as a result of ongoing concerns in the Protestant (Unionist) community about the failure of paramilitary organisations to decommission their weapons.[3]

Under direct rule, the Department of Education (headed by a British Minister for Education) has primary responsibility for securing elementary and secondary education within Northern Ireland.[4] This includes the main responsibility for policy development and programmes of legislative change, albeit that primary legislation is ultimately made by way of Order of the Privy Council at Westminster. The Order in Council process, a key element in Northern Ireland's so-called "democratic deficit," is thought to inhibit both debate on the substance of the legislation and the influence of local politicians.[5]

One consequence of this is that educational reforms are often modelled on previous legislative initiatives in England and Wales.[6] For instance, Northern Ireland has inherited a series of statutory provisions which were designed originally for England and Wales in an effort to increase parental rights and raise educational standards.[7] Yet, there are several areas in which the law is distinctively different.[8] These areas often reflect Northern Ireland's distinct social and educational context and can, in many instances, be attributed to the influence of religion in general, and the local churches in particular, on the education system.[9]

Northern Ireland does not have a traditional written constitution. Moreover, the key piece of constitutional legislation, the Northern Ireland Act 1998, does not provide specifically for education, other than to say that it is a transferred matter, that is one which is devolved to the Northern Ireland Assembly when it is in operation. Instead, constitutional-type rights protections are derived largely from international human rights law, most notably the European Convention on Human Rights (ECHR). The ECHR was incorporated into UK law in 2000, providing students with the opportunity to challenge education law and practice in the domestic courts.[10] It contains many of the fundamental civil rights protections which are otherwise absent from the domestic statutory frameworks, including, for example, rights to freedom of conscience, association, and expression. Not surprisingly, the potential of the ECHR to transform the landscape of children's rights at school was much heralded.[11] Five years later, there has not yet been a case within Northern Ireland where the ECHR has been successfully invoked by a student or by his or her parents.[12]

The Belfast Agreement was founded on principles which include "the protection and vindication of the human rights of all" and "partnership, equality and mutual respect."[13] The Northern Ireland Act 1998, which implements the Belfast Agreement, contains a number of provisions intended to ensure compliance with a range of international human rights standards.[14]

Since the Agreement, several major initiatives have placed emphasis on the implementation of the United Nations Convention on the Rights of the Child (CRC) and the protection of children's rights. The most significant of these is the establishment of the post of NI Commissioner for Children and Young People (NICCY). The Commissioner has the statutory obligation "to safeguard and promote the rights and best interests of children and young persons."[15] On his first day in office, the Commissioner announced plans for a major study of the state of children's rights in Northern Ireland with a view to establishing the main areas of law, policy, and practice where children's rights were being ignored or underplayed. The author of this chapter was a member of the inter-disciplinary team which was commissioned to carry out the research and this chapter incorporates reference to some of the key findings within the sub-theme of "education."[16]

The Right to Receive an Education

The CRC requires its signatories not only to provide free elementary education but to make it compulsory.[17] Education, unlike other aspects of the Convention, is not just a right but an obligation. In Northern Ireland, a child is of compulsory school age between the ages of four and sixteen.[18] The Standing Advisory Commission on Human Rights recommended that the lower age limit should be raised to five on the basis that most children are too young to benefit from the formal curriculum before the age of five.[19] Their recommendation was initially rejected by the government who did not consider that it was substantiated on educational grounds. More recently, schools have been piloting the introduction of an "enriched," that is, less formal, curriculum for under-sevens.[20]

Attendance at School

The CRC requires states to take measures to encourage regular attendance at schools.[21] In Northern Ireland, parents are placed under a statutory duty to secure education for their children. Legislation states that "the parent of every child of compulsory school age shall cause him to receive efficient full-time education suitable to his age, ability and aptitude and to any special educational needs he may have, either by regular school attendance or otherwise."[22] The most common method of complying with the duty in practice is for parents to send their child to a recognized school. Once a child is registered at a school, the parent is under a duty to secure his regular attendance at that school.[23] Regular attendance is not defined in the legislation. However, education authorities normally intervene once absences amount to over 20 percent of the total school days. The legally accepted defenses to non-school attendance include illness, unavoidable cause, and difficulty in securing transport to school.[24]

Levels of attendance at school in Northern Ireland are relatively high.[25] The problem is that a small number of children have high levels of unauthorized absences, with detrimental effects not just for their education but their general life chances. There are various legal options open to a local education authority when a parent fails to comply with his or her duty to secure his child's education. If a child is not registered at a school, the first stage will normally be the serving of an attendance order which requires a parent to register the child at the school named in the order.[26] If the parent does not comply with an attendance order, or if a child who is already registered at a school does not attend school regularly, the education authority can apply to court for an education supervision order, which enables the child's progress to be actively monitored by an education officer.[27] It can also institute criminal proceedings in the Magistrates' Court which may result in fines being imposed on parents.[28]

In the NICCY research, education welfare officers considered that the law had a limited role to play in this area: the effort involved in obtaining an education supervision order in court was not considered to be worth it in most cases and officials were reluctant to institute criminal prosecutions because of the financial impact on families who were often of limited means.[29] Legal enforcement mechanisms were considered to be particularly ineffective in the face of deliberate school-refusal on the part of older children, although it was thought that they were of some value in protecting the right to education of younger children whose parents were apathetic about their attendance at school.

Access to School

Admission to school in Northern Ireland is highly regulated.[30] A system of "open enrolment" has been in operation since 1989 which allows parents to choose a school for their child, subject only to the availability of places. Schools are required by law to publish admissions criteria which determine the allocation of places when a school is over-subscribed and parents have a right to appeal against a decision not to admit if the criteria are not applied correctly.[31] Although the falling birth rate has resulted in a general surplus of places, Northern Ireland retains a grammar, that is, academically selective, system at secondary level and admission to grammar schools is highly competitive.

There are aspects of the admission system which are of concern from a human rights perspective[32] and every year there is a spate of applications to the High Court challenging refusals to admit a child.[33] However, one of the most interesting cases to confront the Northern Ireland courts in recent years focused not on the application of admissions policies but on a physical blockade of a school itself, thereby denying access to registered pupils.

The protest was conducted by local Protestant residents outside a Catholic all-girls primary school in 2001. The police, dressed in full riot gear, provided a human corridor along the route shielding the children from the protestors.

This arrangement continued for twelve weeks, during which time the protestors shouted sectarian insults, blew whistles, and threw missiles at the children (including urine filled balloons and on one occasion, a blast bomb). A mother of one of the children involved in the dispute initiated a legal action against the Police Service of Northern Ireland for its handling of the protests. The plaintiff argued that the decision by the police to allow the protest to continue for over two months breached her daughter's right to life under Article 2 of the ECHR, right to be free from torture, inhuman and degrading treatment under Article 3, and her right to education under Article 2 of the First Protocol.

The High Court judgment, *In Re E's Application*, found that there had not been a breach of any of the provisions of the ECHR.[34] In terms of Article 2, the judge considered that, although the child may have felt that her life was threatened, it had not been proved that the authorities knew or ought to have known at the time of the existence of a real and immediate risk to the applicant's life. The judge was not prepared to hold that the "indignities, threats and naked intimidation" to which the applicant was subjected did not amount to inhuman or degrading treatment, but considered that the policing strategy was within the range of reasonable responses permitted under Article 3. The judge also found that there had not been a breach of Article 2 of the First Protocol, as the children had not been denied their education "because of the sterling efforts of the parents and dedication of the teachers led by their admirable principal." While the judge was unequivocal in his condemnation of the protests, describing it as "one of the most shameful and disgraceful episodes in the recent history of Northern Ireland," he refused to question the legitimacy of the policing strategy. The decision has been appealed to the Court of Appeal.

Home-Schooling

Parents are obliged by law to secure their child's education by "regular school attendance or otherwise." The inclusion of the "or otherwise" leaves open the possibility that parents might educate their children at home. If parents opt to educate a child at home, they must still satisfy the education authorities that the child is receiving "efficient full-time education suitable to his age ability and aptitude and to any special educational needs he may have." Parents do not have to prove that the education their child is receiving is equivalent to or as good as that which they would receive at school.[35] Even so, the content of the Northern Ireland statutory curriculum is undoubtedly an indicator of what might be considered a "suitable" education.[36] In the NICCY research, concern was expressed about the levels of support available to home-schooled children and the fact that the authorities do not always actively inspect the standard of education which children are receiving at home. [37]

Religious Freedom Rights of Students

Northern Ireland's school system is in many respects a product of the wider conflict and religious divisions.[38] Schools are almost completely religiously segregated in terms of their pupil profile. Protestant children generally attend controlled (state) schools that are managed by local education authorities while Catholic pupils generally attend voluntary schools which are fully funded by the state but which are in the ownership of the Catholic Church.[39] Approximately 5 percent of children attend "integrated," or mixed religion, schools. Moreover, with few exceptions, Boards of Governors in Northern Ireland have a significant proportion of their membership drawn from the local clergy or from those whom they have chosen to represent them. These positions are set down in legislation, affording the churches a significant statutory role in school governance.[40]

There is no specific domestic provision on the issue of the students' right to manifest their beliefs in school. In the event of a dispute, the issue would be resolved under Article 9 of the ECHR. This provides a right to manifest religion or belief, subject only to such limitations as are prescribed by law and are necessary in a democratic society in the interests of public safety, for the protection of public order, health, or morals, or for the protection of the rights and freedoms of others. There are currently no restrictions on manifestations of belief in schools which are prescribed by law. Moreover, in practice, there is a high degree of tolerance of personal religious manifestations, such as the wearing of badges and religious clothing.

The curriculum of all publicly funded schools is required by law to include provision for the religious education of all registered pupils.[41] Each school must also have a daily period of collective worship in an assembly or assemblies.[42] Parents have an absolute right to withdraw their children from both religious education and collective worship.[43] The legislation does not give pupils an independent right to decide whether to receive religious education, even where they have attained the age of eighteen.

The parents' absolute right of withdrawal would appear to be in conflict with Article 12 of the CRC which requires its signatories to give due weight to the views of the child in all matters affecting them.[44] Although Article 2 of the First Protocol of the ECHR enshrines the right of parents to have their child educated in accordance with their religious convictions, the child has a separate and individual right to freedom of conscience under Article 9. As yet, the potential conflict between the two articles has not been tested in the European Court of Human Rights or the domestic courts.[45]

Children who have been withdrawn by their parents from religious instruction are given additional protection under the legislation. Religious instruction must be arranged in such a way that the school is open to children of all religious denominations.[46] This effectively requires that religious education be taught in separate classes so that it can be severed from other subjects in the event of an objection. The practicality of this in religious denominational schools was challenged in *In Re Cecil's Application*.[47] The applicant lived on a small island off the coast of Northern Ireland which had one Catholic primary school. The applicant contended that, although his children could be withdrawn from religious classes, Catholicism pervaded the ethos of the school. However, the court considered that a requirement that pupils would not be disadvantaged in any way if withdrawn from religious classes was sufficient to protect his rights. This is in spite of the fact that the Catholic Church's position was essentially as the applicant had described it, that the religious ethos of the school permeates every aspect of school life.[48]

Free Speech Rights of Students

Students do not have a right to freedom of speech in domestic law. Nor is the right protected in constitutional legislation. The only legally enforceable right is contained in Article 10 of the ECHR which affords all persons the right to freedom of expression. In 2002, a student who was suspended from school for having walked out of school to attend a protest about the Iraq War challenged the legality of the suspension on the basis that it breached his rights under Article 10.[49] The case was settled before the court hearing and the student reinstated. There are no other reported cases in which a student has claimed a breach of his or her rights under Article 10. If an action were to arise, it is likely to be in the context of the wearing of badges and emblems of a political nature.

Symbols and emblems which align individuals to political causes and/or paramilitary activities are always controversial within Northern Ireland and it is a matter of time before the issues which already present schools with daily challenges end up in court. It would be for a court to determine whether a ban on badges which might cause offence to other students would constitute a legitimate restriction on freedom of expression as permitted by Article 10(2), for example that it is necessary for the protection of "the reputation or rights of others."

The key initiative in the context of students' free speech rights derives from a different but related human rights obligation, Article 12 of the CRC which requires states to ensure that children have a right to express their views in all matters affecting them, the views to be given due weight in accordance with their age and maturity. In some respects, Article 12 goes beyond the right to freedom of expression because of the inclusion of the additional obligation to give views "due weight." The UK's compliance with Article 12 in schools was criticized by the Committee on the Rights of the Child in 2002.[50] Since then, there have been several initiatives to implement Article 12 such as a statutory requirement to consult pupils on school discipline and bullying policies.[51] Nonetheless, in the NICCY research, the single issue which was of most concern to children and young people in the context of their school lives was that their views were not sought nor respected.[52]

Student Rights and Discipline

The law on school discipline has witnessed rapid change in the past decade. The most significant change from a students' rights perspective was the abolition of corporal punishment in 1987.[53] The change in this instance was brought about as a result of an application to the European Court of Human Rights. In *Campbell and Cosans* v. *UK*, the court found that the use of corporal punishment on pupils against the will of their parents amounted to a breach of Article 2 of the First Protocol of the ECHR.[54] This requires Members States to ensure that education is in conformity with parents' religious and philosophical convictions. Since then, there has been a wave of legislative reforms designed to regulate the circumstances in which the imposition of disciplinary sanctions is lawful.

Physical Restraint

One of the difficulties which teachers faced after the abolition of corporal punishment was knowing when it was lawful for them to have any physical contact with children. In 1998, legislation was introduced which defines the circumstances when a member of staff at a grant-aided school may use physical force on a pupil.[55] It allows a member of staff to use such force as is reasonable in the circumstances for the purpose of preventing the pupil from doing, or continuing to do, any of the following: committing an offence; causing personal injury to, or damage to the property of any person, including the pupil himself; or engaging in any behavior prejudicial to the maintenance of good order and discipline at the school or among any of its pupils, whether that behavior occurs during a teaching session or otherwise.[56] The member of staff's power to restrain does not authorize them to commit any act which would amount to corporal punishment. Yet, it does not preclude them from relying on any other defense such as self-defense.[57]

Detention

Prior to 1998, there was no specific statutory provision on the use of detention as a disciplinary sanction. However, it was clear that detaining a child without parental consent could amount to false imprisonment which is both a criminal offence and can be the basis for a claim for damages.[58] Legislation was introduced which provides that a detention will not be unlawful by virtue of the lack of parental consent provided certain conditions are satisfied.

First, the principal of a school must have previously determined that detention was one of the disciplinary measures employed by the school.[59] Secondly, the detention must be imposed by the principal or another teacher specifically or generally authorized to do so.[60] Finally, a pupil's parents must have been given at least twenty-four hours' notice in writing that the detention was due to take place.[61] The detention must also be reasonable in all the circumstances, including the pupil's age, any special educational needs, any religious requirements affecting him or her, and, where arrangements have to be made for travel, whether suitable alternative arrangements can reasonably be made by his parent.[62]

Searches

Searches of pupils' property and/or person are not regulated in law, an issue which is of concern to both students and teachers. If a pupil is physically searched without a child's consent, the person conducting the search could be prosecuted for assault and sued for damages for trespass to the person. A teacher might be able to raise a defense under the physical restraint provisions outlined above if the reason underlying the search is to prevent the pupil committing an offence or causing personal injury or damage to property such as where a pupil might be carrying a weapon or an illegal substance. Similarly, consent should be obtained for searches to property; otherwise, an action could be taken for trespass to property, assuming that some damage is caused. If a pupil refuses to give his or her consent to a search, schools will normally have to resort to other disciplinary sanctions such as suspensions or, if they believe that the pupil is in possession of something which is illegal, to inform the police which can then conduct the search using statutory police powers.

Exclusion from School

All schools are required to have a scheme for the suspension and expulsion of pupils and are under a series of legal requirements in relation to the procedures which must be followed when a pupil is suspended (temporarily excluded) or expelled (permanently excluded) from school.[63] Pupils can only be suspended by the principal.[64] The initial period for suspension cannot exceed five days and a pupil cannot be expelled for longer than forty-five days in any school year. There is no statutory right of appeal against a decision to suspend a pupil. Even so, challenges have been made by way of an application for judicial review at the High Court.

In *In Re Kean's Application*, a pupil successfully challenged a decision to suspend her immediately on the basis that she had not been given an opportunity to respond to the statements of witnesses.[65] Pupils can only be expelled when they have first served a period of suspension and there has been a consultation meeting at which their future education has been discussed.[66] Parents of pupils who have been expelled, but not the pupils themselves unless they are eighteen, have a right to challenge a decision to permanently exclude in the Expulsion Appeal Tribunal.[67]

The Department of Education recently conducted a review of the suspensions and expulsion procedures used by schools.[68] This found that there were major variations in the approaches in different types of schools and recommended that there should be either a single regional expelling authority or that independent assessors should be appointed to investigate and represent the pupil's interests as a means of ensuring greater consistency across the sector. The review also recommended that pupils should have an independent right to be heard in the Expulsion Appeal Tribunal. It has not, though, recommended the introduction of a right to appeal against suspensions, a gap in the statutory framework which was highlighted by the Committee on the Rights of the Child in 2002.[69] In the NICCY research, concern was also expressed about the adequacy of educational provision for children who have been expelled, many of whom find it difficult to secure a place at an alternative school.[70]

Special Populations

Children with Disabilities

There is an extensive statutory framework which regulates educational provision for children with special educational needs.[71] The key distinction made by the legislation is between children for whom a statement is maintained and children who have special educational needs but for whom no statement is maintained. A statement is a document setting out the child's needs and the educational provision which is required to meet those needs. A statement will only be made where the local education authority considers it necessary for it (rather than the child's school) to assume legal and financial responsibility for the child's educational provision.[72] This applies to approximately 3 percent of schoolchildren, those whose needs are particularly severe or unusual.

Before a statement is issued, an education authority must conduct a formal assessment of the child's needs, taking evidence from teachers, doctors, and social services. In the NICCY research concern was expressed that the statement process was "long, cumbersome, clinical and legalistic," and ultimately led to a document which could be so generally worded as to be meaningless and/or often identified what experienced teachers already knew.[73] At the same time, a statement does act as a passport to a range of other legal rights, in particular a right to appeal to the Special Education and Disability Appeals Tribunal (SENDIST).[74]

The responsibility for the vast majority of children with special educational needs, approximately 18 percent of all pupils, lies with the Boards of Governors in ordinary schools. These children have very limited rights in terms of educational provision and neither they nor their parents have a specific right to appeal to the SENT about the extent or quality of provision made for them.[75] The major difficulty for most children will be in relation to the allocation of resources within the school. Each school receives a financial allocation for special education which is based on the proportion of children receiving free school meals. Despite this allocation, the money is not ring-fenced and there is concern that it can end up being used for other things when school budgets are under pressure. The Northern Ireland Affairs Committee recommended that this money should be kept in a separate budget and that schools should be required by law to account for the expenditure.[76]

New legislation on special education took effect in September 2005.[77] This introduces a prohibition on discrimination on the grounds of disability and will strengthen the right of children to be educated in mainstream schools. Parents now have a right to have their children educated in mainstream schools provided that this is not incompatible with the efficient education of the other children at the school. Further, resource considerations are no longer permitted reasons to deny a child a place in a mainstream school. This emphasis on children receiving education in mainstream schools is very positive from a children's rights perspective. As important as these developments are, in the NICCY research, many of those working in education expressed concern about the new law and in particular the capacity of mainstream schools to cope with increasing numbers of children with learning difficulties.[78]

Ethnic-Minority Children

Northern Ireland has a very small ethnic-minority community, consisting of about 0.85 percent of the total population in the 2001 Census. The Race Relations (NI) Order 1997 prohibits direct and indirect discrimination on the grounds of race in education. The major concerns about inequality of access to education tend to be systemic in nature. For example, it is recognized that there is insufficient emphasis within the statutory curriculum on issues of cultural diversity and also on increasing students' awareness of the nature and negative effects of racism.[79] Moreover, schools are not required by law to have anti-racist bullying strategies even though students have expressed concern about the existence of racist bullying in school and also the racist harassment of minority ethnic pupils as they travel to and from school.[80]

Irish Travellers, a nomadic people indigenous to Ireland, are widely regarded as amongst the most excluded children within Northern Irish society. The majority of Travellers (59 percent) leave school with no qualifications compared with 17 percent in the population as a whole.[81] One of the key difficulties is the lack of appropriate mechanisms to ensure continuity of educational provision for children who uphold a nomadic way of life.[82] For instance, some of the admissions criteria commonly used by state schools such as those which prioritize applicants on the basis of residence in the catchment area or previous rates of school attendance can result in children being denied access to schools.[83] The Travelling community has also expressed concern about both racial bullying by other children and a lack of awareness of and sensitivity toward Travelling culture amongst teachers.[84] In 1999, the Department of Education agreed to implement a series of recommendations made by a special working group on Travellers.[85] Even so, little has happened since then and there is considerable frustration within the Travelling community about the lack of progress in securing change.[86]

Emerging Issues

The Belfast Agreement provided for the production of a Bill of Rights for Northern Ireland, in order to supplement the existing rights in the ECHR. The Northern Ireland Human Rights Commission (NIHRC) was given the task of producing the draft Bill of Rights.[87] It has issued a set of proposals which, if implemented, would alter the constitutional protections afforded to children and would therefore have significant impact on the legal rights of school students.[88] For example, it has suggested that an amended version of Article 2 of the First Protocol of the ECHR would read as follows:

> The State shall . . . ensure the right of parents to choose for their children education in schools with a particular religious ethos, education in integrated schools, education in Irish medium schools or education specializing in the needs of children with disabilities, bearing in mind the best interests of the child and the competence of the child to decide for him- or herself in accordance with his or her age, maturity and understanding.[89]

This formulation, which affords students a say in the process of choosing a school, is intended to better reflect the UK's obligations under Article 12 of the CRC. Moreover, the proposals contain a separate section dedicated to the rights of children which includes a proposal requiring public authorities to "carry out their functions in relation to children in accordance with the provisions of the UN's Convention on the Rights of the Child."[90] This would have the effect of incorporating the CRC into domestic law, enabling students to challenge breaches of the CRC in the domestic courts.

The Bill of Rights process has been fraught with controversy and delay. There is a perception in Northern Ireland that human protections are for the benefit of the Catholic/Nationalist community and there is therefore a considerable degree of hostility toward the Bill of Rights in the Protestant/Unionist Community.[91] It is difficult to see how the Bill of Rights might be implemented if it is not broadly acceptable to both sections of the community. A new Chief Commissioner has been appointed to the NIHRC and pledged to make the implementation of the Bill of Rights a priority when she took up her post in September 2005. Further, in a parallel development, the Irish Republican Army has declared the permanent end to its campaign of violence. It is hoped that this will reinvigorate ongoing efforts to reach a political accommodation which will restore legislative power to the Northern Ireland Assembly and secure other key elements of the Agreement, including the Bill of Rights.

Conclusion

The past ten years have seen significant expansions in students' rights within Northern Ireland, most notably in the context of student discipline and provision for special educational needs. However, the general emphasis of the legislative reform has been on parents' rights and procedural rights rather than the promotion or protection of children's independent civil rights. In the context of Northern Ireland's emerging human rights framework, the emphasis appears to be changing. Several developments, most notably the establishment of the post of Commissioner for Children and Young People, are indicative of a sea change in the government's commitment to the implementation of children's rights, with obvious knock-on effects for students' experiences at school. If this were to be supplemented by the incorporation of the CRC, as is proposed in Northern Ireland's draft Bill of Rights, the jurisdiction might eventually offer some of the most advanced legal protections for schoolchildren in the world.

Notes

1. See B. Dickson, *The Legal System of Northern Ireland,* (4th Ed., Belfast: SLS, 2001).

2. B. Hadfield, *The Constitution of Northern Ireland* (Belfast: SLS, 1990).

3. See Bew and G. Gillespie, *The Northern Ireland Peace Process 1993–1996: A Chronicle,* (London, Serif, 1996); B. Rowan, *The Armed Peace: Life and Death after the Ceasefires,* (Edinburgh: Mainstream Publishing, 2003).

4. Education Reform (NI) Order 1989, Art. 3.

5. B. Hadfield, "Legislating for Northern Ireland: Options for Reform" in *Eighteenth Annual Report of the Standing Advisory Commission for Human Rights* (1992–93) (London: HMSO, 1993) 111–128.

6. L. Lundy, "From Act to Order: The Metamorphosis of Education Legislation" [1998] Vol XX1 *Liverpool Law Review* 63–92.

7. Ibid., 70. See the introduction of statutory curriculum and reporting requirements for school governors.

8. See generally, L. Lundy, *Education Law Policy and Practice in Northern Ireland,* (Belfast: SLS, 2000).

9. Ibid., 4–14.

10. Human Rights Act 1998.

11. A. Bradley, "The Convention Right to Education and the Human Rights Act 1998" (1999) 4 *European Human Rights Law Review* 395.

12. See L. Lundy, "Human Rights and Equality Litigation in Northern Ireland's Schools," [2004] 5/2 *Education Law Journal* 82–90.

13. The Agreement, Declaration of Support (Belfast: 1998) 1.

14. See L. Lundy, "Education Law under Devolution: The Case of Northern Ireland" (2000) *Education Law Journal* 81.

15. Commissioner for Children and Young People (NI) Order 2003, Art. 7.

16. U. Kilkelly, R. Kilpatrick, L. Lundy, L. Moore, Scraton, C. Davey, C. Dwyer, S. McAlister, Children's Rights in Northern Ireland, (Belfast: NICCY, 2005).

17. Article 28.

18. Art. 46(1) of the Education and Libraries (NI) Order 1986. This was substituted by Art. 156 of the Education Reform (NI) Order 1989.

19. The Standing Advisory Commission on Human Rights, Employment Equality: Building for the Future (Belfast, The Stationery Office, 1997) Cm 3684.

20. For an account of the proposals, see Kilkelly et al., infra note 16 at 180.

21. Art. 28(1)(e).

22. Education and Libraries (NI) Order 1986, Art. 45(1).
23. Ibid., Sch.13, para. 3(1).
24. Ibid.
25. Northern Ireland Audit Office, Improving Pupil Attendance at School, (Belfast: The Stationery Office, 2004).
26. Education and Libraries (NI) Order 1986, Sch. 13, para. 1(3).
27. Children (NI) Order 1995, Art. 55.
28. Ibid., Sch. 13, para. 4.
29. See supra note 16 at 158.
30. See supra note 8, 91–128.
31. Education (NI) Order 1997.
32. L. Lundy, Access to Secondary Schools in Northern Ireland, (Belfast: Northern Ireland Human Rights Commission, 2001).
33. See L. Lundy, "Selection on Ability: Lessons from Northern Ireland," (1996) 8 *Education and the Law*, 29.
34. [2004] NIQB 35.
35. Bevan v. Shears [1911] 2 KB 936.
36. Ibid., 941.
37. See infra note 16 at 164.
38. S. Dunn, A Short History of Education in Northern Ireland, 1920–1990, Annex B in the Fifteenth Report of the Standing Advisory Committee on Human Rights (1989–1990)(London: HMSO, 1990), 49–96.
39. See infra note 8, 106–107.
40. Ibid., 65–73.
41. Art. 5(1) of the Education Reform (NI) Order 1989.
42. Education and Libraries (NI) Order 1986, Art. 21(1).
43. Ibid., Article 21(5).
44. The Committee on the Rights of the Child expressed its concern about the failure to respect children's views on issues of religious education in its first periodic report on the UK in 1995. Committee on the Rights of the Child (1995) Concluding Observations of the Committee on the Rights of the Child: United Kingdom of Great Britain and Northern Ireland (UN/CRC/C/15/Add.34), (Geneva: United Nations, 1995).
45. See L. Lundy, (2005) 19 "Family Values in the Classroom: Reconciling Parents' Wishes and Children's Rights in State Schools," *International Journal of Law, Policy and the Family*, 346–372.
46. Art. 21(4) of the Education and Libraries (NI) Order 1986.
47. Unreported decision of the High Court of Northern Ireland, 27 January 1989.
48. See G. Loughran, "The Rationale of Catholic Education," chapter 8 in R.D. Osborne, R.J. Cormack, and R.L. Millar *Education and Policy in Northern* Ireland (Belfast: Policy Research Institute, 1987).
49. See infra note 12 above, 86.
50. Committee on the Rights of the Child, Concluding Observations of the Committee on the Rights of the Child: United Kingdom of Great Britain and Northern Ireland (UN/CRC/C/15/Add.188), (Geneva: United Nations, 2002).

51. Education and Libraries (NI) Order 1993, Art. 19.

52. See infra note 16, 186–191.

53. This was accomplished by the Education (Corporal Punishment) (NI) Order 1987.

54. Campbell and Cosans v. UK [1982] EHHR 293.

55. Education (NI) Order 1998, Art. 4.

56. Ibid., Art. 4(1).

57. Ibid., Art. 4(3).

58. There is authority to the effect that a parent may falsely imprison his or her own child. See R v. Rahman [1985] 81 Cr App. R. 340.

59. Art. 5(3) of the Education (NI) Order 1998.

60. Ibid., Art. 5(3)(b).

61. Ibid., Art. 5(3)(d).

62. Ibid., Art. 5(3)(c).

63. Schools (Suspensions and Expulsions of Pupils) Regulations (NI) 1995.

64. Ibid., Reg. 3(a).

65. Unreported decision of the Northern Ireland High Court, 3 July 1997.

66. See A. Barr, R. Kilpatrick and L. Lundy, "School Exclusions: Lessons from Northern Ireland," (2000) *Education Law Journal* 165–177.

67. Schools (Suspension and Expulsion of Pupils) Regulations (NI) 1994.

68. Department of Education, Suspension and Expulsion Procedures: Proposals for Change (Bangor: Department of Education, 2004).

69. See infra note 50.

70. See infra note 16, 162–163.

71. Education (NI) Order 1996.

72. Ibid., Art. 16(1).

73. See infra note 16, 166–170.

74. Parents can appeal a decision not to statement, the content of the statement, and a decision to withdraw a statement. Education (NI) Order 1996, Arts. 16–22.

75. L. Lundy, "Stating a Case for the Un-statemented: Children with Special Educational Needs in Mainstream Schools," (1998) *Child and Family Law Quarterly* 10(1), 39–53.

76. Northern Ireland Affairs Committee, First report, Public Expenditure in Northern Ireland: Special Needs Education, Report together with the Proceedings of the Committee, Minute of Evidence and Appendices. House of Commons Session 1998–99. (London: HMSO, 1999)

77. Special Education and Disability (NI) Order 2005.

78. See infra note 16, 170.

79. P. Connolly and M. Keenan, Opportunities for All: Minority Ethnic People's Experiences of Education, Training, and Employment in Northern Ireland. (Belfast: Northern Ireland Statistics and Research Agency, 2000).

80. K. Radford, Count Me In, (Belfast: Save the Children, Youth Council Northern Ireland, DE, 2004).

81. Northern Ireland Census 2001.

82. P. Connolly and M. Keenan. "Racist Harassment in the White Hinterlands: The Experiences of Minority Ethnic Children and Parents in Schools in Northern Ireland" (2002) *British Journal of Sociology of Education*, 23 (3): 341–356.

83. L. Lundy, Access to Secondary Schools in Northern Ireland, (Belfast: Northern Ireland Human Rights Commission, 2001).

84. P. Connolly and M. Keenan, Consultation with Travellers on the Recommendations of the Final Report of the Promoting Social Inclusion Working Group on Travellers. (2002) Belfast: Office of the First Minister and Deputy First Minister.

85. Final Report of the Promoting Social Inclusion Working Group on Travellers. Belfast: Office of the First Minister and Deputy First Minister, (1999).

86. See infra note 16, 172–173.

87. Northern Ireland Act 1998, s. 69.

88. Progressing a Bill of Rights for Northern Ireland: an update (Belfast, NIHRC, 2004). For a commentary on its original proposals in relation to education, see E. Craig and L. Lundy, "Education Rights in the Bill of Rights" (2001) 52 *Northern Ireland Legal Quarterly* 325.

89. Ibid., Section 13(2).

90. Ibid., Section 12(1)(c).

91. A. Morgan, "What Bill of Rights?" *Northern Ireland Legal Quarterly* 52 (2001) 234–268.

11

Portugal

António Pedro Barbas Homem

In Portugal, several laws pertain to education. The first of these laws, the Constitution, establishes that "parents have the right and the duty to educate and sustain their children"[1] while guaranteeing the "freedom to learn and to teach."[2] The Constitution also includes various provisions regarding the duties of the State in the field of teaching and education.[3] Under the Constitution, the State shall guarantee everybody the right to universal, free, basic education and the right of opportunity of access to and success in school while creating a network of public educational establishments. Moreover, the Constitution acknowledges that teachers and students have the right to take part in the democratic management of the schools.[4]

According to the Constitution, one of the purposes of the State is to democratise society while providing education and culture, generally affording Portuguese students the right to access the highest levels of education without being hindered by economic reasons or others. As such, cultural democracy is combined with social justice in order to guarantee all Portuguese the opportunity to access to and success in schools.

The Portuguese Parliament has, in the exercise of an exclusive legislative power, approved the Basic Law on Education[5] which develops the applicable principles and constitutional norms. The first aspect of the rights of the students can be found in this legal act. More specifically, this law provides that education shall contribute to assisting students in the full development of their personalities, in the shaping of their character and citizenship, and in preparing them for conscious reflection on spiritual, aesthetic, moral, and civic values. Education shall further ensure the civic and moral education of the young, guaranteeing the right to be different by respecting the individual personalities and life projects. In addition, education shall give due consideration to and value for the different kinds of knowledge and cultures, developing in students the capacity for work. At the same time, students are entitled to a solid general education so that the young may occupy a just place in their working lives, enabling them to contribute to social progress in a manner consistent with their interests, skills, and vocations.

Rights and Duties of Students

The Primary and Secondary Student's Regulation (*Estatuto do Aluno do Ensino não Superior*) was approved by Law 30/2002 (Lei n.º 30/2002) of 20 December. This Regulation sets forth the rights and duties of students and their parents, as well as the responsibilities of the members of the educational community, in particular teachers. The Regulation addresses the students' duty to attend school, with discipline and disciplinary infractions, disciplinary measures, and the competencies to apply them as well as the disciplinary procedures that must be followed and the incorporation of the Regulation in the schools' Rules of Procedures. This set of norms applies to students who attend the public school network as well as vocational training, artistic education, and recurrent education. Insofar as the principles also apply to non-public schools, private and cooperative schools need to establish regulations that incorporate these norms with regard to discipline and school attendance.

The first of the student's rights guaranteed by law is to benefit from quality teaching and education in order to develop their full physical, intellectual, moral, cultural, and civic well-being, the shaping of their personality, self-learning capacity, and conscious criticism of values, knowledge, and aesthetics. Even so, the courts have not drawn any specific consequences of these guarantees.

The Portuguese legislation acknowledges, among others, the right to free expression and to religious orientation. Pursuant to the Civil Code (*Código Civil*), parents shall direct the education of their children[6] and have the right to select the moral and religious education of their children when they are under sixteen years-of-age.[7] However, parents may not intervene in their children's religious and philosophical convictions from the time they are over sixteen.

The Rights of the Students and Discipline

The Student's Regulation distinguishes two types of disciplinary measures: preventive disciplinary and integration measures on the one hand and disciplinary measures that impose sanctions on the other. Perhaps it is more accurate to distinguish between order measures and disciplinary measures. These two measures correspond to different student behaviours, some of which only disturb the regular functioning of the schools but do not hinder the educational services or call them into question while others, given their seriousness, hinder the normal continuation of school activities.

The essential aim of the order measures is to enable teachers and schools to carry on by providing teaching to all the students and to admonish those who hinder order in classes and within schools. The measures involved are admonitions, removals from classes, and integration activities in schools. Conversely, disciplinary measures, namely those designated as sanctions, are reprimands, written reprimands, suspensions, transfers to other schools, and expulsions. Teachers may decide to apply admonitions, removals from classes, reprimands, and written reprimands. Non-teaching staff may admonish students.

Head teachers may apply the following disciplinary measures: admonitions, reprimands, and written reprimands. The chairperson of a school's governing body or head teacher may apply the following disciplinary measures: admonitions, reprimands, written reprimands, and suspensions from schools for periods of up to five working days. Disciplinary class councils may apply the following disciplinary measures: admonitions, reprimands, written reprimands, school integration activities, transfers to other schools, suspensions from schools for periods of six to ten working days, and expulsions from schools.

In disciplining students, the legal and constitutional principles that apply to administration, namely equity, proportionality, justice, impartiality, and good faith, must not be overlooked. Guided by the idea that disciplinary processes relating to students do not have the same nature and importance as the Civil Servants Regulation, the Student's Regulations establish some procedural rules. Accordingly, the application of the following measures require that disciplinary procedures are followed which aim to establish the individual responsibility of students: school integration activities, transfers to other schools, suspensions from school for periods of six to ten working days, and expulsions from schools.

Responsibility is always individual. The application of either order or disciplinary measures to more than one student requires the individualization of the degree of responsibility and the guilt of each student involved. The swiftness that is sought through the application of disciplinary measures, having in view the normal functioning of schools and their pedagogical efficiency, must take into due consideration, in a balanced manner, the guarantees of students in relation with a school's administration.

Students who are charged in disciplinary proceedings have the right to be heard, to be accompanied by their parents or care-givers, and to have legal counsel. At the same time, students can lodge appeals with the regional directors of education (*director regional de educação*) regarding the application of disciplinary measures. Lodging appeals is optional because parents or care-givers, or students who are over the age of eighteen, have the legal right to object to disciplinary measures. Lodgings of second appeals, which go to the Minister of Education (*Ministro da Educação*), are also optional. If the Minister upholds an earlier judgment, there can be no further appeal due to the absence of adverse effect against private persons.

Appeals are possible to competent courts under the law if the internal means provided for them have been exhausted. It is also possible for students to obtain orders, pursuant to the procedural law, temporarily suspending disciplinary measures. The importance of summary procedures, both at disciplinary level and in terms of the corresponding appeals, must be emphasized: The protection of the rights of students is an important matter, both with regard to those who are charged with offences and those who may have suffered damages on account of prohibited behaviours.

Students are responsible for complying with the duties arising from their right to education. This means that students can be criminally liable for their actions from the age of sixteen.[8] In civil terms, parents are liable for their children until they are eighteen. However, when students reach adulthood, at the age of eighteen, they become liable for their own actions.

Conclusion

A detailed Constitution and numerous and comprehensive laws on education do not necessarily mean that educational matters are better protected. Many of these laws, as known from the continental legal tradition, represent political rhetoric which does not entail accurate practical consequences. Further, Portugal does not have a tradition of taking conflicts generated in schools to the courts. As such, it is difficult to strike an accurate balance on the implementation of the laws that establish the rights and duties of students. Most of the conflicts in Portugal have arisen in public schools where teachers and trade unions apply simple and flexible disciplinary procedures.

Notes

1. Article 36, nr. 5.
2. Article 43, nr. 2.

3. Articles 74–75.
4. Article 77.
5. Education (Lei de Bases do Sistema Educativo) (Law nr. 46/86, of 14 October with various amendments).
6. Civil Code (Código Civil), article 1878.
7. Civil Code (Código Civil), article 1886.
8. Article 19 in the Penal Code (Código Penal).

12

The Russian Federation

Igor Rozjkov and Jan De Groof

Article 1 of the Constitution of the Russian Federation, in force since December 25, 1993, stipulates that the Russian Federation is a democratic, federated law-based state. Article 72 of the Constitution attributes general issues of education to the joint competence of the Russian Federation and its members.

General issues relating to upbringing of children, education, science, and culture, physical education, and sport are covered by the joint power of the Russian Federation and its subjects. Within the framework of these joint powers under Article 76, federal laws are passed and norms which are in agreement with them are enacted. In principle, the central government should concern itself solely with general issues such as the principles of policy and nationwide coordination. This means that the Ministry of Education should be organised primarily at the level of the members of the Federation. Yet, neither the Education Law nor the Constitution clarify which matters should be regulated uniformly at the Federation level such as diplomas, admission to schools, and good educational standards.[1]

In its introduction, the Law on Education of the Russian Federation defines the concept of education.[2] However, since this text does not have any enforceable power, the way in which it is interpreted is partly determined by the statutory provisions themselves. This law is supplemented by the rights to education that are identified in Article 43 of the Constitution of the Russian Federation. The main constitutional rights of students and/or their parents as set forth in Articles 43 and 26 of the Constitution are:

- Everyone shall have the right to education;
- General access to free of charge pre-school, basic general and secondary professional education in state or municipal educational establishments and in enterprises is guaranteed;
- Everyone is entitled on a competitive basis to receive higher education free of charge in state or municipal education establishments or in enterprises;
- Basic general education shall be mandatory. Parents shall make provisions for their children to receive basic general education.

Further, Article 26 dictates that: "Everybody has the right to use his native language and to the free choice of language of communication, upbringing, receiving instruction, and creativity." The constitutional rights of students and their parents are further enhanced in the provisions of the Law of the Russian Federation on Education and the Federal Law on Higher and Post-University Professional Education as well as in other legislation.

Scope of Russian Education Law

The definition of education in the law of the Russian Federation corresponds with the terms which are currently in use. The English term "instruction" appears in the first phrase of the first paragraph of the introduction; the term "training" is used in the Ministry's own translation. This includes the entire educational system which is principally oriented toward the transfer of knowledge and skills and toward individual training, from the perspective of its three components: personal, professional, and social training. The English term "education," on the other hand, has the meaning of "upbringing," a task for which the state is only responsible under certain conditions. At the same time, the lack of clarity in the Russian context is exacerbated by the fact that international treaties do not always use the terms "education," "instruction," and "upbringing" clearly.

Objectives of the Law

The law fits in entirely with the desire of the political authorities in Russia for fundamental national reform. The report *Development of Education in Russia*, promulgated by the Minister for Education of the Russian Federation at a UNESCO conference in Geneva in 1992, provides already a great deal of clarification on this subject what still is considered as relevant.[3]

Insofar as legal objectives are not enforceable, it is opportune to set out the general political objectives of the reform within a legal framework with regard to state action dealing with respect to education and its content.[4] All Russian educational institutions thus immediately become partners in the movement toward democratisation and liberalization. Even so, the government assumes the role of both initiator and executor of this operation which immediately exposes weakness: educational reform will be accomplished only if the state is capable of performing this challenging task.

In order to ensure success in reforming the Russian educational system, the era of the state monopoly and bureaucratic control over schooling must come to an end. Instead, the former way of dealing with education must give way to a period where the state makes good on its promise to provide material facilities for schools. Of course, though, governmental control cannot be replaced by a legal vacuum. Otherwise, it will become difficult to achieve the aim of all education called for in Article 14.2, namely to enhance and improve the lawbased state.

Overview of the Law on Education

The Law of the Russian Federation "On Education" identifies various rights:

- to choose an educational establishment and the form of education;[5]
- to receive free elementary general education, general basic education, general secondary (complete) education, elementary vocational education and on a competitive basis to receive secondary vocational education, higher vocational education and postgraduate vocational education in state or municipal educational establishments within the framework of the state educational standards;[6]
- to receive free vocational education as directed by a state employment office, in case of loss of an opportunity to work on a trade or specialty, in case of professional illness and/or disability, and in other cases stipulated by legislation;[7]
- to obtain education in accordance with the state educational standards;[8]
- to receive education within the framework of these standards in the form of an individual study plan, as determined by the charter of an educational establishment;[9]
- to educate one's children (elementary general education, general basic education, general secondary education) within the family;[10]
- to participate in the self-government of an educational establishment in the manner specified by the charter of the educational establishment;[11]
- to respect of one's human dignity;[12]
- to freedom of conscience and information;[13]

- to freedom of expression of opinions and convictions;[14]
- to transfer to another educational establishment with an educational program of the appropriate level, provided that the applicant receives permission from the educational establishment and passes any entrance examination.[15]

In accordance with its Constitution, universally recognised principles and norms of international law and international treaties of the Russian Federation are a constituent part of its legal system. If an international treaty to which the Russian Federation is a party establishes rules other then those provided by Russian law, the rules of the international treaty are to be applied.[16] Russia has signed the International Treaty on Civil and Political Rights, the International Treaty on Economic, Social and Cultural Rights, the Convention of the Rights of the Child, the European Convention for the Protection of Human Rights and Fundamental Freedom (including protocols), the Universal Declaration of Human Rights, and the Declaration of the Rights of the Child.

Article 5 of the Law on Education provides guarantees for the rights of citizens of the Russian Federation in education and the possibility of receiving education in non-state educational institutions. The costs for paid instruction in non-state accredited educational institutions which realize general and vocational educational programs are supposed to be reimbursed to citizens. The costs for paid instruction in non-state, but state-accredited, educational institutions which offer general and vocational educational programs, are also supposed to be reimbursed within the extent of the state norms for the costs of education of the corresponding form and type of state or municipal educational institution.[17] Further, Article 50 of the Law on Education guarantees the right of choice of an educational institution and the form of education.[18]

The Right to Receive an Education

The various aspects to freedom to and right to education are not inherently inter-related. If anything, unless adequate guarantees are provided to enforce it, the right to education remains purely theoretical. The freedom to provide education is an essential part of this element. Various places in the law emphasize the fundamental right to receive an education as it clearly emphasizes both the social dimension of education and its concern for the individuality and personality of each child. This right is repeatedly confirmed from different perspectives: access to the educational system, suitability for every person's educational level.

General education is free with entry examinations used mainly for social reasons to vocational education. In certain cases, entry examinations are provided for[19] and tuition fees are paid,[20] but the selection procedure is based entirely on objective criteria such as the ability of the candidates. This means that students have the right to an education based on official educational standards, to an individual curriculum, to an accelerated educational program, to free use of library and other sources of information, to supplementary educational services by payment, to participation in the administration of the institute, to respect for human dignity, to freedom of conscience, to information, and to freedom of speech and of belief.

An important aspect of the right to receive an education involves the role of parents. To this end, the law acknowledges that parents have the right to choose the institution or type of education for their minor children.[21] Other provisions relate to pre-school education[22] and for dealing with students who fail in general elementary and primary schools.[23] The law, which recognizes the primary responsibility of parents of minor students, is enforced by standards under international law until the pupil reaches the age of majority.

Parents also have a right to be informed about the educational process, the content of courses, and how their children perform in school.[24] Once children are registered in schools, officials must inform parents of a school's charter and all other relevant documents.[25] The charter of every educational institute must include a precise description of the rights and duties of pupils and parents.[26]

Schools must provide facilities for learning.[27] In addition, the law includes detailed provisions aimed at protecting the health of students,[28] but it is unclear whether they can be enforced and/or implemented. The law provides scholarships, exemptions from registration fees for certain levels of schooling, and special financial concessions for the benefit of specified categories of children[29] in order to create the social right to education. However, these are often limited to state or municipal institutions.

Under the law, students cannot be forced to perform work which is not part of their curriculum without the permission of their parents or legal guardians;[30] it is not possible to get around this legal requirement, for instance, by requiring students to perform work disguised as being within the framework of the curriculum in order to help safeguard the financial viability of the institution. Further, students cannot be required to participate in social or social-political organisations (associations) or to participate in propagandistic campaigns and political actions.[31] Yet, students have the right to free participation in activities that do not belong to the curriculum. [32]

An agreement is concluded between non-state schools and students and their parents which defines the level and duration of education. These institutions are entitled to raise money from students.[33] It is necessary to delineate the precise limitations that are imposed by state educational standards. Selection criteria also apply if a maximum number of students is established per institution, depending on the level.[34] From a certain level of education on, admission is regulated, at least in principle, on a competitive basis,[35] particularly in favour of the most capable candidates.[36] With regard to the lower levels of education, the municipal educational institution has an obligation in principle to register every pupil covered by the description of the relevant area. There is obligatory education, but not obligatory school attendance[37] up to the age of fifteen. General primary education and the state attestation sanctioning its completion are obligatory.[38] In contrast to the right to education, some departures from the obligation to study are permitted, provided that schools and parents agree.[39] The law does not contain any further provisions on this topic.

The agencies of local self-government are responsible for ensuring compulsory education.[40] The fact that students have completed other courses does not serve as sufficient grounds for refusing vocational education.[41] The law stipulates a right to take a course of education, regardless of the level or type of education.[42] The "educational voucher" system is expressly rejected.[43] Nevertheless, the idea of financing through a "voucher" system is making progress. On the basis of the cost of a student, calculated in accordance with the minimum standards, the State would provide an allowance in money to the parents which they can then use freely. The preparatory work for this law has yet to be completed.

The voucher system is a clear example of a long-term policy relating to permanent training: every citizen is entitled to a certain period of government-financed training. This raises the question whether the right conditions have already been created in Russia to apply this system of financing, one which is radical even by Western European standards. On the other hand, the law does not stipulate any coercive obligation for the state to provide its own education should gaps appear in the supply of education after "privatisation."[44]

Student Rights

The boldest reformer among Russian education ministers, Eduard Dneprov, sought to democratize the Russian educational system by means of decentralization, de-politicization, de-monopolization, and de-ideologization. He and other reformers had come to believe that a common curriculum and uniform teaching methods no longer could meet the needs of an individualized, diverse, privatized society.[45]

Over the past decade, the legal system of the Russian Federation has gone into detail about the implementation of student rights. Unfortunately, though, the law's treatment of education is a bit disparate. To reiterate, Russian law declares that all citizens have the right to free primary and secondary education, basic vocational education, and on the basis of selection examinations to secondary, higher, and post-academic vocational training in governmental and municipal educational institutes under the official educational standards.[46] Further, if an institute for general education or for basic vocational training closes, its board of governors must guarantee the moving of the students to another equivalent institute, assuming that they have the permission of the parents or the legal representatives.[47]

According to the Law on Education, educational programmes are to be studied in the following forms: at educational institutions, (preferably) not combining education with a job, home education, self-education, and external studies. It is permitted to combine different forms of education. Evening and extern students have the right to supplementary paid vacations, shorter working weeks, and other advantages in accordance with the legislation of the Russian Federation,[48] particularly with its labour laws.[49]

Admission to Schools

Among Russia's educational reforms is a regulation authorizing school officials to expel students fourteen years of age or older who are failing their courses. At the same time, the general requirements with respect to registration of citizens in educational establishments are fixed by Article 16 of the Law on Education. The registration procedure is defined by the founder of an educational establishment and laid down in its charter.

The registration procedure in state and municipal schools is defined in such a way that admission is ensured to all who live within the applicable territory who have a right to the required level of education. According to Article 16 of the Law on Education, "for every level of education, the minimum age and the length of study is determined by the charter of the educational establishment." Under this law, admission to state and municipal general education schools may be refused due to a lack of places or if children are too young for a level of schooling, as spelled out by a school's charter. The Law does not specify that this criterion applies "regardless of ability and level of development," with the result that arbitrary criteria can be employed, leading to a violation of Article 43.2 of the Constitution, guaranteeing equal rights to access to education.

Student Discipline

It is assumed that the maintenance of discipline at school serves the purpose of ensuring that the rights of others are respected. Even so, the right of officials to preserve discipline must not give rise to physical or mental coercion.[50] The sanction of expulsion from school can only be used if a student is over fourteen years of age and can apply only under specific conditions.[51]

Students under the age of eighteen have the right to challenge any action of school officials which they believe violates their rights.[52] In this process, students have the right to enlist the help and support of the proper authorities by their representatives. As such, students have the right to organize meetings for the defence of their rights. The administration of educational institutes cannot obstruct these meetings, even if they take place in the institutes as long as students and/or their representatives have met all of the conditions called for in the law in order to proceed. At the same time, these meetings may not conflict with the current legislation of the Russian Federation with regard to the public order. Moreover, the educational and formation process may not be postponed due to these meetings.

This arrangement is significantly different from the former legislation which stipulated that expulsion was not possible without the agreement of a special local agency called "Commission on the Affairs of Underaged." The practice was that the only students who could have been suspended from school were those who committed criminal acts and were sent to special corrective schools. There used to be a special advisory committee which worked on cases concerning these corrective schools. Yet, this approach was not really effective.

Conclusion

In other European countries, which have a long tradition of contract law, it is generally accepted that a contractual relationship exists between schools and students (with their parents). However, this is not the case in the Russian Federation. Thus, as the system continues to evolve, one can be sure that issues associated with ensuring the rights of students will continue to emerge more prominently.

Notes

1. De Groof, J., "Education: A Matter of Joint Competence. A Brief Analysis of Federalism in Russia," in Siskens, T.J. & Beijlsmit, L.E., *Crossroads in Russia; Experiences in Educational Cooperation*, Leuven, 2000.

2. See The Law of the Russian Federation N° 3266-I of 10.07.1992 Concerning Education of the Federal Law N° 12-03 of 13-01-1996 (with later adjustments); Federal law N° 124-03 of 24-07-1998 Concerning Basic Guarantees of the Children's Rights in

the Russian Federation (with later adjustments). The most exhaustive list of educational rights can be found in Article 50 of N° 3266-1 of 10-04-1992.

3. International Conference on Education, 43rd session.
4. Article 14.
5. Article 50.2.
6. Article 50.7.
7. Article 50.7.
8. Article 50.4.
9. Article 50.4.
10. Article 52.3.
11. Articles 50.4, 52.1.
12. Article 50.4.
13. Article 50.4.
14. Article 50.4.
15. Article 50.19.
16. Article 15.4.
17. Article 5.4, Education Law.
18. De Groof, J. "Analysis of the Legislation on Education of the Russian Federation," in *Comments on the Law on Education of the Russian Federation*, Ed., De Groof, J. Leuven: Acco, 1993; De Groof, Jan Ed. *Educational Policy in Russia and its Constitutional Aspects*, Leuven, Belgium: Acco, 1994; De Groof, Jan, V. Spasskaya, & I. Rozjkov, *Shaping New Legislation on Education in Russia*, Leuven: Acco, 1997; De Groof, J. and G. Lauwers Ed., *A New Framework of Special Education in the Russian Federation*, Belgium: Garant, 2000.
19. Article 5.3 of the law. Russian members of the Joint Committee noted that these examinations are not set for the secondary vocational programs and that they are now only used for specialized courses. Previously, entry examinations were created only for prestigious courses and in the higher years of courses.
20. Article 5.3.
21. Article 50.1-3.
22. Article 18, 1: "Parents are the first educators."
23. Article 17. 4 point. 1.
24. Article 15, para 7.
25. Article 16, para 2.
26. Article 50.1.
27. Article 50.6; see also Article 51.7.
28. Cf. Article 51.
29. Article 40.7, 8; 50.7–12. However, several stipulations have been postponed, including Article 50.11 on "corrective schools."
30. Article 50.14.
31. Article 50.15.
32. Article 50.16.
33. Article 45.1–3.
34. See also Article 32.2. When an official school is privatized, one of the conditions is the preservation of the necessary number of study places complying with the standard requirements throughout its catchment area. Article 39.13.

35. See also Article 42.1.

36. Article 16.3.

37. See also Article 10; Article 19.4, and Article 50.2.

38. Article 19.3–4. This age can be reduced to fourteen but only after the general primary education has been completed.

39. Article 19.6.

40. Article 31.1.

41. Article 20.3.

42. See, e.g., Article 50.4.

43. But see Article 42.

44. There are two reasons for disagreement mentioned by Russian scholars. First, in the reality of the Russian legal system, it is still enough to have some vague or unclear declaration in the written laws (as in Article 2.c and Article 29.1.a) in an attempt to make state and municipal agencies work to achieve their goals by administrative (from above) means. Second, in the Russian legal system there is specific provision in the Act (Article 31.1) obliging municipal authorities to provide basic general education.

45. See Glenn, C. & De Groof, J. *Balancing Freedom, Autonomy, and Accountability in Education*, Volumes 1, 2, and 3, Nijmegen, Netherlands, 2005.

46. Law N° 32661-1 of 10-07-1992. See also Article 50.7.

47. Article 50.17.

48. Article 50.8.

49. Articles 137–177.

50. Article 15.6.

51. Article 19.7.

52. Federal Law N° 124-03 of 24-07-1998 (Article 9.3).

13

South Africa

Rassie Malherbe

LEGAL RIGHTS IN SOUTH AFRICA relating to education derive first and foremost from the Bill of Rights, which forms part of the supreme Constitution of South Africa.[1] These constitutional rights are supplemented by the common law as well as legislation passed since the adoption of the Constitution to turn around the effects of apartheid and give effect to constitutional rights in education. The main feature of the educational provision in South Africa is the government's endeavours to transform the education system in order to improve and extend educational opportunities for all South Africans. Insofar as constitutional rights relating to education form the basis of this policy program, this chapter provides an overview of rights applicable to students.[2]

The South African legal system and tradition was profoundly changed by the commencement of the supreme Constitution.[3] Overnight, every person became entitled to the rights guaranteed in the Bill of Rights.[4] Everybody is, to some extent, at least, also bound by the Bill of Rights.[5] Everybody accordingly has rights as well as duties under the Bill of Rights because insofar as one person is entitled to a right, others have a duty to respect that right. No constitutional right applies absolutely or unqualified, though, and may be limited lawfully in the public interest, for a public purpose, or to protect somebody else's rights. In a conflict over constitutional rights, they need to be balanced, or weighed, in order to determine which should prevail, and to what extent, in a given situation.

Section 36 of the Constitution, the general limitation clause, has to be applied in order to decide whether a limitation of a right is lawful, whether imposed through legislation, executive, or administrative action, or by another individual. Section 36 reads as follows:[6]

> The rights in the Bill of Rights may be limited only in terms of law of general application to the extent that the limitation is reasonable and justifiable in an open and democratic society based on human dignity, equality and freedom, taking into account all relevant factors, including—
> (a) the nature of the right;
> (b) the importance of the purpose of the limitation;
> (c) the nature and extent of the limitation;
> (d) the relation between the limitation and its purpose; and
> (e) less restrictive means to achieve the purpose.

Section 36 recognises that constitutional rights may be limited while providing the requirements for such limits.[7] This has proven to be an invaluable aid to the courts as it provides an explicit test to evaluate how far anyone may go in limiting constitutional rights.[8]

The Bill of Rights contains specific limitation provisions relating to certain rights which must be applied in conjunction with section 36. A specific limitation provision emphasises or qualifies the body that may impose the limitation, the purpose for which, or the conditions or circumstances under which, it may be imposed or the balance that must exist between the limitation and its purpose.[9] Section 36 applies to all constitutional rights, but a specific limitation provision qualifies the application of one or more of these elements in the case of the right in question.[10]

Section 36 is applied in two stages.[11] The applicant has to establish that a particular right has been infringed by the respondent. The burden of proof then shifts to the respondent to show that the limitation imposed on the right complies with section 36 and is thus lawful and constitutional.[12]

Section 36 is significant because it should be appreciated that any violation or restriction of a constitutional right by a school governing body, school principal, or official in an education department, is a limitation as contemplated by section 36. Even if an action is regarded as clearly justified, it still amounts to a limitation to which section 36 applies. Every time a constitutional right is limited by such an action, section 36 must therefore be applied to determine the lawfulness of the limitation. Even when a competent authority goes ahead without expressly considering section 36, it does so on the basis of a reasoning that can be related to section 36, for example that the action or decision is for some reason justified. Thus, it can never be said that section 36 does not apply to every limitation of a constitutional right.

Education is a micro-cosmos of society and many complex and even intimate relationships exist within the educational environment. Accordingly, many constitutional rights apply in the educational context. In the following paragraphs, a selection of student rights is discussed against this background.

The Right to Education

According to the educational guarantees in section 29 of the Constitution:[13]

> (1) Everyone has the right
> (a) to a basic education, including adult basic education; and
> (b) to further education, which the state, through reasonable measures, must make progressively available and accessible.
> (2) Everyone has the right to receive education in the official language of his or her choice in public educational institutions where that education is reasonably practicable. In order to ensure the effective access to, and implementation of, this right, the state must consider all reasonable educational alternatives, including single medium institutions, taking into account
> (a) equity;
> (b) practicability; and
> (c) the need to redress the results of past racially discriminatory laws and practices.
> (3) Everyone has the right to establish and maintain, at their own expense, independent educational institutions that
> (a) do not discriminate on the basis of race;
> (b) are registered with the state; and
> (c) maintain standards that are not inferior to standards at comparable public educational institutions.
> (4) Subsection (3) does not preclude state subsidies for independent educational institutions.

Section 9: Equal Access

Section 29 does not contain an express right to equal access to educational institutions since it is covered by the equality rights guaranteed in section 9.[14] Equal access does not imply total equality, but equal opportunities to education according to every person's abilities and potential. Reasonable and justifiable admission requirements based on performance, language proficiency, and age may in other words be imposed.[15] The Promotion of Equality and Prevention of Unfair Discrimination Act gives further effect to section 9.[16] The Act identifies so-called unfair practices constituting unfair discrimination prohibited by section 9.[17] The following are unfair practices in respect of education:[18]

(a) unfair exclusion of learners from educational institutions, including learners with special needs;
(b) unfair withholding of scholarships, bursaries, or any other form of assistance from learners of particular groups identified by the prohibited grounds;[19] and
(c) the failure to reasonably and practicably accommodate diversity in education.

The equality principle underpins other rights in that it guarantees the full and equal enjoyment of all other rights, and its protective ambit therefore overlaps with those of other rights.[20] The equality principle is thus closely linked to and supportive of other rights and, accordingly, impacts on education in different ways.

Racial, gender, disability, and other forms of discrimination, sexual harassment, and age limitations are contentious issues relating to the equality principle.[21] Gender-specific schools are permitted,[22] but in *Mfolo v. Minister of Education, Bophuthatswana* regulations requiring the obligatory suspension of female students at education colleges who fall pregnant were held to discriminate unfairly on the basis of sex.[23] In *Harris v. Minister of Education*, discrimination on the basis of age was alleged against a ministerial notice in which an age requirement of six years was imposed for admission to school, but the Constitutional Court declined the challenge and chose to strike down the notice on *ultra vires* grounds.[24]

It could be argued that insofar as the state fails to provide quality or adequate education to all learners, especially among the very poor in the townships and rural areas, it violates not only their right to education, but also their right to the equal protection and benefit of the law and therefore amounts to unfair discrimination on the basis of race.[25]

Limitation

Section 9(2) sanctions affirmative action, which is a specific limitation provision, and programs giving preference to the admission of pupils disadvantaged by past discriminatory laws and practices enjoy constitutional protection.[26] In *Motala v. University of Natal*,[27] an exemplary Indian student was refused admission into medical school in favour of a less meritorious African student in terms of an admission policy which limited the number of Indian students in favour of more African students. The court upheld the policy on the ground that Africans were disadvantaged more than Indians under apartheid. Insofar as this left the Indian student still out in the cold, a better approach would have been to review the whole admission policy of the University in order to evaluate whether it was designed to address the position of all victims of past discrimination.[28]

Section 29(1): Basic Education

The right to basic education imposes a duty on the state to provide such education in order for the right to be enjoyed and fulfilled.[29] It is an unqualified right requiring the priority attention of the state, also in respect of budgetary allocations.[30] The right requires the state to provide sufficient schools, educators, and support and other incidental services in order to ensure reasonable access to basic education for everybody.[31] The reference to adult basic education is superfluous, as everyone has the right to a basic education, which means everybody in need of a basic education, irrespective of age.[32]

The right refers to education up to a level of functional literacy, in other words, reading, writing, arithmetic, and an elementary knowledge or awareness of economics, culture, and politics. That is an education probably equivalent to primary education, which in South Africa equals education to the end of the seventh grade.[33] It could also be regarded as an education of a standard that would enable a person to enjoy the rights and fulfil the duties identified with citizenship.[34] In the South African context, "adequate" education could refer to a standard of education that empowers people to rise above the poverty cycle and compete effectively in the labour market, enables people to understand and enjoy their newly acquired democratic values, rights, and freedoms, encourages people to participate in and protect the fledgling democratic system, and enhances their feeling of self-worth as human beings.

Limitations

Limitations on the right to basic education, such as admission requirements,[35] must comply with the general limitation clause.[36] The SA Schools Act prohibits admission tests and, furthermore, a learner may not be refused admission due to the parents' inability to pay the school fees, or because they do not subscribe to the mission statement of the school.[37] Such grounds for the limitation of the right are not regarded as reasonable and justifiable.[38] Of course, refusal on racial grounds is not allowed.[39]

The school fee system, which enables individual schools to augment their allocated state funds, tends to exacerbate the differences between schools in the traditionally white, more affluent, areas and poorer black townships. The system may impede access to education for those learners whose parents cannot afford to pay the prescribed fees, and may thus be an unconstitutional infringement on their right to basic education.[40]

Disciplinary measures such as suspensions and expulsions, or simple dismissals of a learner from class for misbehaviour, also limit the right and must be justified in terms of section 36.[41] Such cases normally require the weighing of, on the one hand, the individual's right to education and, on the other hand, the rights of others to their education, or, put differently, the duty of the relevant institution to maintain order for the sake of protecting the education process.[42]

Further Education

"Further education" has been defined by the state to mean education from grades ten to twelve (the highest school grade), including general and career-specific education provided by technical, vocational, and other colleges and institutions,[43] a definition which excludes higher education.[44] There is no grammatical or legal basis for this restriction of the general inclusiveness of the ordinary dictionary meaning of the word "further."

First, international and foreign law supports a view that further education should include all education above primary education.[45] The narrow South African view seems unfounded in law and out of step with international norms. A better view would be to regard "further education" as an open-ended concept that includes all forms of education above basic education.[46]

Second, the fear that a right to higher education imposes an unbearable burden on the state is unfounded. Section 29(1)(b) provides that the state, through reasonable measures, must make further education progressively available and accessible.[47] This specific limitation provision recognises that the enjoyment of the right to further education depends on state resources. All education above basic education is thus in any case subject to this condition.[48]

It may accordingly be asserted that insofar as higher education is indeed available and an applicant complies with reasonable admission requirements, he or she has a right to higher education at the institution and in the course of their choice, implying that a university cannot arbitrarily refuse anyone admission.[49]

Limitations

The qualification "which the state, through reasonable measures, must make progressively available and accessible" in section 29(1)(b) recognises the shortfall in current education provision and allows the state to move progressively toward full compliance. In dealing with the rights of access to health care services and adequate housing, which contain similar qualifications relating to the availability of resources,[50] the Court confirmed the enforceability of social and economic rights, but took care not to intrude onto the responsibilities of the other branches of government. Yet, the Court expected from the state reasonable policies to fulfil these rights. It found government policies giving effect to the rights to be inadequate in certain respects and therefore not fulfilling the state's reasonable obligations under those rights.[51] Based on the same standard of reasonableness, it might be possible to scrutinise the constitutionality of education provision, especially to the very poor in the townships and rural areas, in similar fashion and to come to a similar conclusion that government policy relating to the provision of education to those South Africans is found wanting.[52]

Section 29(2): Education in One's Preferred Language

Insofar as South Africa is a multilingual nation, section 29(2) guarantees the right of everyone to education in the official language or languages of their choice in public educational institutions where it is reasonably practicable.[53] The right imposes a duty on the state to provide such education wherever reasonably practicable.[54] The right is not confined to existing facilities and may require the establishment of new or additional facilities. The right is not restricted to basic education, and institutions of higher education are also required to provide instruction in the languages preferred by students. The right extends only to the official languages and not to all languages used in South Africa, and although it would accommodate most South Africans, it does not provide for a right to mother-tongue education as such.[55]

Limitations

The right in section 29(2) is subject to the specific limitation provision or condition that education in the preferred language must be reasonably practicable. This is an objective test and whenever it is found to be reasonably practicable to provide such education, the state has a duty to oblige. The phrase "where reasonably practicable" allows for an approach similar to that followed in the Canadian case of *Mahe v. Alberta*, where factors such as student numbers, costs, availability of facilities and educators, and the distance to the nearest similar institution that is able to provide education in the chosen language were used to determine which provision for mother-tongue education should be made for French-speaking students outside of the province of Quebec.[56]

Section 29(2) further provides that the state must consider all reasonable alternatives, including single medium institutions, taking into account equity, practicability and the need to redress the results of past discrimination. This does not provide for a right to single-medium institutions, but it imposes a duty on the state in choosing the appropriate means in general or in a particular case, to consider all reasonable alternatives in a *bona fide* way, taking into account what is educationally appropriate, as well as the listed factors of equity, practicability, and the need for redress.[57] The express reference to single-medium institutions means that within a range of possibilities that may also include dual and parallel medium instruction, at least this alternative must always be considered,[58] and whenever they are found to provide the most effective way to fulfil the right, they should be the first option. The factors of equity, practicability, and the need for redress carry equal weight and must be balanced. The duty imposed by the right applies to existing institutions as well, meaning that when an education department or governing body of an existing facility decides on the medium of instruction, it must comply with section 29(2).

The SA Schools Act provides that the governing body of a school is responsible for the language policy of a school.[59] In *Mikro*, it was held that the provincial Minister of Education therefore could not overturn the policy; furthermore that section 29(2) does not confer an automatic right on learners to be admitted to a school where a language different from their preferred language is used.[60]

Sections 29(3) and (4): Independent Educational Institutions

Section 29(3) provides for a right to establish at one's own expense independent educational institutions that do not discriminate on the basis of race, are registered with the state, and maintain standards not inferior to those at similar public institutions. The right protects people's freedom to establish such institutions and does not impose on the state an obligation to provide them.[61] Such institutions may be established on any reasonable ground or for any reasonable purpose.[62] All levels of education are included, including higher education.

The conditions under which independent institutions may be established are in accordance with international law.[63] As the main provider of education, the state is responsible to monitor private institutions in order to ensure that standards are maintained. The SA Schools Act and the Higher Education Act accordingly provide for the registration and monitoring of independent educational institutions.[64] The prohibition on race discrimination[65] attempts to prevent some people from "buying apartheid," and it is also important that independent educational institutions remain bound by the Bill of Rights in terms of its horisontal application.[66] Private educational institutions cannot, therefore, be used inconsistently with the Bill of Rights as enclaves of apartheid and for the perpetuation of past privilege.

Section 29(4) confirms that although independent institutions must be established and maintained at one's own expense, it does not preclude the state from subsidising such institutions. All over the world, the state subsidises private education. There is no duty on the state,[67] but should the state choose to do so, it will not be allowed to discriminate unfairly between such institutions.

Freedom of Religion

Freedom of religion forms part of section 15, which provides that everyone has the right to freedom of conscience, religion, thought, belief, and opinion. The right to freedom of religion protects one's beliefs, but also one's right to promote, teach, and manifest those beliefs.[68] Included in the right is also the right to join others in manifesting one's beliefs.[69] How is this right exercised in the educational environment?

In *Christian Education SA v. Minister of Education* the constitutionality of the ban on corporal punishment in section 10 of the SA Schools Act was challenged on the basis that it violated the religious freedom of the applicants who administered such punishment in their independent schools as a biblical directive. The Constitutional Court recognised the importance of the right to religious freedom and of corporal punishment as part of the religious beliefs of the applicants, and applied section 36 to the limitation of the right.[70] The Court decided that section 10 intends to promote respect for the dignity and physical and emotional integrity of all children. Any exemption, even on religious grounds, would disturb the symbolic, moral, and pedagogical purpose of the measure, and would undermine the state's duty to protect people from violence. It was reasonable to expect from the applicants to adapt their codes of discipline to non-discriminatory laws. Parents remain free to punish their children according to their beliefs, but they were precluded from authorising teachers, acting on their behalf, to do so at school.

Section 15(2) provides that religious observances may be conducted at state or state-aided institutions, provided that such observances follow rules made by the appropriate authorities, are conducted on an equitable basis, and attendance is free and voluntary. Section 15(2) confirms the right to manifest or observe one's beliefs, by emphasising that it is allowed in state or state-aided institutions, thus putting it beyond doubt that religious observances in public educational facilities are constitutionally protected. Section 15(2) distinguishes South Africa from the United States, where the establishment clause has led to the banning of all forms of religious observances from public institutions like schools.[71] Section

15(2) reflects the traditional South African approach allowing the state to be actively involved in creating favourable conditions for the exercise of religious freedom (without favouring a particular religion, because that would be inconsistent with sections 29[2] and 9).[72]

Religious freedom entails the right to believe privately as one may choose, but also to manifest those beliefs by expressing, confessing, and observing them publicly. It entails that one may individually profess and manifest one's beliefs, but that one may also manifest them collectively by associating with others in worship, confession, and other acts of observance.[73] The right in section 15(2) protects pretty much all this, for example, individual and collective Scripture reading, prayers, moments of silence, worship, messages by clerics and others, campaigns by religious organisations, the display of religious symbols, and the observance of religious dress codes.

In *Antonie v. Governing Body, Settlers High School*[74] a learner who embraced the Rastafarian religion was suspended by the governing body for serious misconduct after she came to school wearing her dreadlocks under a cap. The suspension was set aside since adhering to religious dress codes did not in the eyes of the court amount to serious misconduct under the disciplinary code of the school. This decision stands in stark contrast to the approach in French law which does not allow any distinctive religious attire.

The conditions under which religious observances may be conducted in schools seek to prevent discrimination and protect learners who, in the context of the particular institution, adhere to minority religions, or learners without any religious convictions:

- The observances must follow the rules made by the relevant authorities.[75] Such rules may only regulate and not prohibit religious observances. The observances also do not depend on the existence of such rules.[76]
- Religious observances must be conducted on an equitable basis. This does not mean neutrality as in the United States, because that would be inconsistent with section 15(2),[77] but requires the school governing body to ensure that one religion is not put at an advantage or disadvantage vis-à-vis others. The preferences of students are decisive and it would not make much sense if a religion not practised at a particular school receives similar attention and opportunity as others.[78]
- Attendance at religious observances must be free and voluntary. Nobody may be coerced in attending them, either directly or indirectly. Teachers may not be compelled to lead such observances or participate in them. Pastors and other representatives of churches may lead observances.[79] The preferences of those desiring religious observances should again be the determining factor.[80]

Section 15(2) was involved when the government recently published a policy document providing for the compulsory inclusion in the school curriculum of the study of various religions practised in South Africa, and imposing particular restrictions on religious observances in schools.[81] The policy is in violation of section 15, first because it imposes a state-determined view of religious matters on learners, thereby violating their freedom of religion, and second because it imposes unconstitutional limitations on religious observances guaranteed by section 15(2).[82]

Freedom of Expression

The right to freedom of expression in section 16 protects all forms of communication, including its contents and those to whom it is addressed.[83] The right includes the freedom of the media, the freedom to receive and impart information and ideas, the freedom of artistic creativity, and academic freedom and freedom of scientific research.[84] Expression can take different forms and include not only the written and spoken word, but also music, dress, symbols, gestures, and other forms of conduct by which someone's views are conveyed.[85] It also includes the right of the individual not to express any view, and pressure on a person to express a view on a particular matter would violate her right to freedom of expression. An example would be the general suspension of classes to attend a political meeting, which forces the individual to take a public stand in order to obtain permission to stay away.[86]

Freedom of expression finds application in the education process, which is all about expressing, conveying, and receiving of information and ideas. No one in the education environment should accordingly be prohibited from expressing his or her views and from receiving information, unless it is harmful or can disrupt or otherwise detrimentally affect the education process.[87] The right affects the kind of literature distributed among learners, the kind of books prescribed in the curriculum, and the use of official notice boards on campuses.

The right to freedom of expression may come into conflict with the right to freedom of conscience, religion, thought, and opinion, for example, when learners are confronted with material that offends their personal religious beliefs, or those of their parents or legal guardians.[88] The "Religion and Education" policy document referred to above would be an example. Such cases require the application of section 36 in order to determine which of the competing rights should prevail, and to what extent, under the particular circumstances.

To the extent that there are so many ways to express oneself, there is some overlap between the right to freedom of expression and other constitutional rights such as the right to assemble and demonstrate in section 17, the right to privacy, also of one's communication, in section 14, the right to freedom of religion in section 15,[89] the right to freedom of association in section 18 (which in turn is linked to the right to use the language of one's choice in section 30, and to form associations with others using the same language in section 31), and the right of access to information in section 32. The example of the right to assemble and to demonstrate would suffice, as the right includes the right of demonstrators to express themselves.

In *Acting Superintendent-General of Education v. Ngubo*,[90] demonstrators against the quality of teacher training staged a sit-in on a college campus. When they went further than merely stating their case, and began to vandalise facilities, intimidate fellow students, conduct themselves disorderly, and in general disrupt educational activities, the educational authorities applied for an interdict against the students. The students' defence was that the interdict would violate their right to assemble and to demonstrate. They received little sympathy from the court, however, on the basis that their actions exceeded the scope of the interests and conduct protected by their rights and substantially interfered with the orderly conduct of campus activities.[91] The court seems to have adopted the justification often advanced for limitations on constitutional rights in the educational environment, namely the protection or restoration of the educational process.

Just Administrative Action

Section 33 provides that everyone has the right to administrative action that is lawful, reasonable, and procedurally fair, and that everyone whose rights have been adversely affected by administrative action has the right to be given written reasons.[92] The Promotion of Administrative Justice Act 3 of 2000 gives further effect to section 33.[93]

Section 33 applies to any administrative action, which can be described as any action in which rules of law are applied to an individual instance.[94] Administrative action covers a wide field of actions, activities, and functions as well as all official actions performed by education departments, school governing bodies, principals, and staff members can be classified as administrative actions. An example is the allocation of subsidies to independent schools in terms of legislation authorising such subsidies.[95] Another illustration is the general rules (delegated legislation) made by an administrative body under powers delegated by a legislature.[96] Thus, a code of conduct or other household rules made by a school constitute administrative action to which the right to administrative justice applies.[97]

Section 33 and the Act apply to all bodies performing administrative actions. These include all executive and administrative organs of state,[98] but also private persons and bodies involved in unequal relationships or relationships based on the exercise of authority.[99] All education departments, school governing bodies, principals, and staff members are therefore bound by section 33 and the Act. To the extent that private juristic persons are bound by the right,[100] section 33 and the Act also apply to the governing bodies and staff members of independent schools.

Section 33 means that executive and administrative bodies may perform only actions that have been authorised by law.[101] Second, these administrative actions must be reasonable in terms of the Constitution.[102] Third, an administrative action must be procedurally fair, which primarily means that the rules of natural justice must be followed whenever in the performance of an administrative action, somebody's rights or legitimate expectations are affected.[103] The rules of natural justice comprise the following:[104]

- The person affected by the action, or proposed action, must be afforded the opportunity to state his or her case.[105] This includes fair prior notice.[106]
- All information that may detrimentally affect the person, and about which he or she does not, within reason, have information, must be furnished.[107]
- The body performing the action may not be prejudiced or biased.[108]
- Written reasons for the action must be provided.[109]

Public educational institutions act in terms of the law and are thus required to comply with these rules.[110] To the extent that private juristic persons are bound by section 33 and the Act, independent institutions must also follow the rules. Section 33 and the Act obviously impact significantly on how schools go about their daily business.

The right to administrative justice is particularly relevant in disciplinary cases. In *Maritzburg College v. Dlamini*, three learners were suspended temporarily by a school on account of serious misconduct.[111] In terms of the SA Schools Act, the next step, expulsion, could be effected only with the approval of the head of the provincial education department.[112] Several attempts at obtaining an answer from the Head of Department came to no avail, with the result that the learners stayed on at the school. The court found that the school at all times acted lawfully and in accordance with the procedures and requirements of the relevant legislation, and in the unreasonable absence of the Head of Department's decision on the proposed expulsion, granted the application for expulsion. In the Mpumalanga case, the court held that the education authorities acted procedurally unfairly by not allowing the relevant schools the opportunity to state their case before the state summarily withdrew subsidies for hostels on the basis of which the schools already budgeted for the current financial year.[113]

Special Needs Students

The different rights discussed above impact the issue of special needs in various ways. The equality principle,[114] in particular, has a direct bearing on the position of students with special needs. Moreover, the provisions for affirmative action in section 9, designed to rectify past inequalities, have been mentioned.[115] Measures imposed also address, for example, the position of women and persons being discriminated against on the basis of their sexual orientation. Section 29(2) is aimed at the protection and accommodation of language communities who wish to be educated in their own language.[116]

Insofar as the awareness of special needs has increased, more and more attention is being paid to the educational needs and circumstances of people with disabilities, if not through educational policies, statutes, and directives, then through the application of the Promotion of Equality and Prevention of Unfair Discrimination Act referred to above.[117] The SA Schools Act provides that where reasonably practicable, education for learners with disabilities, including support services, must be provided at ordinary public schools.[118] Otherwise, special schools for those students must be provided.

Emerging Issues

The challenges to education in South Africa are numerous. Eradicating the inequalities of the past, combating the impact of HIV/AIDS and crime in the educational environment, and the provision of quality education to all South Africans are intimidating enough, mainly due to limited resources. As is evident from the above discussion, developing a human rights culture in education and effectively protecting student rights is another challenge. For this reason, various other rights need to be nurtured in the educational environment.

Human Dignity

As mentioned, human dignity is closely related to the right to equality and the Constitutional Court regards the impairment of human dignity as an indication of unfair discrimination.[119] Human dignity underpins all other rights, is an extremely vulnerable right in any new democracy, and is clearly a critical component of the multifarious relationships obtaining in the educational environment, especially because so many minors or otherwise vulnerable and defenseless persons are involved. Human dignity may be violated in disciplinary proceedings, the daily interaction between educators and learners (which is inherently an unequal relationship), initiation programs for newcomers to an institution, informal interaction on the playground where bullying is an imminent and ever growing threat, and any other relationship in which the degrading treatment of people is a temptation. The effective protection of the right to human dignity is one of the most important and daunting challenges facing the South African education system.

Freedom and Security of the Person

The right to freedom and security of the person includes the right to be free from all forms of violence, not to be tortured, and not to be treated or punished in a cruel, inhuman, or degrading way,[120] and is particularly significant in the educational environment. The right is closely related to human dignity and any infringement of one's bodily or psychological integrity will invariably affect one's dignity. The right impacts on punishment in schools. Corporal punishment was outlawed as a form of punishment for learners by the SA Schools Act,[121] and in *Christian Education South Africa v. Minister of Education*, the constitutionality of this ban also in the case of independent schools was upheld.[122]

Any other punishment or correction should be examined equally carefully. Expulsion of learners and placing of offenders in reform schools are examples of corrective measures that need close scrutiny. Any form of discipline contains some element of humiliation or degradation, but certainly not all disciplinary measures are so excessive that they cannot be justified lawfully. Forms of community service, such as cleaning of classrooms and cloakrooms and picking up litter, are disciplinary measures which can be justified under most circumstances. Disciplinary measures that limit the learner's right to education, such as suspensions or expulsions, must always be administered with extra care.

Also affected are initiation practices and ceremonies at educational institutions, which unfortunately often entail physical and other forms of abuse. Even when official orientation programs for newcomers pass constitutional muster, the informal activities invariably running alongside are often grossly out of line. Such irregularities place all initiation practices under suspicion and educational institutions bear the responsibility to eliminate any action that may lead to abuse.

Privacy

The right to privacy[123] has a direct impact on schools. Rules regarding school uniforms, dress codes for educators, hair codes, and other rules on appearance such as the wearing of jewellery may be regarded as limitations on the right to privacy which have to be justified in terms of section 36. A suggested approach is not to interfere with such school rules unless they are arbitrary and unreasonable.[124] The right also affects disciplinary codes generally.[125] Other issues concern the publication of examination and test results, drug searches, and the mandatory furnishing of health information.[126] In such cases, limitations should be justified by a rational educational purpose, which could result in a less strict standard of justification being imposed by the courts on schools than on other bodies.

An example is personal searches for drugs, firearms, or other contraband. In the case of ordinary police searches, a search warrant is required, unless the person searched gives consent, or there are reasonable grounds to believe that a warrant would have been issued had there been time to apply for one.[127] In the educational environment, much more leeway should be allowed as long as reasonable pedagogical considerations can be advanced, such as the protection of the educational process or the rights or safety of other learners. For example, the insistence on a search warrant should not be enforced as strictly as in the case of ordinary police searches, and surprise and even preventative searches can be acceptable in appropriate circumstances. Parents expect from a school to take special care of their children, for their education, as well as their protection from harm during those hours when they are under the authority and care of the school.

Conclusion

Students do not only have rights but also the duty to respect the rights of others. Constitutional rights are therefore not a licence for a disregard of the rights of others and for ill discipline by students or, for that matter, teachers. Unruly behaviour, swearing, bad manners, vandalism, assault, and the possession of drugs or weapons on school premises are not protected by the Bill of Rights. Such conduct may in some cases constitute common law or statutory offences for which severe sentences may be imposed. No school should tolerate such behaviour, and education departments should actively support schools in combating crime and the increasing lack of discipline. Laziness, drunkenness, sexual harassment, and child molesting by teachers are also not protected by the Bill of Rights, and should be treated equally decisively and severely.

The purpose of constitutional rights is to regulate the peaceful and orderly co-existence of people in a way that respects and enhances everybody's human dignity. Students have the duty to exercise their rights and conduct themselves generally in a way conducive to this objective. Behaviour in schools that breaks down human dignity and the orderly educational process does not serve the Bill of Rights or the development of a human rights culture. Students need to understand that the culture of rights that they help create today will determine their children's enjoyment of constitutional rights tomorrow.

Notes

1. Ch 2 of the Constitution of the Republic of South Africa, 1996. For a brief exposition, see Rautenbach and Malherbe, *What Does the Constitution Say?* (1998).
2. Reference is made where appropriate to the common law and various legislative instruments. See also Visser "Educational Rights in South Africa" 2004 *International Journal for Education Law and Policy* 84–94.
3. The interim Constitution of 1993 took effect on 27 April 1994, the day on which the first non-racial, democratic elections took place, and the final Constitution, adopted by a constitutional assembly consisting of the members of Parliament elected in those first elections, took effect on 4 February 1997. This transformed South Africa from a system of parliamentary sovereignty to a democratic system of constitutional supremacy.
4. S 8 of the Constitution.
5. S 8(2) of the Constitution.
6. S 36 is strongly influenced by s 2 of the Canadian Constitution, but is more comprehensive.
7. Davis, Cheadle, and Haysom Ed. *Fundamental Rights in the Constitution: Commentary and Cases* (1997) 304–305 regards s 36 as "an express constitutional route to reconcile individual rights with a majoritarian imperative of a parliamentary legislative programme." See also Cheadle, Davis, and Haysom *South African Constitutional Law: The Bill of Rights* (2002) 694–695.
8. Woolman S. "Limitation" in Chaskalson et al. *Constitutional Law of South Africa* (1998) 12-1-2 calls it a reasonably precise guideline that alleviates the counter-majoritarian problem where an unelected judiciary must review the actions of the elected government.
9. Rautenbach and Malherbe *Constitutional Law* (2004) 326. See also Carpenter G. "Internal Modifiers and other Qualifications in Bills of Rights—Some Problems of Interpretation" 1995 *SA Public Law* 260.
10. Examples of specific limitation provisions are the affirmative action provision in s 9 which protects the equality rights, the provision for the expropriation of property in s 25 which guarantees property rights, and the qualification in ss 26 and 27 in terms of which the state must take reasonable measures within its available resources to realise the rights of access to adequate housing and health care.

11. The courts adopted this approach developed by the Canadian courts even before the adoption of the final Constitution—S v. Makwanyane 1995 6 BCLR 665 (CC) para 102. See also Cheadle et al. (n 7) 697ff.; De Waal et al. The Bill of Rights Handbook (2001) 113–114. But see Rautenbach IM "Die Konstitusionele Hof se riglyne vir die toepassing van die reg op gelykheid" 2001 *TSAR* 329–340 for a discussion of the extent to which the Court itself incorrectly applies the criteria of s 36 during the first stage of the enquiry to determine whether a right has been infringed, instead of during the second stage to determine whether the infringement was constitutional.

12. For a discussion of the actual application of s 36, see Rautenbach and Malherbe (n 9) 321–326.

13. See Malherbe "Reflections on the Background and Contents of the Education Clause in the South African Bill of Rights" 1997 *TSAR* 85, 91–95. See also Kriel "Education" in Chaskalson et al. (n 8) 38. The provision does not refer to all universally accepted education rights. Several international law instruments provide for educational rights; see, e.g., the International Convention on Economic, Social, and Cultural Rights (Art 13[1]), African Charter on Human and Peoples' Rights (Art 17), European Convention on the Protection of Human Rights and Fundamental Freedoms (Protocol 1 Art 2) and especially the Convention against Discrimination in Education. See also, De Groof "Some Comments and Questions on Rights Dealing with Education in South Africa" in De Groof and Bray Ed. *Education under the New Constitution in South Africa* (1996) 55. Compulsory education is not part of the right (although s 3[1] of the SA Schools Act 84 of 1996 compels learners to attend school from the age of seven years until the age of fifteen years, or the ninth grade, whichever comes first). S 29 also does not guarantee a right to free education.

14. Malherbe "Die Onderwysbepalings van die 1993 Grondwet" 1995 *TSAR* 1, 2–3. This view is shared by Cheadle et al. (n 7) 537. See also Malherbe "Equal Educational Opportunities in South Africa: the Constitutional Framework" 2004 *TSAR* 427–447.

15. According to the School Education Act of Gauteng (Act 6 of 1995), for example, admission requirements may not discriminate unfairly on the basis of race, sex, belief, and language. This should not be interpreted to mean that boy and girl schools are inadmissible or even that learners may not be refused because they do not understand the medium of instruction at a particular school. See also item 2 of the Schedule to the Promotion of Equality and Prevention of Unfair Discrimination Act 4 of 2000.

16. Act 4 of 2000, made in pursuance of s 9(4). See also the Employment Equity Act 55 of 1998 and the Restitution of Land Rights Act 22 of 1994 and related legislation dealing with the issue of land.

17. S 29(1) and (2), read with the schedule to the Act.

18. Item 2 of the schedule to the Act.

19. The prohibited grounds are those mentioned in s 9(3) of the Constitution—see s 1(xxii) of the Act, which in fact extends the grounds mentioned in s 9(3).

20. See, e.g., National Coalition for Gay and Lesbian Equality v. Minister of Justice 1998 12 BCLR 1517 (CC), 1999 1 SA 6 (CC) par 32, 112. See generally the discussions by De Waal et al. (n 11) 197ff.; Cheadle et al. (n 7) 51ff., Chaskalson et al. (n 8) 14-1ff. Also note the close relationship between equality and human dignity—the Constitu-

tional Court defined unfair discrimination for the purposes of the application of the equality principle inter alia as the unequal treatment of a person that impairs that person's human dignity (Prinsloo v. Van der Linde 1997 6 BCLR 708 [CC], 1997 3 SA 1012 [CC] par 33). On its impact in education see Bray "Constitutional Values and Human Dignity: Its Value in Education" 2004 *Perspectives in Education* 37–47.

21. Imber and Van Geel *Education Law* (2000) 217ff. See in the case of racial discrimination in South Africa, Matukane v. Laerskool Potgietersrus 1996 3 SA 223 (T).

22. S 12(6) of the SA Schools Act.

23. 1994 1 BCLR 136 (B).

24. Minister of Education v. Harris 2001 11 BCLR 1157 (CC). See the discussion of the case by Bertelsmann in 2001 *Perspectives in Education* 29–34.

25. Berger "The Right to Education under the South African Constitution" 2003 *Columbia Law Review* 614, 640–641 avers that it should be easier to establish the former than the latter, in other words that the equality principle is being violated, rather than one's education rights.

26. See the discussions of this provision by Cheadle et al. (n 7) 76ff.; De Waal et al. (n 11) 223ff. S 9(2) has been reiterated without further explanation in s 14(1) of the Promotion of Equality and Prevention of Unfair Discrimination Act 4 of 2000.

27. 1995 3 BCLR 374 (D).

28. See De Waal et al. (n 11) 224–225. Cheadle et al. (n 7) 83 is less critical of the judgment.

29. "In re: The School Education Bill of 1995" (Gauteng) 1996 4 BCLR 537 (CC), 1996 3 SA 165 (CC) par 8–9. See s 7(2) of the Constitution which provides that "the state must respect, protect, promote, and fulfil the rights in the Bill of Rights."

30. Significantly, the specific limitation provision allowing the state in the case of the right to further education to move progressively toward full compliance (s 29[1][b]) does not apply here and the state is expected to fulfil this right fully and immediately.

31. Cheadle et al. (n 7) 536.

32. As adult illiteracy remains a tremendous problem in many parts of the country, the emphasis on adult basic education can nevertheless be appreciated. The Adult Basic Education and Training Act provides in detail for the delivery of education to illiterate adults, fleshing out this constitutional right in innovative ways. See Act 52 of 2000.

33. In the White Paper on Education and Training, it was suggested that basic education refers to education to the ninth grade. See also the comments in Cheadle et al. (n 7) 535.

34. This is also the approach followed in the United States; San Antonio Sch. Dist. v. Rodriguez 411 US 1 (1973). Van Dijk and Van Hoof *Theory and Practice of the European Convention on Human Rights* (1990) 467 refer to "the existence and maintenance of a minimum of education provided by the State, since otherwise the right would be illusory, in particular for those who have insufficient means." In whatever way it is defined, the right requires the state to provide education of an "adequate" standard, or an education that provides "a base or foundation for ongoing personal development, civic activity and employment" (Chaskalson et al. [n 8] 38-3), or that is

"directed to the full development of the human personality" (art 13 of the International Covenant on Economic, Social and Cultural Rights which must be considered in determining the content of the right—s 39[1][b] of the Constitution). See also Article 29 of the Convention on the Rights of the Child, and Article 11 of the African Charter on the Rights and Welfare of the Child.

35. See e.g. Visser "The Admission of Learners to Public Schools: Who Makes the Decisions?" 1998 *THRHR* 487–491.

36. S 36; see Chaskalson et al. (n 8) 38–10.

37. S 5 of Act 84 of 1996. See Governing Body, Gene Louw Primary School v. Roodtman 2004 1 SA 45 (C) in which the non-custodian parent was held not to be liable for the school fees of his minor child.

38. This does not condone non-payment of school fees, or non-subscription to a school's mission statement, but these duties of parents must be enforced through other means than to refuse the child admission which would limit the child's right to education.

39. Matukane v. Laerskool Potgietersrus 1996 3 SA 223 (T). See the comments by Visser and Zivanovic "Discrimination in Admissions Practices Unfair and Unconstitutional" 1999 *Education & Law Journal* 307–313.

40. Roithmayr "Access, Adequacy, and Equality: The Constitutionality of School Fee Financing in Public Education" 2003 *SAJHR* 382, 397. It is also contended that school fees are furthermore unconstitutional as it requires the poor to spend an inordinate portion of their income on the education of their children (397). Another contention is that the fee system creates differentiation on the basis of the wealth or poverty of a community, which is still inextricably linked to race, and thus amounts to indirect (unintentional) unfair discrimination in terms of section 9(3)(Roithmayr 410). On the other hand, the supplementary nature of school fees possibly weakens its discriminatory effect.

41. Chaskalson et al. (n 8) 38–10. On the proper procedures to be followed in such cases, see s 33 of the Constitution, and the Promotion of Administrative Justice Act 3 of 2000, as discussed by Malherbe "Administrative Justice and Access to Information: Implications for Schools" 2001 *Perspectives in Education* 65.

42. This test, namely to protect the educational process or prevent its disruption, is widely used in the United States and seems to be appropriate for South Africa as well. See e.g. Acting Superintendent-General of Educ. v. Ngubo 1996 3 BCLR 369 (N).

43. See the White Paper on Education and Training GG 16312 of 15 March 1995 26. S 1(viii) of the Further Education and Training Act 98 of 1998 defines further education as all learning programmes leading to qualifications from levels 2 to 4 of the National Qualifications Framework, or their equivalent of grades 10 to 12 in the school system.

44. S 1(xiii) of the Higher Education Act 101 of 1997 defines higher education as all those learning programmes leading to qualifications higher than grade twelve or its equivalent in terms of the National Qualifications Framework. The White Paper (35) referred to higher education as education provided by professional colleges, technikons, and universities, which is not very helpful.

45. Most international human rights instruments accept that there is at least a right of equal access to higher education. Art 26(1) of the Universal Declaration of Human Rights provides that "higher education shall be equally accessible to all on the basis of merit" (see the comments by Arajärvi "Article 26" in Eide et al. *The Universal Declaration of Human Rights: A Commentary* [1992] 405ff.; Nowak "The right to education" in Eide et al. *Economic, Social and Cultural Rights: A Textbook* (1995) 189ff.; Sieghart *The International Law of Human Rights* [1983] 247). (Art 4[a] of the Convention against Discrimination in Education contains a similar provision.) Art 13(2)(c) of the International Covenant on Economic, Social, and Cultural Rights provides that "higher education shall be made equally accessible to all, on the basis of capacity, by every appropriate means, and in particular by the progressive introduction of free education." In terms of Art II.10(1) of the European Social Charter, states undertake "to grant facilities for access to higher technical and university education, based solely on individual aptitude." The European Convention on Human Rights and Fundamental Freedoms is interpreted to mean that one has a right to any education provided at a given time, which naturally includes higher education if provided. Art 2 of Protocol 1 provides that "no person shall be denied the right to education." See also Kempees *A Systematic Guide to the Case-law of the European Court of Human Rights Vol II* (1996) 1311–1312. See also BVerfGE 39, 276; 43, 47. No international instrument or foreign constitution uses the term "further education," referring instead to "secondary education," which indicates a particular category of education, namely between primary and tertiary schools.

46. See e.g. Van Raemdonck and Verheyde "The Right to Education in South Africa and Belgium: A Comparative Perspective" in De Groof and Malherbe Eds. *Human Rights in South African Education: From the Constitutional Drawing Board to the Chalkboard* (1997) 247, 266.

47. See the Grootboom and Treatment Action Campaign cases referred to below (n 50) on the meaning of this phrase. The significance of the fact that the qualification in s 29(1)(b) does not contain the phrase "within its available resources" which appears both in s 26(2) (housing) and s 27(2) (health care), may be considered further. It may e.g. mean that in the case of further education, a lack of resources is not, as in the case of housing and health care, a ground on which the state may plead inability to comply. However, even if it does not signify that difference, it would not affect the argument advanced here.

48. This matter is argued further below.

49. Cheadle et al. (n 7) 538 simply states, "In line with international standards, further education should be interpreted to include primary education (to the extent that it is not covered by the right to a basic education), secondary and higher education, as well as technical and vocational education." See also Malherbe "'Handves' van regte en onderwys" 1993 *TSAR* 686, 691.

50. Soobramoney v. Minister of Health Care, KwaZulu-Natal 1997 12 BCLR 1696 (CC), 1998 1 SA 765 (CC); Government of the RSA v. Grootboom 2000 11 BCLR 1169 (CC), 2001 1 SA 46 (CC); Minister of Health v. Treatment Action Campaign (1) 2002 10 BCLR 1033 (CC). These cases have been discussed at length; see e.g. Moellendorf

"Reasoning about Resources: Soobramoney and the Future of Socio-economic Rights Claims" 1998 *SAJHR* 327; Scott and Alston "Adjudicating Constitutional Priorities in a Transnational Context: A Comment on Soobramoney's Legacy and Grootboom's Promise" 2000 *SAJHR* 206ff.; Blackbeard "Renal Failure—Right to Haemodialysis Denied" 1999 *THRHR* 304; Mubangizi "Public Health: The South African Bill of Rights and the Socio-economic Polemic" 2002 *TSAR* 343; Liebenberg "The Right to Social Assistance: The Implications of Grootboom for Policy Reform in South Africa" 2001 *SAJHR* 232; Sloth-Nielsen "The Child's Right to Social Services, the Right to Social Security, and Primary Prevention of Child Abuse: Some Conclusions in the Aftermath of Grootboom" 2001 *SAJHR* 210; De Vos "Grootboom: The Right of Access to Housing and Substantive Equality as Contextual Fairness" 2001 *SAJHR* 258; Klug "Access to Health Care: Judging Implementation in the Context of AIDS" 2002 *SAJHR* 114.

51. Note that the qualification that the state must take measures "within its available resources" which appears in s 26 (housing) and 27 (health care), does not appear in s 29(1)(b).

52. See Berger (n 25) 635–640. Berger is of course incorrect when he alleges (637) that since the Constitutional Court did not refer to s 36 in the Grootboom case, "limitations are not at the center of constitutional interpretation of socioeconomic rights." The fact that the Court did not apply s 36 expressly does not mean that it did not in fact conduct a "limitations analysis," albeit by implication.

53. S 29(2).

54. The right goes further than Art 2 of Protocol I of the European Convention on Human Rights and Fundamental Freedoms as it was interpreted and applied in the Belgian Linguistic Cases (1 EHHR 241). See comments by Van Dijk and Van Hooft (n 34) 467.

55. It has been proven that the mother tongue is the preferred medium of education, especially in the early phases; see e.g. "SA Law Commission, Project 58: Group and Human Rights: Interim Report" (1991) 189ff., and see the more recent research by Heugh "Bilingual and Multilingual Education in South Africa," paper read at a parliamentary conference on multilingualism, Cape Town 23 February 2004.

56. Mahe v. Alberta 1 SCR 342 (1990). The reference in section 23(3)(a) of the Canadian Constitution to student numbers was further held to establish a sliding scale of steps that must be taken by the state to fulfil the right. See the comments by Hogg P.W. *Constitutional Law of Canada* (1992) 1224–1225.

57. Cheadle et al. (n 7) 540–541.

58. Cheadle et al. (n 7) 540.

59. S 7 of Act 84 of 1996.

60. Governing Body of Mikro Primary School v. Western Cape Minister of Education 2005 2 All SA 37 (C); Western Cape Minister of Education v. Governing Body of Mikro Primary School 2005 10 BCLR 973 (SCA). A similar approach was followed in Laerskool Middelburg v. Departementshoof, Mpumalanga Departement van Onderwys 2003 4 SA 160 (T).

61. In the context of the interim Constitution, Mahomed J. in "In re: The School Education Bill of 1995" (Gauteng) 1996 4 *BCLR* 537 (CC), 1996 3 SA 165 (CC) called this a "defensive right" (par 7, 9).

62. The grounds on which such institutions may be established are left unspecified, but the interim Constitution referred to a common culture, language, or religion, which led to the question why other grounds like educational grounds, gender, or disability, or a simple purpose like commercial profit, were excluded (see Malherbe [n 14]4).

63. See Currie "Minority Rights: Education, Culture, and Language" in Chaskalson et al. (n 8) 35–27.

64. See ss 45–50 of the SA Schools Act 84 of 1995 and ss 50–64 of the Higher Education Act 101 of 1997.

65. In any case, this is covered by s 9.

66. Section 8(2) of the Constitution expressly provides that the Bill of Rights binds natural and juristic persons—see e.g. Cheadle et al. (n 7) 45ff.

67. Cheadle et al. (n 7) 542–543.

68. Malherbe "Die grondwetlike beskerming van godsdiensvryheid" 1998 *TSAR* 680.

69. This aspect of the right is covered by s 18, which provides for freedom of association, but even more expressly by s 31, which provides inter alia that members of a religious community may practise their religion together with other members of the group.

70. Christian Educ. South Africa v. Minister of Educ. 2000 10 BCLR 1051 (CC). See also the judgment of the court a quo, which held that even if it was a biblical injunction for parents to administer corporal punishment to their children, it could not be shown to be a sincere religious belief that parents should empower teachers and schools to administer corporal punishment to learners; Christian Education SA v. Minister of Education of the Government of the RSA 1999 9 BCLR 951 (SE) 959D.

71. See e.g. Chandler et al. *Constitutional Law Deskbook: Individual Rights* (1993) 90ff.; Witte J. and Green "The American Constitutional Experiment in Religious Human Rights: The Perennial Search for Principles" in Van der Vyver J.D. and Witte J. Ed. *I Religious Human Rights in Global Perspective* (1996) 497ff.; Van der Vyver J.D. "Introduction" in Van der Vyver and Witte xi–xlvii; Witte J. "The South African Experiment in Religious Human Rights" 1993 *Journal for Juridical Science* 1ff.; Underkuffler-Freund LS "Religious Guarantees in a Pluralistic Society: Values, Problems and Limits" 1997 SA Public Law 32ff. The Constitutional Court is actually of the opinion that the South African Constitution rejects the strict wall of separation doctrine present in the United States (S v. Lawrence; S v. Negal; S v. Solberg 1997 10 BCLR 1348 [CC] paras 100–102; 116–118).

72. The position in South Africa is more similar to the German Constitution which imposes a duty on the state to further religious observances in schools (Malherbe [n 68] 703). See in respect of Germany Jarass H.D. and Pieroth P. Gründgesetz für die Bundesrepublik Deutschland (1995) 220ff.

73. See Malherbe (n 68) 679–681.

74. 2002 4 SA 738 (C). See the comments by Roos "The Physical Appearance of Learners in Public Schools: Antonie v. Settlers High School 2002 4 SA 738 (C)" 2003 *TSAR* 792.

75. According to s 7 of the SA Schools Act 84 of 1996, this refers to school governing bodies.

76. In the absence of rules one would still be entitled to conduct such observances. Otherwise, a school could effectively thwart the exercise of this right by simply failing to make the rules.

77. See O'Regan J. in S v. Lawrence; S v. Negal; S v. Solberg (n 71) para 116.

78. The doubt expressed by some commentators (Smith N. "Freedom of Religion" in Chaskalson et al. [n 5] 19–20; Meyerson D. *Rights Limited: Freedom of Expression, Religion and the South African Constitution* [1997] 10ff) whether religious observances could ever be equitable from the point of view of minorities or non-believers must be rejected. It is the very purpose of rules of law to find equitable solutions between conflicting rights or interests, which is the point of departure underlying section 15(2) as well. It would not be a solution to ban religion from schools simply because equity seems difficult to attain. Apart from being directly inconsistent with section 15(2), it would be a cop-out and would simply turn around any unfairness that may exist on those who do wish to conduct religious observances. The challenge is for every institution to devise mechanisms and procedures that will ensure that the right can be exercised as fairly as possible within the context of the particular institution.

79. As long as a particular church is not favoured or prejudiced in the context of the particular school.

80. It is significant that in German case law the free and voluntary nature of the observances has been regarded as an indication whether the arrangements of the particular school were equitable. See BVerfGE 52, 223 (1979); BVerfGE 41, 29 (1975).

81. National Policy on Religion and Education, Government Notice 1307 GG 25459 12 September 2003.

82. See e.g. Malherbe "The Constitutionality of Government Policy Relating to the Conduct of Religious Observances in Public Schools" 2002 *TSAR* 391–418; Malherbe "The Unconstitutionality of Government Policy Relating to Religion and Education" paper read at the eighth international conference of SAELPA on "Legal Risk Management at School: Education Law and Policy Issues," 31 August–2 September 2003, Magoebaskloof, Limpopo Province; Malherbe "The Right to Freedom of Religion in South African Schools: Recent Disturbing Developments" 2004 *International J. for Educ. Law and Pol'y* 248–257.

83. The right does not protect so-called hate speech and section 16(2) provides that the right does not extend to propaganda for war, incitement of imminent violence, and advocacy of hatred based on race, ethnicity, gender, or religion, and that constitutes incitement to cause harm.

84. See the discussion of the latter rights e.g. by Malherbe "Die regsbeskerming van akademiese vryheid en universiteitsoutonomie in 'n nuwe Suid-Afrika" 1993 *TSAR* 359; "Die onderwysbepalings van die 1993 Grondwet" 1995 *TSAR* 1; "A Constitutional Perspective on Higher Education" 1999 *Stell LR* 328; "A Fresh Start II: Issues and Challenges of Education Law in South Africa" 2000 *European Journal of Education Law and Policy* 57; "The Erosion of Academic Freedom in South Africa: Reflections on a Battle Forfeited" 2003 *TSAR* 213; Malherbe and Berkhout "The National Qualifications Framework and the Unconstitutional Limitation of Academic Freedom" 2001 *South African J. of Higher Educ.* 62; Dlamini "Academic Freedom and Institutional Auton-

omy in South Africa" 1999 *THRHR* 3; Smith "Constitutional Academic Freedom" 1995 *SALJ* 678.

85. See e.g. the famous case Tinker v. Des Moines Independent Community School District (1969) 393 US 503, in which a ban on the wearing of armbands in protest against the Vietnam War was held to be unconstitutional. See De Waal et al. (n 11) 311.

86. See e.g. Nistad v. Board of Educ. (1969) 304 N.Y. Supp.2d 971.

87. The tendency in the United States to avoid general bans on freedom of expression in favour of limitations imposed on an individual basis should be noted.

88. Board of Education, Island Trees Union Free School District No 26 v. Pico, 457 U.S. 853 (1982).

89. See par 3.

90. 1996 3 BCLR 369 (N). See also Vista University (Bloemfontein Campus) v. Student Representative Campus Vista 1998 4 BCLR 514 (O).

91. 374C.

92. Section 33 encompasses the main features of the rules of administrative law relating to administrative action and forms the constitutional basis of South African administrative law (Rautenbach and Malherbe [n 9] 229). See also Burns Y. *Administrative Law under the 1996 Constitution* (1998) 78.

93. See in general on s 33 and its application Burns (n 92); Klaaren J. "Administrative Justice" in Chaskalson et al. (n 8) para 25-1ff.

94. Excluding adjudication by the courts which is governed by its own rules (Rautenbach and Malherbe [n 9] 225). But see the definition in s 1 of the Act.

95. Permanent Secretary, Department of Education, Eastern Cape v. Ed-U-College (PE)(s 21) Inc 2001 2 BCLR 118 (CC), 2001 2 SA 1 (CC).

96. Fedsure Life Assurance Ltd v. Greater Johannesburg Transitional Metropolitan Council 1998 12 BCLR 1458 (CC) par 45.

97. See, on the legal requirements for codes of conduct in schools, Visser "Some Ideas on the Legal Aspects of a Code of Conduct for Learners in Public Schools" 1999 *De Jure* 146. Visser regards a code of conduct as subordinate or delegated legislation (148).

98. Note that in President of the RSA v. SARFU 1999 10 BCLR 1059 (CC) paras 140–148 the Constitutional Court held that "the test for determining whether conduct constitutes 'administrative action' is not the question whether the action concerned is performed by a member of the executive arm of government. What matters is not so much the functionary as the function. The question is whether the task itself is administrative or not" (para 141).

99. This is an old principle of administrative law—Wiechers Administrative Law (1985) 4 and 70. Burns (n 12) 57 refers to private bodies with an internal hierarchy and relationships based on authority.

100. In terms of s 8(2) of the Constitution.

101. This implies inter alia that the conferral of wide discretionary powers on an administrative body without the legislature providing guidelines as to the way in which the powers should be exercised, may constitute a violation of the right to lawful administrative action. See e.g., Janse van Rensburg NO v. Minister of Trade and Industry NO 2000 11 BCLR 1235 (CC) in which a provision of the Consumer Affairs

(Unfair Business Practices) Act 71 of 1988 was declared unconstitutional on this basis.

102. In this regard it has been held inter alia that the action must be justifiable in relation to the reasons given for it; Fedsure Life Assurance Ltd v. Greater Johannesburg Transitional Metropolitan Council 1998 12 BCLR 1458 (CC). See also Roman v. Williams NO 1997 9 BCLR 1267 (C).

103. Yet, the right to procedural fairness is more comprehensive than the rules of natural justice.

104. The rules have been included in and elaborated on in the Promotion of Administrative Justice Act 3 of 2000. See the discussion by Burns (n 92) 165ff.

105. The so-called audi alteram partem rule.

106. See e.g. Premier, Province of Mpumalanga v. Executive Committee of the Association of Governing Bodies of State-Aided Schools: Eastern Transvaal 1999 2 BCLR 151 (CC); Oranje Vrystaatse Vereniging vir Staatsondersteunde Skole v. Premier van die Provinsie Vrystaat 1996 2 BCLR 248 (O); Cekeshe v. Premier for the Province of the Eastern Cape 1997 12 BCLR 1746 (Tk).

107. See e.g. Van der Merwe v. Slabbert NO 1998 6 BCLR 697 (N).

108. The nemo iudex in sua causa rule.

109. See, e.g., De Ville J. "The Right to Administrative Justice: An Examination of Section 24 of the Interim Constitution" 1995 *SAJHR* 268, 270–272. The fact that this latter rule has been included explicitly in the Constitution and that the others are referred to only by implication has no practical significance. It also does not matter that according to s 33 written reasons are required only when a person's rights have been adversely affected, whereas no such qualification is included in respect of the other rules. The rules of natural justice have been followed only when a person's rights have been affected.

110. See the application of the right to education by Malherbe "Administrative Justice and Access to Information: Implications for Schools" 2001 *Perspectives in Education* 65–87.

111. Case no 2089/2004 NPD.

112. S 9(1)(b) of Act 84 of 1996.

113. Premier, Mpumalanga v. Executive Committee, Association of State-Aided Schools, Eastern Transvaal 1999 2 SA 91 (CC). See also Permanent Secretary, Department of Education and Welfare, Eastern Cape v. Ed-U-College (PE) (Section 21) Inc 2001 2 SA 1 (CC). In Bel Porto School Governing Body v. Premier, Western Cape the court dismissed a claim that an education restructuring scheme violated the right to administrative justice (2002 9 BCLR 891 [CC], 2002 3 SA 265 [CC]). The majority held that the mere unfair results of an administrative decision did not constitute a ground for review.

114. Section 9.

115. Par 2.1.

116. Par 2.4.

117. Act 4 of 2000. See par 2.1.

118. S 12(4) of Act 84 of 1996.

119. Par 2.2.

120. S 12(1). See the discussion by De Waal et al. (n 11) 246ff.

121. S 10 of Act 84 of 1997. This followed on S v. Williams 1995 7 BCLR 861 (CC), 1995 3 SA 632 (CC) in which corporal punishment for juvenile offenders was held unconstitutional.

122. Christian Education SA v. Minister of Education of the Government of the RSA 1999 9 BCLR 951 (SE). See the discussion in par 3.

123. S 14. The right includes the right not to have their person, property, or homes searched, their possessions seized, or the privacy of their communications infringed. The right protects control over access to information about the individual's personal matters and closely relates to the common law right to privacy, which forms part of a person's "dignitas." An invasion of someone's personal privacy, or a disclosure of private facts about a person, violates the right.

124. See in the United States, Kelley v. Johnson, 425 US 238 (1976).

125. S 8 of the SA Schools Act.

126. The right of access to information is guaranteed in s 32 of the Constitution, and given further effect by the Promotion of Access to Information Act 2 of 2000. See generally Klaaren J. "Access to information" in Chaskalson et al. (n 8) para 24-1ff.; De Waal et al. (n 11) 437ff. For the application of the right in education, see Malherbe (n 110) 65–87.

127. See ch 2 of the Criminal Procedure Act 51 of 1977. See also the strict approach followed by the courts in the case of all legislative authorisations of searches and seizures, e.g. in Mistry v. Interim Medical and Dental Council of South Africa 1998 4 SA 1127 (CC); Park-Ross v. Director, Office for Serious Economic Offences 1995 2 BCLR 198 (C); Investigating Directorate: Serious Economic Offences v. Hyundai Motor Distributors 2000 10 BCLR 1079 (CC).

14

United States

Charles J. Russo and Ralph D. Mawdsley

THE RIGHTS OF STUDENTS IN AMERICAN public schools[1] are governed by a complex array of state and federal laws.[2] As such, this chapter begins with a brief over-view of the legal system in the United States before examining a variety of issues governing the substantive and procedural due process rights of students in elementary and secondary schools.

The American Legal System

The United States Constitution is the law of the land. As the primary source of American law, the Constitution provides the framework within which the entire legal system operates. To this end, all actions taken by the federal, state, and local governments, including state constitutions, statutes, regulations, and common law, are subject to the Constitution as interpreted by the Supreme Court.

As important as education is, it is not mentioned in the Constitution. Under the Tenth Amendment, according to which "[t]he powers not delegated to the United States by the Constitution, nor prohibited by it to the States, are reserved to the States respectively, or to the people," education is primarily the concern of individual states. Federal courts can intervene in educational disputes if a federal right is at issue such as in *Brown v. Board of Education* (*Brown*).[3] In *Brown*, the Supreme Court struck down state-sanctioned racial segregation on the basis that officials in public school violated the students' rights to equal protection under the Fourteenth Amendment to the United States Constitution.

Along with delineating the rights of Americans, the Constitution establishes the three coequal branches of government. The legislative, executive, and judicial branches of government, in turn, give rise to the three other sources of law. The legislative branch "makes the law." While federal statutes have become increasingly important in recent years, most education laws are made at the state level. Once a bill completes the legislative process, it is signed into law by a Chief Executive, who has the authority to enforce it by means of regulations. Put another way, since statutes are typically silent on such matters as the content of the curriculum and length of the school day, these items are addressed in regulations that are developed by personnel at administrative agencies who are experts in education.

The fourth and final source of law is judge-made or common law. Common law requires judges to "interpret the law," examining issues that may have been overlooked in the legislative or regulatory process or that may not have been anticipated when a statute was enacted. Common law gives rise to the concept of precedent, the concept that a majority ruling of the highest court in a given jurisdiction is binding on all lower courts within its jurisdiction. As such, a ruling of the United States Supreme Court is binding throughout the nation, while a decision of a state supreme court is binding only in a given state.

The federal judiciary and most state court systems consist of three levels: trial courts, intermediate appellate courts, and courts of last resort. In the federal system, trial courts are known as federal district courts; state trial courts use a variety of names. Each state has at least one federal district court and some densely populated states, such as California and New York, have as many as four. Trial courts typically involve a judge and a jury. The role of the judge, as trier of law, is to apply the law by deciding, for instance, whether evidence is admissible and instructs the jury on how the law should be applied in a case. Federal intermediate appellate courts are known as Circuit Courts of Appeal; there are thirteen circuit courts; state intermediate appellate courts employ a variety of names. The highest court in the United States is the Supreme Court; while most states refer to their high courts as supreme courts, a variety of titles are in use.

Few school-related cases are directly under the jurisdiction of the federal courts. The vast majority of federal cases dealing with education involve a federal question, meaning that a dispute must be over the interpretation of the United States Constitution, a federal statute, or a federal regulation. A party not satisfied with a ruling can appeal. Insofar as the Supreme Court receives in excess of 7,000 petitions per year and takes, on average, less than 100 cases, it is clearly difficult for a case to reach the Supreme Court.[4] It is easier for an appeal in a state court to reach the court of last resort, especially where a state law is at issue.

The Right to Receive an Education

Following the development of compulsory education laws in the United States beginning in Massachusetts in 1852,[5] all states passed laws requiring children to attend school. In fact, under the Tenth Amendment to the United States Constitution, despite growing federal incursions in the area, education is the responsibility of individual states rather than the federal government.[6]

Insofar as American public schools were not always hospitable to all children, Roman Catholic schools underwent a major expansion beginning in the 1880s. In perhaps the most significant exception to compulsory attendance laws, *Pierce v. Society of the Sisters of the Holy Names of Jesus and Mary (Pierce)*,[7] the Supreme Court ruled that parents were to send their children to the schools of their choice.[8] In light of *Pierce*, over the past twenty-five years, more than thirty states passed laws, and all others have made it legal by regulation, to permit parents to home-school their children. While *Pierce* also recognized the right of non-public schools to exist, a later line of cases, under the Establishment Clause in the First Amendment to the United States, placed significant limits on the amount of aid that the government, whether federal or state, could provide for children who attended religious schools.

Even as all states had compulsory attendance statutes, the laws were silent with regard to the equality of educational opportunities. As such, in 1954, *Brown v. Board of Education*, the Supreme Court's most important education case of all time, wherein it struck down segregation in public schools based on race, ushered in an era of equal education opportunities guaranteeing the rights of all children to attend school regardless of their race, sex, disabling conditions, and/or the immigration status of their parents. In other words, were it not for *Brown*, it is unlikely that laws guaranteeing equal educational opportunities for females[9] and the disabled[10] would have emerged when they did.

In *Plyler v. Doe (Plyler)*,[11] the Supreme Court declared that Texas could not deny a free public school education to children whose parents were undocumented aliens. In applying the right to equal protection to the children, the Court determined that the constitutionality of a classification depended on whether it could be viewed as furthering a substantial state interest. The Court was of the view that the uniqueness of education distinguishes it from general forms of social welfare, thereby triggering the necessity for a state to support withholding it by more substantial justification than required by the rational relationship test. The Court also thought both that the state's reasons for the statute failed to meet this test and that since the children were innocent of the conduct of their parents, the law severely punished them as long as they were in the United States.

A year later, in a second case from Texas, *Martinez v. Bynum*, the Supreme Court rejected a challenge to constitutionality of a statutory-residency requirement that denied tuition-free admission to public schools to minors who lived apart from their parents if they were in districts primarily to obtain a free education. In affirming that the statute violated neither the Fourteenth Amendment nor interfered with the constitutional right of interstate travel, the Court held that "[a] bona fide residence requirement, appropriately defined and uniformly applied, furthers the substantial state interest in assuring that services provided for its residents are enjoyed only by residents."[12]

Religious Freedom of Students

Insofar as disputes involving religion involve two distinct arenas, state aid to students who attend religiously affiliated non-public schools and prayer and religious activity in public schools, this section examines both separately.

State Aid to Students who Attend Religiously Affiliated Non-Public Schools

The Supreme Court's modern Establishment Clause jurisprudence with regard to state aid in the context of K-12 education, sometimes referred to as *parochiaid*, evolved through three phases. During the first stage, which began in 1947 with *Everson v. Board of Education*,[13] and ended in 1968 with *Board of Education v. Allen*,[14] the Court enunciated the Child Benefit Test, a legal construct that permits an array of publicly funded aid on the ground that it assists children rather than their religiously affiliated non-public schools. The years between the Court's 1971 judgment in *Lemon v. Kurtzman*,[15] arguably the Court's most significant case in this area, and *Aguilar v. Felton*[16] in 1985 were static with regard to the Child Benefit Test as the Court largely refused to move beyond the limits it created in *Everson* and *Allen*.

Starting with its 1993 ruling in *Zobrest v. Catalina Foothills School District*,[17] the Supreme Court breathed new life into the Child Benefit Test that extends through the present day. For example, in *Agostini v. Felton (Agostini)*,[18] the Supreme Court largely vitiated *Aguilar v. Felton* by modifying the *Lemon* test by reviewing only its first two parts, purpose and effect, while recasting entanglement as one criterion in evaluating a statute's effect. As such, the Court upheld the constitutionality of a federal law that permitted the on-site delivery of supplemental, remedial instruction and counseling services to disadvantaged children on a neutral basis since there were safeguards in place to avoid impermissible governmental aid to religion. Subsequently, in further extending the reach of the Child Benefit text, the Court upheld the use of vouchers that permitted poor students in Cleveland, Ohio, to attend the schools of their choice.[19]

Prayer and Religious Activities in Public Schools

Unlike its evolving attitude toward aid to students who attend religiously affiliated non-public schools, ever since its first case involving religion in the schools, the Court has largely adopted the Jeffersonian metaphor calling for "building a wall of separation between Church and state,"[20] language that is not in the constitution. In its first case involving religion in public schools, *People of State of Illinois ex rel. McCollum v. Board of Education of School District No. 71, Champaign County*,[21] the Court invalidated a program that allowed religious leaders to enter schools to provide religious instruction for students whose parents agreed to have their children attend the classes. The Court ruled that since public schools could not be used to disseminate religious doctrine, officials acted impermissibly in affording religious groups invaluable aid in helping them to provide students via the state's compulsory education machinery.

In *Engel v. Vitale*,[22] its first case on point, the Supreme Court struck down a prayer from the New York State Board of Regents for suggested use in public schools; the prayer was intended to inculcate moral and spiritual values in students. The Court held that the daily classroom practice of having students recite prayer was a religious activity wholly inconsistent with the Establishment Clause.

A year later, in the companion cases of *School District of Abington Township v. Schempp* and *Murray v. Curtlett*,[23] the Court addressed Bible reading and/or the use of the Lord's Prayer/Our Father in public schools in Pennsylvania and Maryland, respectively. The Court vitiated both programs in light of its test which maintained that in order "to withstand the strictures of the Establishment Clause there must be a secular legislative purpose and a primary effect that neither advances nor inhibits religion."[24] The Court later struck down the posting of the Ten Commandments in public schools[25] and a statute that would have required a "moment of silence" in every public school classroom.[26] More recently, the Court reached mixed results on the posting of the Ten Commandments in public places, prohibiting the practice in a courtroom in Kentucky,[27] but allowing a display to remain on the grounds of the state capitol in Texas.[28]

In *Board of Education of Westside Community Schools v. Mergens*,[29] the Court upheld a federal statute that permits student sponsored prayer and/or Bible study clubs to meet during non-instructional time. The Court expanded its rationale in granting non-school groups access to public school facilities in

Lamb's Chapel v. Center Moriches Union Free School District[30] and *Good News Club v. Milford Central School.*[31]

Lee v. Weisman (Lee)[32] was the Supreme Court's first, and only case on school-sponsored prayer at graduation ceremonies. In *Lee*, a middle school student and her father objected to prayer at her graduation where school officials invited a rabbi to deliver the invocation and benediction. In striking the prayers down as violating the Establishment Clause, the Court argued that the state, through school officials, had a pervasive role not only by selecting who would pray but also by directing its content. The Court held that prayer was an unconstitutional form of psychological coercion since students were a captive audience that was forced to participate, possibly against their wishes, insofar as they were not free to absent themselves from the ceremony.

Later, in *Santa Fe Independent School District v. Doe*[33] the Court invalidated student-sponsored prayer prior to the start of high school football games. However, rather than rely on the psychological coercion test, the Court argued that by letting students choose to pray, officials granted impermissible governmental approval or endorsement of religion.

The Supreme Court sidestepped a challenge to the inclusion of the term "under God" in the Pledge of Allegiance. Rather than address the constitutionality of the term, the Court held that a non-custodial father lacked standing, or the legal ability, to file such a challenge.[34]

Free Speech Rights of Students

Perhaps the most cherished of all American rights, the Supreme Court first addressed student free speech in schools in *Tinker v. Des Moines Independent Community School District* (*Tinker*).[35] In *Tinker* the Court invalidated a two-day-old board policy from Iowa which sought to prohibit students from wearing black armbands to school in protest of American activity in Vietnam. In acknowledging that "[i]t can hardly be argued that either students or teachers shed their constitutional rights to freedom of speech or expression at the schoolhouse gate,"[36] the Court sought an acceptable middle ground to balance the rights of students against the needs of school officials to maintain order and discipline.

In *Tinker*, the Court ruled that the case involved "direct, primary First Amendment rights akin to 'pure speech' [that did not concern] . . . speech or action that intrudes upon the work of the school or the rights of other students."[37] According to the Court, in order to prohibit students from expressing particular points of view, school officials had to be able to show that their actions were motivated by "more than a desire to avoid the discomfort and unpleasantness that always accompany an unpopular viewpoint. Certainly where there is no finding and no showing that engaging in the forbidden conduct would 'materially and substantially interfere with the requirements of appropriate discipline in the operation of the school,' the prohibition cannot be sustained."[38] Where officials can reasonably forecast that serious disturbances might arise, courts typically rule in their favour.

On a related matter, the Supreme Court examined the limits of student expression in a dispute from Washington where a speaker delivered a lewd speech at a school assembly. The speech included elaborate, graphic, and explicit sexual metaphors that caused a substantial disruption. Ignoring warnings from two teachers that he not deliver the speech, the student was suspended for three days and had his name removed from the list of possible speakers at his graduation. Even so, the student was elected by a write-in vote to serve as a speaker. On further review of a judgment in favor of the student, in *Bethel School District No. 403 v. Fraser* (*Fraser*),[39] the Court reversed in favor of the school board. The Court reasoned that officials had the authority to discipline the student for violating school rules because he delivered the speech after being advised not to do so. The Court distinguished the speech from *Tinker* where the armbands were a passive, non-disruptive expression of a political position, rather than a lewd and obscene speech totally lacking in any political viewpoint, incident to a student election that was delivered to an unsuspecting captive audience. In explaining that educators have the duty to inculcate habits and manners of civility and teach students the boundaries of socially appropriate behavior, the Court concluded that "[t]he determination of what manner of speech in the classroom or in school assembly is inappropriate properly rests with the school board."[40]

Hazelwood School District v. Kuhlmeier (Hazelwood)[41] is the Court's only case involving school-sponsored publications. The dispute arose after a principal in Missouri deleted two articles, one on teenage pregnancy, and the other about the divorce of a student's father, from a newspaper that was written and edited by members of a journalism class that was part of the school's curriculum. The Court found that the principal acted reasonably in light of factors such as possible identification of unnamed pregnant students, references to sexual activity and birth control that were inappropriate for some of the younger students in the first article, and a student's unilateral criticism of her father in the second article.

The Court distinguished *Hazelwood* from *Tinker* insofar as the issue was not so much the right of students to speak on specific topics as it was the duty of educators not to promote particular speech. The latter area concerns the authority of school officials over school-sponsored publications, theatrical productions, and other expressive activities that could reasonably be perceived to bear a school's imprimatur. In key language, the Court noted that "educators do not offend the First Amendment by exercising editorial control over the style and content of student speech in school-sponsored expressive activities so long as their actions are reasonably related to legitimate pedagogical concerns."[42]

Student Rights and Discipline

Courts generally defer to educators who use reasonable forms of discipline as long as the punishments are appropriate in relation to the severity of the misbehavior at issue and students receive notice. Cases thus often hinge on whether officials provided students with adequate procedural due process protections. While due process does not require educators to afford students all of the safeguards that are present in criminal, or, for that matter, civil, proceedings, essential elements depend on the circumstances and gravity of potential punishments. At the very least, students who are subject to significant disciplinary penalties are entitled to notice,[43] the nature of the evidence that they face,[44] and opportunities to respond in the presence of fair and impartial third-party decision-makers.

Suspension and Expulsion

Suspension and expulsion are the most serious penalties that school officials can impose on students. Allowing for variations in terminology from one jurisdiction to another, suspensions generally refer to temporary exclusions for specified periods or until students and their parents satisfy specific conditions while expulsions indicate permanent removals from school.

In *Goss v. Lopez* (*Goss*),[45] the Supreme Court set out the minimum constitutional rules for student suspensions of ten days or less. In a dispute from Ohio, students who did not receive a hearing challenged their ten-day suspensions for allegedly disruptive conduct. Ruling in favor of the students, the Court mandated that due process requires that they be given "oral or written notice of the charges against [them] and, if [they] denies them, an explanation of the evidence the authorities have and an opportunity to present [their] side of the story."[46] The Court remarked that there is no need for a delay between officials' giving students notice and the time of their hearings. The Court acknowledged that in most cases, educators may informally discuss students' alleged misconduct with them shortly after they occurred. The Court added that if the presence of students constitutes threats of disruption, they may be removed immediately with the due process requirements to be fulfilled as soon as practicable.

The *Goss* Court expressly rejected the notion that students should be represented by counsel, be able to present witnesses, and be able to confront and cross-examine adverse witnesses in short-term exclusions from school. The Court emphasized that "[l]onger suspensions or expulsions for the remainder of the school term, or permanently, may require more formal procedures . . . [and that] in unusual situations, although involving only a short suspension, something more than the rudimentary procedures will be required."[47] States have followed the Court's suggestion and have developed statutory guidelines when students are subject to long-term suspensions and/or expulsions.

Incident to hearings, most courts decided that students are not entitled to have attorneys present as trial counsel,[48] or to know the identity of[49] and/or to confront witnesses,[50] especially where there may be clear and serious danger to student witnesses.[51] Yet, some courts ruled that students do have a right to have an attorney present[52] and to cross-examine witnesses.[53]

Searches

Although not strictly disciplinary per se, educators typically perform searches in attempts to maintain schools as safe and orderly learning environments and punish students who are discovered to be in possession of contraband such as drugs and/or weapons. Searches fall under two broad headings, those of students and their property and those involving testing for drugs and other substances.

Searches of students and their property

The spread of violence, coupled with the presence of contraband such as weapons and drugs in schools, has led to litigation over the extent to which educators can search students and their property in attempting to keep schools safe. According to the Fourth Amendment, "The right of the people to be secure in their persons, houses, papers, and effects, against unreasonable searches and seizures, shall not be violated."

The Supreme Court first addressed the Fourth Amendment in a school setting in *New Jersey v. T.L.O. (T.L.O.)*.[54] When a first-year high school student, identified as T.L.O., and a friend were accused of violating school rules by smoking cigarettes in a school lavatory, the latter, who admitted to smoking, was not brought to the office for a search. Insofar as T.L.O. denied smoking and claimed that she did not smoke at all, the teacher who confronted her brought her to the assistant principal's office. On opening T.L.O.'s purse, since the assistant principal saw her cigarettes "in plain view," a term of art borrowed from criminal law, he removed them and accused her of lying. Continuing with the search, the assistant principal discovered a great deal of evidence implicating T.L.O. in dealing marijuana. Although T.L.O. was adjudicated delinquent, the Supreme Court of New Jersey ultimately struck down the search of her purse as a violation of the Fourth Amendment.[55]

On appeal, in *New Jersey v. T.L.O.*, the Supreme Court reversed in favor of the State of New Jersey. Finding that the Fourth Amendment's prohibition against unreasonable searches and seizures applies in public schools, the Court devised a two-part test to evaluate the legality of a search: "First, one must consider 'whether the . . . action was justified at its inception'; second, one must determine whether the search as actually conducted 'was reasonably related in scope to the circumstances which justified the interference in the first place.'"[56] The Court added that "a search will be permissible in its scope when the measures adopted are reasonably related to the objectives of the search and not excessively intrusive in light of the age and sex of the student and the nature of the infraction."[57]

The Court clarified that a search is justified at its inception when there are reasonable grounds for suspecting that the search will turn up evidence that the student has "violated or is violating either the law or the rules of the school."[58] Inasmuch as school, also known as administrative, searches are designed to ensure school safety where there are generally large numbers of young people and relatively few adults present, educators need only articulable justification in order to proceed.

A related concern in addressing the totality of circumstances is that school officials may have to depend on the reliability of witnesses in considering whether to search. In assessing the sufficiency of cause to conduct a search, courts consider such factors as the source(s) of information, a student's record, the seriousness and prevalence of a problem, and the urgency of making a search without delay. As such, courts have upheld searches based on information supplied by students,[59] parents,[60] school employees,[61] and the police.[62] Further, recognizing that different types of searches involve varying levels of intrusiveness, courts have generally sustained searches of students' cars,[63] lockers,[64] and backpacks[65] for routine administrative purposes connected with maintaining school safety. Courts have thus generally upheld the use of metal detectors,[66] including those that are hand-held and used in random searches[67] and trained dogs to sniff, or detect, the presence of contraband in educational settings.[68]

An even more intrusive form of searches involves strip searches. Following *T.L.O.*, most,[69] but not all,[70] cases have struck down strip searches for personal items rather than drugs or other forms of contraband. In a related concern, most,[71] but not all, courts[72] refused to impose personal liability on educators for unreasonable strip searches since case law did not clearly establish that their actions were unconstitutional under the circumstances.

Drug testing

A dispute from Indiana became the first case directly addressing drug testing of student-athletes. After high school baseball players tested positive for marijuana, their school board implemented a random drug testing policy for student-athletes and cheerleaders. The Seventh Circuit affirmed the validity of testing on the grounds that it was reasonable under the Fourth Amendment and that school officials instituted sufficient safeguards to protect student privacy.[73]

Ten years after *T.L.O.*, the Supreme Court addressed mass suspicionless drug testing of student-athletes in *Vernonia School District 47J v. Acton (Acton)*.[74] In *Acton*, the Court applied a three-part balancing test in affirming the policy's constitutionality. First, the Court held that students have a lesser expectation of privacy than ordinary citizens do. The Court explained that student-athletes in particular experience diminished privacy rights not only because they are subject to physical examinations before becoming eligible to play but also because they dress in open areas of locker rooms. Second, the Court posited that the urinalysis testing was minimally intrusive since it was coupled with safeguards that allowed little encroachment on the students' privacy. Third, given the perception of increased drug use, the Court agreed with school officials and parents that there was a significant need for the policy.

Seven years after *Acton*, the Supreme Court re-examined the legality of a policy that called for drug testing of students who were involved in athletics and other extracurricular activities. In practice, though, the policy applied only to student-athletes; in *Board of Education of Independent School District No. 92 of Pottawatomie v. Earls (Earls)*,[75] the Court reversed in favor of the board. In applying the same test as in *Acton*, but for arguably making it easier for school officials to pass the third part of the test, the Court upheld the policy in question. Yet, even in concluding that drug testing was a reasonably effective means of addressing the board's legitimate concerns in preventing, deterring, and detecting drug use, the Court "express[ed] no opinion as to its wisdom."[76] While the amount of litigation involving drug testing does not match that involving students and their property, courts continue to uphold drug testing of student-athletes.

Special Populations

Following the Supreme Court's monumental ruling in *Brown v. Board of Education*, educational leaders, politicians, and policy-makers worked to provide equal educational opportunities for all students. Of the so-called special populations, three stand out: children with special needs, the gifted, and children who are of limited English proficiency. As such, this section examines the rights of all of these students.

Students with Disabilities

The educational rights of students with disabilities are governed primarily by two federal statutes: Section 504 of the Rehabilitation Act (Section 504) and the Individuals with Disabilities Education Act.[77] Prior to the enactment of these laws, many states overlooked the educational needs of children with disabilities.[78]

Section 504 of the Rehabilitation Act of 1973

Section 504 of the Rehabilitation Act of 1973 is the oldest federal law dealing with the needs of the disabled. Pursuant to Section 504: "No otherwise qualified individual with a disability in the United States . . . shall, solely by reason of her or his disability, be excluded from the participation in, be denied the benefits of, or be subjected to discrimination under any program or activity receiving [f]ederal financial assistance."[79] Section 504 differs significantly from the IDEA. For example, while Section 504 applies to school systems that receive federal financial assistance in the form of money, books, free lunches, or the like, they do not receive additional funds under its provisions as do boards that serve children who qualify for IDEA services. Also, Section 504 protects individuals under the broader notion of impairment rather than the IDEA's reliance on the statutorily concept of disability and has no age limitation. Moreover, Section 504 covers students, employees, and others, including parents, while the IDEA focuses on the rights of children.

Section 504 defines an individual with a disability as one "who (i) has a physical or mental impairment which substantially limits one or more of such person's major life activities, (ii) has a record of such an impairment, or (iii) is regarded as having such an impairment."[80] In order to have "a record of impairment," one must have a history of, or been identified as having, a mental or physical impairment that substantially limits one or more major life activities, including learning and working.[81] Once an individual is identified as having an impairment, educators must consider whether the child is "otherwise qualified." Unlike the IDEA, Section 504 requires neither that individuals submit to psychological, or other, examinations, nor does it afford as extensive due process protections.

In order to be "otherwise qualified," persons must be "(i) of an age during which non-handicapped persons are provided such services, (ii) of any age during which it is mandatory under state law to provide such services to handicapped persons, or (iii) [one] to whom a state is required to provide a free appropriate public education [under the IDEA]."[82] Individuals who are "otherwise qualified," meaning that they are eligible to participate in programs or activities despite their impairments, must be permitted to partake as long as they can be provided with "reasonable accommodations."

Even if one appears to be "otherwise qualified," educators can rely on three defenses to avoid being charged with non-compliance of Section 504, another major difference between Section 504 and the IDEA since the latter does not recognize defenses. First, educators can be excused from making accommodations that would result in "a fundamental alteration in the nature of [a] program."[83] The second defense allows educators to avoid making a modification if it imposes an "undue financial burden."[84] The third defense is that otherwise qualified individuals can be excluded from programs if their presence creates a substantial risk of injury to themselves or others.[85]

Individuals with Disabilities Education Act

After being enacted in 1975 as the Education for All Handicapped Children Act, the IDEA was re-authorized and revised in 1986, 1990, 1997, and 2004. Even so, the IDEA is still sometimes referred to as P.L. (Public Law) 94-142, indicating that it was the one hundred and forty-second piece of legislation introduced during the Ninety-Fourth Congress. The IDEA, and its regulations, requires states, through local educational agencies or school boards, to identify, locate, evaluate, and serve all children with disabilities, including those in non-public schools, regardless of the severity of their needs. Insofar as the child find provisions are included as a related service in the IDEA's regulations, many school systems screen pre-school children to assist in the early identification of students with disabilities.

In order to be covered by the IDEA, children must meet three requirements. First, students must be between the ages of three and twenty-one.[86] Second, students must have a specifically identified disability.[87] Third, they must be in need of special education and related services,[88] meaning that the children must be in need of a free appropriate education[89] in the least restrictive environment that is directed by an individualized education program (IEP).[90] Related include developmental, supportive, or corrective services as transportation, speech pathology, audiology, psychological services, physical therapy, occupational therapy, recreation (including therapeutic recreation), social work services, and counseling services (including rehabilitation counseling), among others. As children near graduation or begin to age out of special education, school officials must develop individualized transition services plans to promote their movement to post-school activities.[91]

IEPs must describe students' current levels of educational performance, annual goals and short term objectives, the specific services that they will receive, the extent to which they can take part in general education, the date services are to begin and how long they will be offered for, and criteria to evaluate whether they are achieving their goals.[92] IEPs must also discuss how students' disabilities affect their ability to be involved in and progress in inclusive settings and necessary modifications to allow them to take part in the general curriculum.

The IDEA includes extensive due process protections to protect the rights of students,[93] particularly when dealing with disciplining students with disabilities and determining whether their misbehavior is a manifestation of their disability. Among other protections, parents have the right to take part in developing IEPs that direct the education of their children.[94] At the same time, officials must provide parents with notice and obtain their consent prior to evaluating or placing children.[95] Once students are placed in special education, school officials must notify parents before trying to change their placements.[96] The IDEA also includes provisions, supplemented by the Family Education Rights and Privacy Act[97] protecting the confidentiality of all information used in the evaluation, placement, and education of students.[98]

At the heart of the IDEA is the requirement that all children with disabilities receive a free appropriate public education in the least restrictive environment. Yet, since neither the IDEA nor its regulations include a definition of appropriate, it was necessary to seek judicial help for such an understanding. In *Board of Education of the Hendrick Hudson Central School District v. Rowley (Rowley)*,[99] its first case involving the IDEA, the Supreme Court interpreted appropriate as providing a floor of opportunities rather than as a vehicle to maximize a child's potential. The Court ruled that an appropriate education was one that met the IDEA's procedures and was "sufficient to confer some educational benefit"[100] on the child. Insofar as the Court was convinced that the child received "some educational benefit" without the sign-language interpreter, the Court concluded that she was not entitled to one even though she might have achieved at a higher level had officials provided her with such assistance.

Rowley's interpreting the IDEA as having set a minimum level of appropriateness does not prevent states from setting higher standards. To date, courts have upheld higher state requirements in such jurisdictions as California, Massachusetts, Michigan, Missouri, New Jersey, and North Carolina. Some of these courts acknowledged that the higher state standards replaced the federal requirements since the IDEA expects special education programs to meet "the standards of state educational agencies."

The IDEA's goal of full inclusion aside, not all students with disabilities must be placed in regular classes. Courts have approved more restrictive placements where students could not function in regular classes, even with supplementary aids and services, or where inclusion did not work.

Gifted Students

Unlike students with disabilities, the law does not afford much protection for children who are gifted. The only applicable federal statute, the Jacob K. Javits Gifted and Talented Act, encourages local school boards to create programs, but does not provide funds to do so.[101] While states are free to offer programs for children who are gifted and talented, a case from the Supreme Court of Connecticut reflects the general rule.[102] The court unanimously affirmed that a gifted child's state constitutional right to a free public education did not include the right to special education. The court specified that the legislature's failure to mandate a program for a gifted child did not violate their rights under the equal rights and equal protection provisions of the state constitution. Conversely, the Supreme Court of Pennsylvania unanimously affirmed that pursuant to a commonwealth statute and regulations requiring an Individualized Education Program (IEP) for each gifted student a child had a right to gifted education.[103]

Language Minorities

In *Lau v. Nichols (Lau),*[104] its only case involving bilingual education for students who were of limited English proficiency, the Supreme Court acknowledged that a class of non-English speaking students of Chinese origin in San Francisco were entitled to relief from the school board's policy of providing special English instruction for only about 1,000 of the more than 2,800 eligible children. In rejecting the board's claim that it lacked the funds to implement a program, the Court indicated that students who did not understand English and who did not receive specialized instruction were effectively precluded from obtaining a meaningful education. Rather than base its judgment on equal protection, the Court relied on the Civil Rights Act of 1964, which bars discrimination under federally assisted programs on a ground of "race, color, or national origin."[105] The Court pointed out that federal guidelines required instruction for correction of language deficiencies and that the board contractually agreed to abide by them in order to receive federal funds.

In a recent case from Illinois, a federal trial court rejected a school board's motion to dismiss a class action suit claiming that it failed to address the needs of these children by eliminating existing language barriers.[106] The court permitted the case to proceed since it agreed that the plaintiffs demonstrated the existence of language barriers, the board's failure to take appropriate action to overcome these barriers, and the resulting impediment to the ability of the students to participate equally in instructional programs.

Emerging Issues

Amid the ever evolving landscape of education law in the United States, and growing federal intervention in this important arena, in 2002 Congress enacted the No Child Left Behind Act (NCLB), perhaps the most controversial of all federal education statutes.[107] Ultimately designed to improve student achievement, under the NCLB's far-ranging provisions, states that receive federal financial assistance must take steps to improve academic achievement among students who are economically disadvantaged; assist in preparing, training, and recruiting "highly qualified" teachers (and principals); provide improved language instruction for children of limited English proficiency; make school systems accountable for student achievement, particularly by imposing standards for annual yearly progress for students and districts; require school systems to rely on teaching methods that are research based and that have been proven effective; and afford parents better choices while creating innovative educational programs, especially if local school systems are unresponsive to their needs.

As litigation begins to emerge with regard to the NCLB, two federal trial courts rejected claims that the statute created private rights of actions in parents and private service providers, respectively, who opposed its provisions[108] while a third dismissed a suit alleging that it was an unfunded federal mandate.[109] In another case that may indicate things to come under the NCLB, an appellate court in Pennsylvania affirmed that it was it was not practicable for the Commonwealth's Department of Education to provide native language testing.[110] The court specified that since native language testing is not mandatory under the NCLB and should be provided only to the extent that it is practicable, the Department did not violate the law, especially since it was trying to determine which of the 125 native languages that are spoken in Pennsylvania it would be feasible to use in testing.

Other areas that bear watching include the spread of litigation to oversee student use of the Internet[111] and to eliminate bullying in schools.

Conclusion

The ancient adage of Heracleitus,[112] that one cannot step twice into the same river because change is constant certainly applies to American education law.

More to the point, to the extent that new and emerging issues continue to arise in American schools, then about the only thing about which one can be certain is that the legal issues associated with schooling will continue to evolve.

Notes

1. To the extent that non-public schools, which do not receive public funds, are governed largely by the law of contracts, this chapter largely focuses on issues in American public schools.

2. For a discussion of Education Law in the United States, see, e.g., Charles J. Russo (2006). *Reutter's The Law of Public Education*, 6th Ed. New York, NY: Foundation Press.

3. 347 U.S. 483 (1054).

4. See www.supremecourtus.gov/publicinfo/year-end/2005year-endreport.pdf at 7 (end of year report by Chief Justice Roberts).

5. Mass. Gen. Laws Ann. 76 § 1 (historical notes St.1852, c. 240, §§ 1, 2, 4).

6. See San Antonio Indep. Sch. Dist. v. Rodriguez, 411 U.S. 1, 35 (1973) (noting that "[e]ducation, of course, is not among the rights afforded explicit protection under our Federal Constitution. Nor do we find any basis for saying it is implicitly so protected").

7. 268 U.S. 510 (1925). For the Court's other early case involving students in non-public schools, see Cochran v. Louisiana State Bd. of Educ., 281 U.S. 370 (1930) (upholding a statute from Louisiana that provided free textbooks for all students in the state, regardless of where they attended school).

8. See Wisconsin v. Yoder, 406 U.S. 205, (1972) (granting an exemption to Amish children on the basis that their parents and communities provided them with the education that they needed).

9. Title IX, 20 U.S.C.A. § 1681, originally enacted to enure equal opportunities for women in intercollegiate athletics, was later interpreted as forbidding teacher-on-student and peer-to-peer sexual harassment. See Franklin v. Gwinnett County Pub. Schs., 503 U.S. 60 (1992), on remand, 969 F.2d 1022 (11th Cir.1992) (acknowledging that Title IX could be used in a case of teacher-on-student sexual harassment); Gebser v. Lago Vista Indep. Sch. Dist., 524 U.S. 274 (1998) (setting limits on board liability in cases of student-on-teacher sexual harassment); Davis v. Monroe County Bd. of Educ., 526 U.S. 629 (1999), on remand, 206 F.3d 1377 (11th Cir.2000) (establishing guidelines for dealing with peer-to-peer sexual harassment).

10. See the Individuals with Disabilities Education Act, 20 U.S.C.A. §§ 1400 et seq.

11. 457 U.S. 202 (1982), reh'g denied, 458 U.S. 1131 (1982).

12. 461 U.S. 321 (1983).

13. 330 U.S. 1 (1947) (permitting parents in New Jersey to be reimbursed for the cost of transporting their children to non-public schools).

14. 392 U.S. 236 (1968) (upholding a statute from New York that permitted the loaning of textbooks for secular subjects to students in non-public schools).

15. 403 U.S. 602, 612–613 (1971). Under the Lemon test, every analysis in this area must begin with consideration of the cumulative criteria developed by the Court over many years. Three such tests may be gleaned from our cases. First, the statute must have a secular legislative purpose; second, its principal or primary effect must be one that neither advances nor inhibits religion; finally, the statute must not foster "an excessive government entanglement with religion" (internal citations omitted).

16. 473 U.S. 402 (1985) (striking down the on-site delivery of auxiliary services to students in non-public schools in New York on the ground that doing so created excessive entanglement between the religious schools and the state).

17. 509 U.S. 1 (1993) (permitting a sign language interpreter to provide services for a deaf student at his Catholic high school in Arizona).

18. 521 U.S. 203 (1997).

19. Zelman v. Simmons-Harris, 536 U.S. 639 (2002). See also Mitchell v. Hems, 530 U.S. 793 (2000), reh'g denied, 530 U.S. 1296 (2000), on remand sub nom. Helms v. Picard, 229 F.3d 467 (5th Cir. 2000)(a plurality upholding the constitutionality of a federal law that permits the loans of instructional materials including library books, computers, television sets, tape recorders, and maps to non-public schools.

20. *16 Writings of Thomas Jefferson* 281 (Andrew A., Ed. 1903).

21. 333 U.S. 203 (1948).

22. 370 U.S. 421 (1962).

23. 374 U.S. 203 (1963).

24. Id. at 222.

25. 449 U.S. 39 (1980).

26. 472 U.S. 38 (1985).

27. McCreary County, Ky., v. American Civil Liberties Union of Ky., 125 S. Ct. 2722 (2005).

28. Van Orden v. Perry, 125 S. Ct. 2854 (2005).

29. 496 U.S. 226 (1990).

30. 508 U.S. 384 (1993).

31. 533 U.S. 98 (2001).

32. 505 U.S. 577 (1992).

33. 530 U.S. 290 (2000).

34. 542 U.S. 1 (2004), reh'g denied, 125 S.Ct. 21 (2004).

35. 393 U.S. 503 (1969).

36. Id. at 506.

37. Id. at 508–509.

38. Id. at 509 citing Burnside v. Byars, 363 F.2d 744, 749 (5th Cir.1966).

39. 478 U.S. 675 (1986).

40. Id. at 683.

41. 484 U.S. 260 (1988).

42. Id. at 273.

43. See, e.g., Bivins v. Albuquerque Pub. Schs., 899 F. Supp. 556 (D.N.M.1995); Donovan v. Ritchie, 68 F.3d 14 (1st Cir.1995); Hammock ex rel. Hammock v. Keys, 93 F. Supp.2d 1222 (S.D. Ala.2000).

44. C.B. By and Through Breeding v. Driscoll, 82 F.3d 383 (11th Cir.1996).

45. 419 U.S. 565 (1975).

46. Id. at 581.

47. Id. at 584.

48. See, e.g., Osteen v. Henley, 13 F.3d 221 (7th Cir.1993); Lake Central Sch. Corp. v. Scartozzi, 759 N.E.2d 1185 (Ind. Ct. App. 2001).

49. See, e.g., Brewer v. Austin Indep. School Dist., 779 F.2d 260 (5th Cir.1985); Coplin v. Conejo Valley Unified Sch. Dist., 903 F. Supp. 1377 (C.D. Cal.1995), aff'd in an unpublished opinion, 116 F.3d 483 (9th Cir.1997).

50. Newsome v. Batavia Local Sch. Dist., 842 F.2d 920 (6th Cir.1988).

51. Dillon v. Pulaski County Special Sch. Dist., 468 F. Supp. 54 (E.D. Ark.1978); John A. v. San Bernardino City Unified Sch. Dist., 654 2d 242 (Cal.1982).

52. Givens v. Poe, 346 F. Supp. 202 (W.D.N.C.1972); Gonzales v. McEuen, 435 F.Supp. 460 (C.D. Cal.1977).

53. Colquitt v. Rich Township High Sch. Dist. No. 227, 699 N.E.2d 1109 (Ill. App. Ct.1998).

54. 469 U.S. 325 (1985).

55. In re T.L.O., 463 A.2d 934 (N.J.1983).

56. New Jersey v. T.L.O., 469 U.S. 325, 341 (1985).

57. Id. at 342.

58. Id.

59. See, e.g., Wofford v. Evans, 390 F.3d 318 (4th Cir. 2004); State v. J.H., 898 So.2d 240 (Fla. Dist. Ct.App.2005).

60. See, e.g., United States v. Aguilera, 287 F. Supp.2d. 1204 (E.D. Cal.2003); In re Joseph G., 38 Cal.Rptr.2d 902 (Cal. Ct. App.1995).

61. See, e.g., Cornfield v. Consolidated High Sch. Dist. No. 230, 991 F.2d 1316 (7th Cir.1993).

62. See, e.g., In re D.E.M., 727 A.2d 570 (Pa. Super. Ct.1999).

63. See, e.g., Anders ex rel. Anders v. Fort Wayne Community Schs., 124 F.Supp.2d 618 (N.D. Ind. 2000); Covington County v. G.W., 767 So.2d 187 (Miss.2000).

64. See, e.g., Zamora v. Pomeroy, 639 F.2d 662 (10th Cir.1981); Commonwealth v. Carey, 554 N.E.2d 1199 (Mass.1990); In Interest of Isiah B., 500 N.W.2d 637 (Wis.1993), cert. denied, 510 U.S. 884 (1993); In re F.B., 726 A.2d 361 (Pa.1999).

65. See, e.g., In re F.B., 726 A.2d 361 (Pa.1999); In re Murray, 525 S.E.2d 496 (N.C. Ct. App.2000).

66. See, e.g., Thompson v. Carthage Sch. Dist., 87 F.3d 979 (8th Cir.1996); In re F.B., 726 A.2d 361 (Pa.1999); cert. denied sub nom; F.B. v. Pennsylvania, 528 U.S. 1060 (1999); People v. Dukes, 580 N.Y.S.2d 850 (N.Y. Crim. Ct.1992).

67. See, e.g., State v. J.A., 679 So.2d 316 (Fla. Dist. Ct. App.1996), reh'g denied (1996), review denied, 689 So.2d 1069 (Fla. 1997), cert. denied, 522 U.S. 831 (1997).

68. See, e.g., Doe v. Renfrow, 475 F. Supp. 1012 (N.D. Ind.1979), rev'd in part on other grounds, 631 F.2d 91 (7th Cir.1980), cert. denied, 451 U.S. 1022 (1981); Commonwealth v. Cass, 709 A.2d 350 (Pa. 1998), cert. denied, 525 U.S. 833 (1998); Marner v. Eufaula City Sch. Bd., 204 F.Supp.2d 1318 (M.D. Ala. 2002). But see B.C. v. Plumas Unified Sch. Dist., 192 F.3d 1260 (9th Cir.1999) (striking down the use of a sniff dog).

69. See, e.g., State ex rel. Galford v. Mark Anthony B., 433 S.E.2d 41 (W.Va.1993); Kennedy v. Dexter Consol. Schs., 10 3d 115 (N.M. 2000); Thomas ex rel. Thomas v. Roberts, 261 F.3d 1160 (11th Cir.2001).

70. See, e.g., Williams ex rel. Williams v. Ellington, 936 F.2d 881 (6th Cir.1991); Cornfield by Lewis v. Consolidated High Sch. Dist. No. 230, 991 F.2d 1316 (7th Cir.1993); Jenkins v. Talladega City Bd. of Educ., 115 F.3d 821 (11th Cir.1997), cert. denied, sub nom., Jenkins by Hall v. Herring, 522 U.S. 966 (1997).

71. See, e.g., Williams ex rel. Williams v. Ellington, 936 F.2d 881 (6th Cir.1991); Jenkins v. Talladega City Bd. of Educ., 115 F.3d 821 (11th Cir.1997), cert. denied sub nom. Jenkins by Hall v. Herring, 522 U.S. 966 (1997).

72. See, e.g., Kennedy v. Dexter Consol. Schs., 10 3d 115 (N.M. 2000); Fewless v. Board of Educ., 208 F. Supp.2d 806 (W.D. Mich. 2002).

73. Schaill v. Tippecanoe County Sch. Corp., 864 F.2d 1309 (7th Cir.1988).

74. 515 U.S. 646 (1995).

75. 536 U.S. 822 (2002), on remand, 300 F.3d 1222 (10th Cir.2002).

76. Id. at 838.

77. A third law, the Americans with Disabilities Act, 42 U.S.C.A. §§ 12101 et seq., which extends similar protections to individuals in the private sector which has limited application for public schools, is beyond the scope of this chapter.

78. For a thorough discussion of education law in the United States, see e.g. Allan G. Osborne & Charles J. Russo (in press). *Special Education and the Law: A Guide for Practitioners*, 2nd Ed. Thousand Oaks, CA: Corwin Press.

79. 29 U.S.C.A. § 794(a).

80. 29 U.S.C.A. § 706(7)(B).

81. 45 C.F.R. § 84.3(j)(2)(i).

82. 45 C.F.R. § 84.3(k)(2).

83. Southeastern Community College v. Davis, 442 U.S. 397, 410 (1979).

84. Id. at 412.

85. School Bd. of Nassau County v. Arline, 480 U.S. 273, 287–88 (1987).

86. 20 U.S.C.A. § 1412(a)(A).

87. 20 U.S.C.A. § 1401 (3)(A)(i).

88. 20 U.S.C.A. § § 1401 (3)(A)(i), (ii).

89. 20 U.S.C.A. § 1401(8)(A).

90. 20 U.S.C.A. § 1401 (14).

91. 20 U.S.C.A. § 1414(d)(1)(A)(vii)(II); 20 U.S.C.A. § 1401(30).

92. 20 U.S.C.A. § 1414(d)(1)(A).

93. 20 U.S.C.A. § 1415.

94. 20 U.S.C.A. §§ 1414(d)(1)(B)(I), (f)).

95. 20 U.S.C.A. §§ 1414(a)(1)(2), (b)(3).

96. 20 U.S.C.A. § 1415(b)(3)(A).

97. 29 U.S.C.A. § 1232g.

98. 20 U.S.C.A. § 1417 (c).

99. 458 U.S. 176 (1982).

100. Id. at 200.

101. 20 U.S.C.A. § 7253. States often follow an approach such as the one used in Ohio which requires school board officials to identify, but not serve, students who are gifted. Ohio Rev. Code Ann. § 3324.04.

102. Broadley v. Board of Educ. of City of Meriden, 639 A.2d 502 (Conn.1994).

103. Centennial Sch. Dist. v. Commonwealth, Dep't of Educ., 539 A.2d 785 (Pa.1988). See also York Suburban Dist. v. S.P., 872 A.2d 1285 (Pa. Cmwlth. Ct. 2005) (affirmed that a school board was required to provide an education sufficient to confer a benefit on a gifted student that was tailored to his unique needs pursuant to an IEP).

104. 414 U.S. 563 (1974).

105. 42 U.S.C. §§ 2000d et seq.

106. Leslie v. Board of Educ. for Ill. Sch. Dist. U-46, 379 F. Supp.2d 952 (N.D. Ill. 2005).

107. 20 U.S.C.A. §§ 6301 et seq.

108. See Association of Community Org. v. New York, 269 F. Supp.2d 338 (S.D.N.Y. 2003); Fresh Start Academy v. Toledo Bd. of Educ., 363 F. Supp.2d 910 (N.D. Ohio 2005).

109. School Dist. of the City of Pontiac v. Spellings, 2005 WL 3149545 (E.D. Mich. 2005).

110. Reading School Dist. v. Department of Educ., 855 A.2d 166 (Pa. Commw. Ct. 2004), appeal denied, 877 A.2d 463 (Pa. 2005).

111. For cases striking down discipline of students for inappropriate use of the Internet, typically on the ground that rules were vague and/or overbroad, see, e.g., Flaherty v. Keystone Oaks Sch. Dist., 247 F. Supp.2d 698 (W.D. Pa.2003); Coy v. Board of Educ., 205 F. Supp.2d 791 (N.D. Ohio2002). Beussink ex rel. Beussink v. Woodland R–IV Sch. Dist., 30 F. Supp.2d 1175 (E.D. Mo.1998); Killion v. Franklin Reg'l Sch. Dist., 136 F. Supp.2d 446 (W.D. Pa.2001). But see J.S. v. Bethlehem Area Sch. Dist., 807 A.2d 847 (Pa.2002) (upholding a student's expulsion for making derogatory on-line remarks about his algebra teacher, asking for collections to pay a hit man to kill her).

112. According to Heracleitus, "You could not step twice into the same river; for other waters are ever flowing on to you." Hippocrates, Heracleitus. (1979) (W.H.S. Jones, Trans.) *In on the Universe*, XLI 483. Cambridge, MA: Harvard University Press.

15

Analysis and Reflections

Jan De Groof, Charles J. Russo, and Douglas J. Stewart

Analysis

THE RIGHT TO EDUCATION is internationally recognized as a basic human right. In many countries, rights in and to education are protected by national laws which are often based on or inspired by international legislation. The chapters in this book reveal that in many nations, the right to basic education is fully, or nearly fully, achieved in many aspects. The chapters also demonstrate that many educational topics are implemented by national legislation such as free enrolment at schools, compulsory education, the possibility to establish private schools, and freedom of speech and religion. Although these countries have shown interest in many common educational topics, differences in national legislation, of course, still remain.

Under European jurisprudence, the right to education, by its very nature, is based on state regulations which may vary in time and place according to the needs and resources of the community and of individuals. Further, pursuant to European jurisprudence, the right to education is, by its very nature, subject to regulation by the state. As such, the amount and degree of regulation may vary in time and place according to the needs and resources of the community and of individuals. This perspective is not significantly different from the American perspective that states have the authority to regulate education. It is, of course, different insofar as in the United States, education is primarily, although as witnessed by increasing federal intervention in recent years, not exclusively, a province of state governments.

All of the countries reviewed in this book have compulsory education which is free of charge. In China and the United States, attendance at school is obliged, in Northern Ireland regular attendance at school is encouraged. In Australia, although education from ages five to sixteen is compulsory, there is no expressed legal right, except in New South Wales, to an education. This is reflected in their legislation.

Many times, there is a disparity between legal theory and actual practice. In China, the involvement of party policies may endanger the legitimacy and consistency of law concerning educational topics. Some of the administrative rules enacted by the Ministry of Education lack a constitutional and statutory basis. Moreover, since schools are not a part of government in China, they are legal entities that bear their own liabilities, meaning that students may have little redress if their rights are not satisfied. In New Zealand, as in England, there is no written constitution. Even though civil liberties and equality are certainly as well protected in New Zealand as they are in countries with constitutional rights, students' rights "have not yet loomed large."

It is legally possible, in practically all of the countries discussed in this book, to establish private or independent schools. These schools are registered and generally must maintain standards which are comparable to public educational institutions. In addition, parents can freely choose the school that they wish their children to attend and can, in varying degrees, have their children excused from specific subjects in the curriculum to which they object for pedagogical and philosophical reasons.

In England for instance, religious education is part of the basic curriculum in all state schools. Each student has to participate in a daily act of collective worship. In Germany, there is religious instruction in public and private schools. However, parents may withdraw their children from this religious instruction; these students must then take part in alternative courses in philosophy or ethics. Every publicly funded school in Northern Ireland must have a daily period of collective worship as well. This is required by law. Parents can, as in Germany, withdraw their child from this kind of education. The religious education is moreover taught in separate classes to make sure the school is open to children of all religious denominations.

According to the legal system in the United States, which has erected the judicially created so-called "wall of separation" between Church and State, there can be no school-sponsored prayer or religious activity in public schools; as discussed in the chapter on the United States, student-sponsored religious activity may be permitted under some circumstances. Yet, this barrier may be weakening in the United States as the courts have recognized the rights of religious groups to use school facilities after school hours as long as other groups have the same right to do so. In non-public schools, most of which are religiously affiliated and receive no direct aid from the government, American students are free to engage in prayer and other religious activities.

Article 10 of the European Convention on Human Rights protects freedom of expression, including freedom of speech. This is relevant for both students and teachers. In general, the freedom of expression is protected by law. In Northern Ireland, students have the right to freedom of speech in domestic law. In Germany, freedom of speech means students can express opinions of all kinds; they can ask questions and make judgements. Students have the right to freedom of expression. This means that students can freely express ideas, beliefs, and thoughts.

The right to freedom of expression in South Africa protects all kinds of communication, its content, and those to whom it is addressed. Students have the freedom to receive and impart information and ideas and they also have the freedom of artistic creativity. This expression is not limited to the oral and written expressions. Music, clothing, symbols, gestures, and other forms of conduct are allowed. A student also has the right not to express his ideas. In England, students may be punished when their verbal or other forms of expression are considered to be offensive or disruptive to the educational process. While students clearly have an expansive right to freedom of speech and expression in American public schools, educators can limit their ability to speak out if their doing so would create a reasonable forecast of material and substantial disruption in schools.

In Australia, Belgium, Northern Ireland, the Netherlands, and the United States, home-schooling is allowed. In Belgium, home teaching can be organised by the parents or in unsubsidized private schools. The government stipulates the formal conditions which must be fulfilled. The inspectorate checks whether the supplied home tuition meets the objectives and examines whether the development targets (which need to be the same as the education organised in schools) are being achieved. In Northern Ireland, parents do not have to prove the education that is given at home meets the standards of the education the child would receive at school. The education must be suitable to a child's age, attitude, and special needs he may have. In the Netherlands, home teaching is only allowed when parents refuse to enrol their child in any schools in their neighbourhoods for reasons of conscience.

Schools pay attention to children from ethnic minorities or deprived families. In Malaysia, the indigenous population gets special privileges, as there are positions in the public service, scholarships, educational, and training privileges. In educational institutions, places are reserved for indigenous persons. In South Africa, programs give preference to the admission of pupils disadvantaged by past discriminatory laws and practices; similar programs exist in the United States but they tend to focus on higher education.

Children with special needs or disabilities have the same right to education as other students and can receive educational services that are adjusted to their individualized needs. Schools must ensure that students with disabilities are not disadvantaged. According to article 9 of the United Nations Convention on the Rights of the Child, all students have the right to expect and receive education in safe and accommodating learning environments. In Australia, England, Germany, New Zealand, and the United States, among others, inclusion of children with special needs in regular classrooms is possible. Most disabled children in other nations attend school in special institutions. In Belgium, the number of schools for special education established by the government must not only be sufficient, but also geographically spread.

Corporal punishment is prohibited in most countries. However, in Australia and the United States, corporal punishment is permitted in certain circumstances. School regulations must provide safeguards to exclude excessive punishment. In Malaysia corporal punishment, which is permitted on male students only, is regarded as educational and deterrent in nature. The school principal is responsible to ensure this measure will not be abused. Excessive force is prohibited. Under some circumstances, students can take legal action against their teachers, school, or its staff.

All of the nations reviewed in this book prevent discrimination against students on the grounds of their gender, marital or family status, religion, colour, race, ethnic or national origin, nationality, disability, political opinion, and sexual orientation.

In Belgium and England, parents have to sign a declaration to show they agree with the school regulations when their children are being enrolled. In Belgium, the school governing board is obliged to inform the student and his parents about the school regulations and the pedagogical project. South African students may not be refused when they want to enrol if their parents do not subscribe to the mission statements of the schools.

Students can be excluded or expelled from school for a fixed period or permanently for serious violations of school rules or the law. In most countries, this is provided for under specific regulations set by the relevant educational authority. In Belgium and Germany there is an explicit students' right to participate in the proceedings as they form part of their schools' councils. While the rules of student participation are not as formal in the United States, students have the right to be present at disciplinary proceedings that might impact their ability to continue to attend classes.

In most nations, with the United States, and apparently Malaysia, being the most significant exceptions in this book, non-public or private schools receive financial subsidies from governments. In the Netherlands schools with a large number of students with a deprived socio-economic background, receive more funding. Special public schools for pupils with behavioural or learning problems receive limited extra budget in just about all of the nations reviewed herein.

Reflections

All of the nations discussed in this book are party to and have ratified various human rights conventions that identify education as a basic human right. More specifically, Article 28 of the Universal Declaration of Human Rights recognises that children have a right to education. Further, as reflected herein, many countries have already incorporated this indispensable basic right into national legislation and legal systems. Political commitments and policies have been made in order to ensure the effective implementation into national legislation.

Unfortunately, the right to education as a fundamental right is not recognised in many countries that were not included in this book. Ensuring the right to education is an obligation of governments that need to translate their international commitments into constitutions and domestic legislation. Otherwise, it will be most difficult to develop and enforce policies calling for equal educational opportunities for all children.

The principles specified in the Declaration as well as in national constitutions and other legal documents need to be translated into concrete rights and duties, all of which are subject to protection via judicial action. When the right to education is reflected in national legislation, it is not automatically achieved in real terms since systemic disparities between legislation and practices often remain in place. This means that the enforcement of educational rights can sometimes be hampered. Put another way, it is difficult to prevent discrimination absent a legislative or regulatory foundation that can establish norms to permit officials to take the necessary measures to protect the educational rights of students.

At the national, state, and local levels, governments must continuously develop policies to improve the quality of education and equality principle within their school systems. All of the countries examined in this book require a compulsory period of basic free education in public or private schools. Primary education, at the very least, should be free of charge, available, accessible, and compulsory all over the world. Nations should seek to extend this right through secondary and/or vocational education while also making higher education, admittedly beyond the scope of this book, available to all who are qualified. To reiterate, it is the core responsibility of governments to develop sound educational systems while ensuring that all necessary steps are being taken to achieve this goal.

The promotion and protection of students' rights and the equality principle are crucial. Governments must give consideration to the interests, skills, knowledge, and talents of students even as they guarantee equality of opportunity for all students to avoid educational and social segregation. In an attempt to effectuate the ideals of the Convention, one of the objectives of the World Education Forum in April 2000 was to universalize primary education worldwide by 2015. The right to education is essential to and can help to effectuate other human rights; it can, for instance, lift children out of poverty while simultaneously promoting democracy and common values.

It is a great challenge to achieve the right to education for all. In South Africa, for example, this right is not limited by age. It is necessary to guarantee access to education for persons who did not or could not complete at least their formal education in primary schools. Governments should encourage and intensify programs to educate adults who did not receive an appropriate education when they were younger.

At the same time, legal, administrative, social, and educational measures are needed to protect children against physical and mental violence, abuse, and maltreatment. The physical and mental integrity of children should be a national priority in each nation. To this end, most of the nations addressed in this book have prohibited the use of corporal punishment in schools.

As to another matter, as stipulated in article 26 of the Universal Declaration of Human Rights (UDHR), education shall be directed to the full development of the human personality. Articles 13 and 14 of the International Covenant on Economic, Social, and Cultural Rights add to article 26 of the UDHR that education shall be directed to the human personality's sense of dignity, that it shall enable persons to participate effectively in a free society, and that it shall promote understanding among ethnic, racial, and religious groups in all nations.

The establishment of educational policy and educational management systems is certainly a challenging task. Education is a complex enterprise because it must represent a broad range of interests for different stakeholders including students, teachers, parents, school staff, and governing boards. Many of these stakeholders are affected by the policies and decisions of the educational enterprise. Moreover, it is not easy to foresee the effects of certain policies. The approach of schools must meet the democratically agreed on objectives of their education systems and internationally enforced, or enforceable, learning outcomes. International multilateral and bilateral cooperation agencies such as UNESCO are contributing financially and/or technically to such programmes of educational development.

Through national laws and policies, the right to education and acquiring the necessary qualifications to participate in a nation's economy must be given concrete shape in terms of educational programs and curricula. It is important to adapt schooling to new emerging problems. Demographic, cultural, and social changes in society can have a strong influence on educational systems. The right to education must develop respect for the values of children and of others. As difficult as change can be, as reflected by the United States Supreme Court's monumental decision in *Brown v. Board of Education*, invalidating segregation in schools based on race, educational systems sometimes need to be reformed in order to face social, political, cultural, and technological changes. Curricula must reflect the contemporary needs of students in an ever-changing world. Yet, at the same time, governments are responsible for maintaining credibility of their schools' curricula in terms of internal sustainability and continuity despite political, social, and institutional changes.

Many children are, unfortunately, still denied equal educational opportunities. In order to ensure that underprivileged students are not discriminated against due to their socio-economic status, governments can provide financial support to them by means of study grants. This assumes, of course, that there are no decisive financial constraints within these countries related to educational development. However, many governments are faced with the problem of regulating the restrained budgets and at the same time avoiding discrimination and disruption.

The education of young women, minorities, and children with disabilities are just some of the important aspects of educational rights for governments to take into account. Other important concerns for students include issues associated with protecting their rights to due process when facing disciplinary actions, freedom of speech, privacy, religion, and to participate in decision-making that impacts their lives.

Students with disabilities and children from deprived social, cultural, ethnic, or financial backgrounds should have equal educational access. No child can be denied the access to quality education. Education cannot be limited by sex; this sensitivity recognizes that all students have the same learning chances and are treated on an equal basis. The rights-based promotion of gender equality is an important priority. Refugees or children with another nationality who reside in a country should not suffer any discrimination in access to learning opportunities either.

There is a necessity for a sufficient number of schools that are equipped with all of the necessary materials and facilities to guarantee high standards of education and appropriate, safe learning environments. This also means that governments must ensure the presence of well-trained teachers whose professional freedom to speech, religion, and academic freedom are as well assured as those of their students. Of course, there is a variety in the kinds of curricula in different schools. The standards of education in all public schools of the same level are mostly equivalent as well as the conditions relating to the quality of the provided education. Even so, a variety of questions remains. Should this be an obligation? Do governments have the right to prescribe by law the quality standards of a private school and the right to decide which approach meets best certain qualifications and learning outcomes? In many countries, this question has been answered affirmative.

Should there be a focus on the promotion of linguistic diversity at all levels of education? Can, or should, parents in a multilingual country decide whether their children are to be educated in the official language or in the language they prefer even if the latter impedes social integration? How much difference should there be between public and private schools if both are state funded? How much difference can, or should, there be in countries like the United States where there is no direct government funding for private, religious schools? Does a government have to take measures to make education culturally appropriate for minorities or just for indigenous children? Comparative educational law offers several examples of "best practices" for just about all of these perplexing questions.

All over the world, there is a diversification of educational systems. Will the quest for globalization focus on equal, quality education? Currently, the quality of education in each country can be monitored by the government, the minister of education, or appropriate state agencies on national, regional, and/or local levels. Does the government have to choose the method of instruction or determine its content? Is it possible to compare the educational systems in for instance the United States of America and various European nations? Do nations need frameworks to measure and compare different learning outcomes? Who is accountable for the quality of the provided education? What is the appropriate instruction? This book reveals that all countries are confronted with these questions.

Another important question concerns whether parental choices for educating their children can be limited by family income. Sadly, in reality, this is often the case. Can schools admit students or teachers according to certain criteria? Again, national legislation can be an inspiring source of domestic law in another country.

Conclusion

Human dignity is closely related to the protection of the physical and mental integrity of students as they grow to become productive adult members of their societies. Human dignity can be violated in the educational environment, for instance, in disciplinary procedures. Quality education for all children is the key to the reduction and elimination of adult illiteracy in future generations. Improvements in basic education are a prerequisite to sustainable personal and social development. None of the social, civil, economic, and political rights can be exercised by individuals, unless they have received a basic education. Education is a lasting investment in the future of children, indeed of society itself, and sustainable development and social progress in general. Insofar as education is critical to improving the lives of people by helping them both to break the cycle of poverty and to lead lives of participation in democratic societies, it cannot be in short supply. If anything, it is an essential governmental responsibility to ensure that the educational rights of students remain protected, rights that are compatible with human rights provisions.

The editors of this book and all of the chapter authors are dedicated to achieving universal access to basic quality education for all children as well as to eliminating gender disparities and other forms of discrimination. In fact, we all recognize that achieving the right to basic education for all is one of the biggest moral challenges of our times. To this end, the editors and chapter authors hope that our work will begin discussions that will culminate in ensuring the educational rights of all children throughout the world without regard to their races, creeds, genders, or socio-economic status.

APPENDIX

Educational and Social Issues by Nation

	Compulsory Education	*Free Expression, Freedom of Speech*	*Religious Freedom of Students*	*Corporal Punishment*	*Legal Basis to Establish Private Schools*	*Home-Schooling*	*Education is Free of Charge*
Australia	yes	yes	yes	yes—but	yes	yes	yes
Belgium Flemish Community	yes	yes	yes	no	yes	yes	yes
China	yes	unclear	yes	no	yes	unclear	no
Germany	yes	yes	yes	no	yes	no	yes
England	yes	yes	yes	no	yes	yes	yes
Malaysia	yes	yes	yes	yes	yes	yes	yes
Northern Ireland	yes	yes	yes	no	yes	yes	yes
Netherlands	yes	yes	yes	no	yes	yes	yes
New Zealand	yes	yes	yes	no	yes	yes	yes
Portugal	yes	yes	yes	no	yes	yes	yes
Russia	yes	yes	yes	unclear	yes	yes	yes
South Africa	yes	yes	yes	no	yes	unclear	yes
United States	yes	yes	yes—but	depends	yes	yes	yes

(*continued*)

Educational and Social Issues by Nation (*continued*)

	Parents Can Have their Children Excused from Specific Subjects to Which They Object for Pedagogical or Philosophical Reasons	*Special Care for Children with Special Educational Needs*	*Mandatory Religious Education*	*Free Enrolment*
Australia	no	yes	no	yes*
Belgium Flemish Community	yes	yes	yes for moral education	yes
China	unclear	yes	no	yes
Germany	yes	yes	yes	yes*
England	partly—statutory right of excusal for sex education, religious education, and collective worship only	yes	yes—but parents can opt child out	yes*
Malaysia	unclear	yes	yes—if parents agree	yes
Northern Ireland	yes	yes	yes—but parents can opt child out	yes*
Netherlands	yes	yes	no	yes—in public shcools
New Zealand	yes	yes	no	yes*
Portugal	yes	yes	no	yes*
Russia	yes	yes	no	yes*
South Africa	yes	yes	no	yes*
United States	no	yes	no	yes*

*In most countries, there are admission policies based on the religious denomination, spoken language, or living place of the pupil.

Source: The content is partly based on the book *Finding the Right Balance: Freedom, Autonomy, and Accountability in Education*, Glenn, C., De Groof, J., Lemma Publishers, 2002, pp. 336–341.

About the Contributors

Jan De Groof

Jan De Groof is founder and chairman of both the European Association for Education Law and Policy and of the Interuniversity Centre for Education Law; he is also a co-founder of the Russian and the South African Associations for Education Law and Policy. One of the leading education law specialists worldwide, he helped organize and chaired the First World Conference on the Right to Education, in 2004. De Groof is professor at the College of Europe in Bruges, Belgium, and the University of Tilburg, Netherlands; formerly, he was professor at Ghent University in Belgium. He is also government commissioner for the universities of the Flemish community in Belgium. Previously, he was Chief of Cabinet of the Flemish Minister for Education and Training. He is often entrusted with international assignments and acted as an expert for OECD, EU, Council of Europe, and UNESCO while also fulfilling missions with Max Van Der Stoel, former High Commissioner for National Minorities of the OVSE, chiefly in the Balkan region. He publishes extensively in the field of international law, public law, education rights, education law and policy, and is author or co-author of books, chapters, and academic articles. He is also visiting professor at several universities worldwide and is often invited as a guest speaker at international symposia on educational rights and policy. De Groof is founder and editor in chief of the *European Journal for Education Law and Policy*, now transformed into the *International Journal for Education Law and Policy*.

Neville Harris

Neville Harris, LL.B., LL.M., Ph.D., Barrister, is professor of law at the University of Manchester, UK. He is the general editor of *Education Law Journal* and *Education Law Reports* and co-editor of the *Journal of Social Security Law*. His books include *Law and Education: Regulation, Consumerism and the Education System* (1993); *The Law relating to Schools* (1995); *Special Educational Needs and Access to Justice* (1997); (as lead author) *Social Security Law in Context* (2000); (as co-author) *Challenges to School Exclusion* (2000); and *Halsbury's Laws: Vol 15* (Education) (2001). His latest book is *Education, Law and Diversity*, due for publication in the fall of 2006.

Tie Fatt Hee

Tie Fatt Hee is an associate professor at the University of Malaya in Kuala Lumpur, Malaysia. He teaches education law at the post graduate level at the Faculty of Education and at the Institute of Principalship Studies. He is as an advocate and solicitor of the High Court of Malaya. His academic qualifications include Bachelor of Arts (Malaya); Diploma in Education (Malaya); Master in Education (Malaya); Bachelor of Laws (London); Certificate in Legal Practice (Malaya); Master of Law (Malaya); and Doctor of Legal Science (Bond, Australia).

António Pedro Barbas Homem

António Pedro Barbas Homem, LL.M, Ph.D., is professor of law, faculty of law, Lisbon University, Portugal, and a lawyer. He publishes numerous textbooks, articles, and case notes in the fields of education law, theory of law, history, and philosophy of law. He is the general editor of *Education and the Law* (Educação e Direito). His books include *Laws of Education.*

Laura Lundy

Laura Lundy is a reader in the Graduate School of Education at Queen's University, Belfast, and a Barrister at Law. She is the author of *Education Law, Policy and Practice in Northern Ireland* (Belfast: SLS, 2000) and was chairperson of the Northern Ireland Human Rights Commission's Working Party on Education Rights for the Bill of Rights (2001). In 2004–2005, she was the principal investigator in an inter-disciplinary team which completed a major research project on children's rights for the Northern Ireland Commissioner on Children and Young People.

Rassie Malherbe

Rassie Malherbe is professor of public law at the University of Johannesburg, South Africa, and specialises in constitutional law, human rights, education law, and statutory interpretation. He publishes widely, both nationally and internationally, and is the author and co-author of numerous textbooks, articles, and case notes in the fields of constitutional law, human rights, and education law. He is an executive member of the South African Education Law and Policy Association and of the Inter-University Education Law and Policy Centre in Pretoria, and is a member of the editorial committee of the *Journal for South African Law.* He served as an adviser during the South African constitution-making process of the early nineties.

Ralph D. Mawdsley

Ralph D. Mawdsley, M.Div., J.D., Ph.D., is professor of educational administration in the College of Education and Human Services, Cleveland State University, and adjunct professor of law, Regent University College of Law. He is co-director of an Education Law Project cosponsored by the United States Embassy in South Africa, the University of Pretoria, and Cleveland State University to develop capacity building among South African administrators for understanding the rights and responsibilities of education stakeholders. Dr. Mawdsley was the 2001 president of the Education Law Association and the 2004 recipient of its McGhehey Award for outstanding achievement in education law. He has in excess of five-hundred publications and is active in the American Education Law Association, the South Africa Education Law and Policy Association, and the Australia/New Zealand Education Law Association where he is a regular speaker at their conferences.

C. (Niels) W. Noorlander

C. (Niels) W. Noorlander, LL.M., Ph.D., wrote his dissertation on the legal position of pupils and parents (*Recht doen aan leerlingen en ouders,* Nijmegen,

2005) and several papers and articles on education law at the Vrije Universiteit Amsterdam. He is currently working at the Education Inspectorate.

Ingo Richter

Ingo Richter, president of the Irmgard Coninx Foundation, studied law at the universities of Göttingen, Munich, Hamburg, and Paris. He earned his Doctorate in Law at Hamburg University (1965) and his Docteur de l'Université de Paris (1966). He has served as head of the Department of Law and Administration at the Max-Planck-Institute for Educational Research, Berlin; as professor of law at the Free University of Berlin; and as professor of public law at the University of Hamburg. He also taught at the universities of Bordeaux, Rostock, Hastings, and Chicago. He was chairman and head of Deutsches Jugend Institut in Munich and also was chairman of the 11th Government Commission on Children and Youth. He has been editor of the educational-law journal *Recht der Jugend und des Bildungswesens.*

Paul Rishworth

Paul Rishworth is a professor of law and dean of the faculty of law at the University of Auckland, New Zealand. He was a founding member of the New Zealand chapter of the Australia and New Zealand Education Law Association. He is a joint author of *The New Zealand Bill of Rights* (2003) and has written extensively on human rights law and education law in New Zealand.

Igor Rozjkov

Igor Rozjkov, Ph.D., is a senior researcher of the department on the Jurisprudence of Education Systems, in the Institute for Teacher-Training in Moscow. He is a co-founder of the Russian League for Education Law and Policy and assisted at several European Education Law Association meetings over the past decade. He is author of the handbook *Education Law in Russia.*

Charles J. Russo

Charles J. Russo, M.Div., J.D., Ed.D., is the Joseph Panzer Chair in Education in the School of Education and Allied Professions and adjunct professor in the

School of Law at the University of Dayton. The 1998–1999 president of the Education Law Association and 2002 recipient of its McGhehey (Achievement) Award, he has almost 600 publications including twenty-four books. He speaks on issues in education law in the United States and at Education Law Conferences in Australia-New Zealand, Canada, Europe, and South Africa. He worked in Sarajevo, Bosnia, and Herzegovina, with the Office of the Ombudsman on matters pertaining to civil rights and religious freedom as well as with the Faculty of Education on improving schooling in Bosnia. In addition to speaking in nineteen nations on six continents, he taught summer courses in England and Spain (for the College of New Jersey) and served as a visiting professor at Queensland University of Technology in Brisbane, Australia (and will do so at the law faculty of the University of Newcastle, Australia); the University of Sarajevo, Bosnia; South East European University, Macedonia; the Potchefstroom Campus of Northwest University in Potchefstroom, South Africa; and the University of Malaya in Kuala Lumpur, Malaysia. In May 2004, he received the award Philosophiae Doctor, Honoris Causa, from Potchefstroom University, now the Potchefstroom Campus of North-West University, in recognition of his contribution to the study of education law. Before joining the faculty at the University of Dayton as professor and chair of the Department of Educational Administration, he taught at the University of Kentucky in Lexington, Kentucky, and at Fordham University in his native New York City.

Douglas J. Stewart

Douglas J. Stewart is a senior lecturer, faculty of education, Queensland University of Technology. His major research and teaching interests are in preventive legal risk management. He presents papers at national and international conferences, has co-authored four books, contributed chapters to several others, and has published widely in both professional and academic journals.

Ben P. Vermeulen

Ben P. Vermeulen, LL.M., M.A., Ph.D., is professor of constitutional and administrative law at the Vrije Universiteit, Amsterdam; professor of education law, Vrije Universiteit, Amsterdam, and Radboud Universiteit, Nijmegen; member of the Onderwijsraad (Education Council), the permanent advisory board of the Minister of Education; and member of the Adviescomissie

Vreemdelingenzaken (Immigration Council), the permanent advisory board of the Minister of Immigration and Integration. He has written extensively on fundamental rights, constitutional freedoms, education law, and asylum law.

Ran Zhang

Ran Zhang is a Ph.D. student in Educational Policy Studies and Educational Psychology at Indiana University. She received her undergraduate degrees in law and economics at Beijing University in China. In her doctoral program at Indiana, she has been doing research on educational law, comparative education, and research methodology. She is co-editing an issue of *Chinese Education and Society* on legal issues involving students' rights in China.

www.ingramcontent.com/pod-product-compliance
Ingram Content Group UK Ltd.
Pitfield, Milton Keynes, MK11 3LW, UK
UKHW012037150926
475560UK00001B/46

9 781578 865093